TEACH YOURSELF BOOKS

Beginner's
JAPANESE

Anne M. Hooghart
アニー・ホガート 亜仁 歩賀人

8 Vernon
Battle Creek,
MI 49017
(616)965-2326

D1364988

About the author

Helen Gilhooly has lived and worked in Japan, and has extensive experience of teaching Japanese and writing teaching materials at secondary school and adult level. She has an MA and a PGCE in Japanese and is the Co-ordinator of Derbyshire County Council's Japanese Resources Centre. She is also a teacher trainer of Japanese at Nottingham University.

Acknowledgements

Many thanks to all those people who have supported me in the writing of this book. In particular, thanks to Chizumi Fallon for her patient work in checking the drafts and contributing to the dialogues; to Mavis Pilbeam for her invaluable help with proof-reading and input into the text; to Masae Sugahara for her advice and for taking part in the recording; to Robert Gilhooly for his help in seeking out authentic materials; and to Kate Jarratt and Sarah Mitchell for reading and commenting on the lessons and audio-script. But most of all, to John Rogers for his untiring support and encouragement.

Language adviser: Chizumi Fallon

The publishers and author would like to thank the following for the use of material in this book: Japan National Tourist Office, UK; NTT Europe; the Japanese Inn Group; East Group Japan Rail; Ministry of Post and Telecommunications; Shibuya Seibu department store; Domino's pizza, Tokyo; and Tama City International Center.

Beginner's
JAPANESE

AN EASY INTRODUCTION

Helen Gilhooly

TEACH YOURSELF BOOKS

Long-renowned as the authoritative source for self-guided learning – with more than 30 million copies sold worldwide – the *Teach Yourself* series includes over 200 titles in the fields of languages, crafts, hobbies, sports, and other leisure activities.

British Library Cataloguing in Publication Data
A catalogue record for this title is available from the British Library

Library of Congress Catalog Card Number: 95–71315

First published in UK 1996 by Hodder Headline Plc, 338 Euston Road, London NW1 3BH

First published in US 1996 by NTC Publishing Group, 4255 West Touhy Avenue, Lincolnwood (Chicago), Illinois 60646 – 1975 U.S.A.

Typeset by Transet Limited, Coventry, Warwickshire.
Printed in Great Britain by Cox & Wyman Ltd, Reading, Berkshire.

Impression number   10 9 8 7 6 5 4 3
Year   1999 1998 1997

CONTENTS

INTRODUCTION

────────── **About the course** ──────────

Japanese has become increasingly popular as a language to learn in recent years, and a growing awareness of Japan has been created through industry, television, newspaper articles, Japanese events and exhibitions. However, Japanese is still regarded as an 'exotic' language by many people and believed to be 'too difficult to learn'. Nothing could be further from the truth – Japanese is a very accessible language and can be a great deal of fun to learn. The language itself can teach you many interesting things about Japanese life and culture, and this book seeks to give you an understanding both of the language and the culture behind that language, and so demystify something of the 'exotic' in order to give you a clearer view.

Teach Yourself Beginner's Japanese is the right course for you if you are a complete beginner or want to make a fresh start. It is a self-study course which will help you to understand and speak Japanese and apply what you have learnt to business and social situations both in Japan and in this country. There is even an opportunity for you to learn some of the basics of reading Japanese.

Two key elements

This book has two main parts. Units 1–12 introduce you to the basic structures and grammatical points you'll need in everyday situations. These units should be taken in order as each builds on the previous ones.

Units 14–20 involve you in everyday situations such as shopping, eating out, travelling, meeting a Japanese business person and entertaining a Japanese person in your home. In these units you have the opportunity to put into practice the language you have learnt in the first 12 units. You can take these units in any order.

The course is best used together with the accompanying 90-minute audio cassette, but is not dependent upon it. You are recommended to obtain the cassette if possible because it will help you to pronounce Japanese correctly and to acquire an authentic accent. The recorded dialogues and activities will also give you plenty of practice in understanding and responding to spoken Japanese. The *Pronunciation guide* and the new words in the first few units are also recorded on the cassette to help you speak Japanese correctly in the important early stages of your study. Readers without the cassette will find that there are some units which contain an activity that cannot be done with the book alone, but in such cases the material is always covered by other activities in that unit.

Introducing the main characters

There is a storyline running throughout the book which involves the following characters.

The Yamaguchi family:

* Reiko Yamaguchi, Mother and housewife, she works part-time;
* Masaki Yamaguchi, Father and company employee at the Tokyo Bank, he does business with foreign companies;
* Emi Yamaguchi, daughter, aged 19 and a student at Tokyo University. She is planning a trip to England during the university holidays;
* Takeshi Yamaguchi, son, aged 15 and at High School;
* Anne Jenkins (pronounced **An Jenkinsu** in Japanese), aged 22, she is coming to Tokyo to stay with the Yamaguchi family and learn Japanese at a local foreign language school.

Language school characters:

* Han is from China;
* Scott (pronounced Sukotto in Japanese) is from America;
* Tani is from France;
* Heidi (pronounced Haidi) is from Germany;
* Satō-sensei, the teacher.

You'll learn more about these characters as you progress through the book.

About Units 1–12

Each unit covers approximately 8–10 pages.

The first page tells you what you are going to learn in that unit and is called **Hajime ni** (*Introduction*). There is then an easy activity **Hanashimashō** (*Let's talk*) to get you speaking straightaway.

Tango-hyō (*Vocabulary list*) contains the most important words and phrases from the unit. Try to learn them by heart. They will be used in that unit and in later units. There are various tips throughout the book to help you with learning new words.

Kaiwa (*Conversation*). Progress to the conversation once you are at least familiar with the new words. The conversations will show you how the words are used and will reinforce the new words in your memory. If you have the cassette listen to the conversation once or twice without stopping the tape; if not, read through it without looking anything up. This will help you to develop the skill of listening or reading for gist or general meaning. You don't have to understand every word to understand the overall meaning. There are also extra words (**Tango**) under each conversation to aid your understanding.

Next, use the pause button on your cassette recorder to divide the conversation into smaller chunks and try repeating each phrase out loud. This will help you gain a more authentic accent. If you don't have the cassette, use a piece of paper or book marker to cover part of the dialogue so that you can concentrate on a small part at a time. The important thing in either case is to *speak out aloud* because this will help you to gain confidence in speaking Japanese. If you have a tape recorder, try recording yourself sometimes. If you have the cassette, you could compare your recording with the cassette to help you improve your pronunciation. Or if you have Japanese friends, practise on them! This and further advice will be reiterated through the book.

Hinto (*Hints*) are special sections which give you advice on developing techniques to improve your learning skills: hints on mastering a particular structure or grammar point; hints on remembering vocabulary; hints for developing your confidence, and so on.

Setsumei (*Explanations*). This section concentrates on the main grammar and structures for that unit and gives you lots of examples. You can either read the examples first and see if you can work out the rule for yourself, or read the **Setsumei** first. Once you feel confident with the explanations try making up your own examples.

Rei (*Examples*). This word is used in some units when examples are given in the **Setsumei** and activity sections.

Renshū (*Practice*). This section consists of various activities to help you practise what you have learnt in the unit. Some activities are labelled **Kiku-renshū** (*Listening practice*). For these you will need to listen to the cassette. It is not essential to have the cassette in order to complete the course and most activities are not dependent on it. However, listening to the cassette will make your learning much easier and more varied.

Tesuto (*Test*). At the end of each unit you can test yourself on what you have learnt up to that point. At the end of Unit 6 there is a **Fukushū** (*Review*) section which gives you the opportunity to look back at the first six units before proceeding further. At the end of Unit 10 there is a **Fukushū tesuto** (*Revision test*) which challenges you to test yourself on everything you have learn in Units 1–10. And finally, at the end of Unit 12 the **Fukushū tesuto** tests you on points from all the units in the learning section.

Nihon ni tsuite (*About Japan*). These short notes, in English, offer you an insight into different aspects of Japanese society and culture, and are usually linked to the situations you are learning about in each unit.

About Units 14–20

These units give you the opportunity to practise what you have learnt in meaningful and useful situations.

The first page tells you what you are going to learn, and under **Fukushū** (*Revision*) there is a checklist and page number for the structures you have already learnt which you will need in that unit. This gives you the opportunity to refer back to these and so feel fully confident before beginning the unit.

Tango-hyō gives you the basic vocabulary that you will need when dealing, in real life, with practical situations such as introducing yourself to a Japanese person, booking a room, making a phone call, ordering a meal, buying a train ticket.

There are several different **Kaiwa**, sometimes linked with different sets of **Tango**, each dealing with different aspects of a topic. Remember to listen to the dialogues first and use the pause button to practise new phrases out aloud (or read the dialogue out aloud).

Renshū. These are based on real Japanese situations and sometimes use authentic material, so you can develop a real feel for how things work in Japan.

Tesuto and **Fukushū Tesuto**. As in Units 1–12.

Kotae (*Answers*). The answers to all the **Hanashimashō**, **Renshū** and **Tesuto** can be found at the back of the book.

Unit 13 – an introduction to reading Japanese

Contrary to popular opinion, Japanese is not a difficult language to speak, particularly at beginner's level. Pronunciation is fairly straightforward without any complicated rules, and the grammar is fairly simple and easy to grasp. Where Japanese does offer a more serious challenge to the learner is in its reading and writing. However, that can be fun to learn too, and is very interesting. This book is written in our script (known as **rōmaji** or roman letters, in Japanese) so that the learner can get straight down to speaking Japanese without the barrier of an unknown form of writing. However, Unit 13 is a special unit. It gives the learner the opportunity to find out something about reading Japanese, and in the **Yomimashō** (*Let's read*) sections in this unit, you will find yourself actually reading some Japanese, including an authentic menu! This unit is designed as a one-off so that learners who would rather concentrate solely on listening and speaking skills can miss it out without it affecting their understanding of other units. However, in Unit 15 there is a menu written both in Japanese writing and **rōmaji** so that those who have read Unit 13 can have the chance to revise and practise what they learnt.

A note on using the cassette

If you have obtained the audio cassette which accompanies this book here are some tips for getting the best possible use out of it.

- Try to use it in a quiet room or environment so that you can concentrate and listen to what is being said. Using a Walkman or headphones is ideal for this.
- Before you listen to a dialogue or activity, put the number counter, if you have one on your machine, back to 0. In this way you will easily be able to find the beginning of the dialogue and your learning will progress more smoothly.
- When you first listen to a dialogue or activity, give yourself an overall picture by listening to it all the way through once or twice. You won't get all the information the first time but it will help you to develop the skill of picking out the essential points and processing them in your brain more quickly. This in turn will help you to increase the speed of your listening and understanding.
- Once you have listened to a whole activity once or twice, break it down into manageable chunks if necessary, using the pause button, so that you can complete the information required. Also, use the pause button when you are practising chunks of dialogue. This will help you to focus on accurate pronunciation and thus to develop your Japanese accent. Use it too when memorising new words or dialogue – you will get better results if you work on small chunks at a time.

How to be successful at learning Japanese

- A little, often, is far more effective than a long session every now and then. So try and put in about 20–30 minutes' study each day, if possible, or two or three times per week. If you study at a regular time, for example, before you go to bed, or during lunchtime, it will be easier to get into the habit of studying a little, often.
- Find a balance between moving through the book and revising what you have already learnt. If you move forward too quickly, you will find later units difficult because you haven't built effectively on your learning. Equally, however, if you keep going over the points you have learnt, you will feel frustrated at not moving forward. Set aside one session every now and again (maybe once every five sessions) when you look back at previous units to remind yourself of what you have learnt. A good place to start is with the test at the end of the unit – if you have difficulties with a certain structure, refer back to its explanations and examples.

- Study in a quiet room where you can speak out aloud. People develop different studying habits – some people like to study with music in the background, for example, while others need complete silence. The difference with learning a language is that you need to build up your speaking and listening skills, and so you need somewhere where you can concentrate and, literally, hear yourself speak.
- Don't be too harsh on yourself! Learning a language is a gradual and cumulative process, and everyone makes mistakes. You mustn't expect to be perfect straight away, and you can't be expected to remember every item of vocabulary and every new structure. Learn slowly and surely, and don't be impatient with yourself.
- Seek out opportunities to use your Japanese. You don't have to go to Japan to do this. There are many opportunities these days to experience Japan in this country, and there are quite a number of Japanese people living here. Find out about Japanese societies, join a Japanese class, go to a Japanese restaurant and practise ordering in Japanese (but be careful – people working in Japanese restaurants are not always Japanese) or visit some of the Japanese department stores, bookshops or supermarkets, especially in London, where you will hear Japanese being spoken all around you.

There are many tips to help your learning provided throughout the book in the **Hinto** sections. They often repeat this advice and add to it – take heed of it, and most of all remember that learning and using a foreign language is *fun*!

At the back of the book

At the back of the book is a reference section which contains:

- Answers;
- A Japanese–English vocabulary list containing all the words in the course;
- A complete list of numbers in Japanese;
- An index to enable you to look things up in the book.

About symbols and abbreviations

This indicates that the cassette is needed for the following section. (But often there is an alternative way of completing the section if you don't have the cassette.)

This indicates a dialogue.

This indicates activities – where you can practise using the language.

This indicates key words or phrases.

This indicates grammar or explanations – the nuts and bolts of the language.

This draws your attention to points to be noted.

This indicates a reading passage (used in Units 14–20).

(Lit.) literally

Pronunciation guide

The Japanese 'alphabet' is made up of a number of sounds created by combining the five vowels (**a, e, i, o, u**) with a consonant (letters which are not vowels). These vowel sounds are always pronounced in the same way. So whereas in English, for example, the sound **a** can vary as follows:

m**a**t   m**a**te   m**a**yor (etc.)

The sound **a** in japanese is always pronounced as in *mat*.

The five Japanese vowels in order are:

a   as in m*a*t
i   as in m*ea*t
u   as in m*oo*d
e   as in *e*nd
o   as in h*o*t

This sentence will help you to remember these sounds:

M**a** **e**ats tw**o** **e**ggs and **o**ranges.
    a i   u e   o

How to pronounce syllables

Below is a sound chart of the Japanese syllables. If you have the cassette tape, switch it on at the beginning, and you will hear some of the sounds below being spoken. Listen to each exercise a line at a time, starting with *a, i, u, e, o*, then pause the tape and say these sounds yourself. Continue like this until you reach exercise 6 on the cassette, then switch the tape off (or repeat the process for extra practice). The cassette will now be in the right place for the next pronunciation exercise below. If you don't have the tape, bear in mind the pronunciation of the five vowels as explained above and work through the chart line by line, saying the sounds out aloud. Pronunciation of Japanese is very straightforward, and there are pointers at the side of the chart to help you.

Sound chart

a	i	u	e	o	
ka	ki	ku	ke	ko	
sa	shi	su	se	so	
ta	chi	tsu	te	to	**Tsu** is an unfamiliar sound for English speakers; it is only one syllable (or beat); squash the **t** and **s** together as you say them
na	ni	nu	ne	no	
ha	hi	fu	he	ho	**Fu** is a soft sound, between **f** and **h**. Your front teeth don't touch your lips as you say it; air is let out between your teeth and lips
ma	mi	mu	me	mo	
ya		yu		yo	
ra	ri	ru	re	ro	**R** is a soft sound, somewhere between **r** and **l**, and not like the French **r** sound
wa				n	**N** has a full beat. There are examples in *How to pronounce words* below
ga	gi	gu	ge	go	**G** as in *get* not *gin*
za	ji	zu	ze	zo	
ba	bi	bu	be	bo	There is no **V** sound in Japanese, and **b** is substituted for foreign words. For example, *Valerie* becomes *Ba-ra-ri-i*
pa	pi	pu	pe	po	
da			de	do	

The final set of sounds in the *Sound chart* consist of a consonant plus **ya**, **yu**, or **yo**. These also have a single beat (i.e. they are one syllable), although English-speaking people sometimes mistakenly pronounce these sounds with two beats. For example, the first sound of the city name **Kyoto** is sometimes wrongly pronounced **Ki-yo** instead of **kyō**.

Practise saying these sounds carefully.

kya	kyu	kyo	
sha	shu	sho	
cha	chu	cho	**ch** as in *chance* not *character*
nya	nyu	nyo	
hya	hyu	hyo	
mya	myu	myo	
rya	ryu	ryo	
gya	gyu	gyo	
ja	ju	jo	**ja** as in *jam* (not the German *ja*)
bya	byu	byo	
pya	pyu	pyo	

How to pronounce words

(a) Every syllable in Japanese is given equal stress, whereas in English we give more stress to some parts of the words than others. Look at this example:

English	A-**me**-ri-ca	The stress is on **me**.
Japanese	A-me-ri-ka	Each syllable has equal stress.

English-speaking people often add stress to Japanese words. For example:

Hi-ro-**shi**-ma   The stress is on **shi** whereas it should sound like this: Hi-ro-shi-ma. (Listen to it being spoken on your cassette.)

To make your accent sound more authentic, try not to stress parts of words as you do in English; instead give equal stress to each syllable.

(b) Long syllables

In this book, a macron is used over vowels to indicate where the sound is a long sound. Here is an example to illustrate this:

Tōkyō   You hold the sounds with macrons for about twice the normal length: To-o-kyo-o. (Listen to it on your cassette.) The word should be spoken smoothly.

However, macrons are not used in the case of place names when the name appears as part of an English text, only as part of a Japanese dialogue.

(c) **N** is a syllable by itself. Look at this example of *hello* in Japanese.

ko-n-ni-chi-wa   (Listen to it on your cassette.)

When **n** is followed by **p, b** or **m** its sound softens to **m**:

gambatte   *good luck*

sampaku   *three nights* (Listen to these examples on your cassette.)

Where **n** is followed by a vowel, an apostrophe is inserted between them to distinguish the sound **n** from the sounds **na, ni, nu, ne, no**, as in this example: **ten'in** (*shopkeeper*) has four syllables **te-n-i-n**; it is not pronounced **te-ni-n**.

(d) Double consonants

A double consonant indicates that you should pause slightly before saying it, as you would in these English examples (say them out aloud):

headdress   (pause after *hea* – not *head dress*)
bookcase   (pause after *boo*)

You will come across these double consonants in Japanese – **kk, ss, tt, tc, pp**. Here are some examples:

ga mba**tte**   *good luck*
Ho**kk**aidō   North island of Japan
Sa**pp**oro   capital of Hokkaidō
ma**ss**ugu   *straight on* (Listen to them on the tape.)

You *always* add this pause in the case of Japanese double consonants.

(e) Silent vowels

Sometimes **i** and **u** become almost unvoiced. This is indicated below by bracketing the vowel. Read (and listen to) these examples:

des(u)	*it is*
s(u)ki	*I like*
ikimas(u)	*I go*
hajimemash(i)te	*How do you do?*

This will be pointed out to you as you come across such words in the units.

(f) Pronunciation of non-Japanese words

Foreign words have to be adapted to the Japanese sound system. You have already seen one example of this above (the name *Valerie*). Here are some more examples of names:

Sukotto	*Scott*
Sumisu	*Smith*
Furansu	*France*
Satchā	*Thatcher* (Listen to them on your cassette.)

There is no *th* sound in Japanese and *s* is used instead.

Renshū *Practice*

Below is a map of Japan with the four main islands and some of the main cities marked on it. Moving from north to south (1–12) say each place out aloud, then check with the cassette or pronunciation guide before moving on to the next one. Particular points to look out for are in bold type:

1

HAJIMEMASHITE
How do you do?

In this unit you will learn

- how to introduce yourself
- how to say *hello* and *goodbye*
- how to say *excuse me* and *thank you*
- how to introduce a friend or business colleague

Hajime ni   *Introduction*

You have already met the main characters in the book in the *Introduction*. You will be following their stories throughout the 20 units. Before you start this unit, look back over the pronunciation guide and practise it with the cassette tape.

Also look at the *Study guide* on page 6. Learning by yourself requires discipline but can be very rewarding and means that you can progress *at your own pace*.

Try to set aside a regular time when you can put in half an hour's study rather than trying to do too much less regularly. You will then progress more smoothly, and you will be able to build more quickly on your learning.

—— # Hanashimashō *Let's talk* ——

Do you know any Japanese greetings already? People often know the word for *goodbye* – **sayōnara**, and sometimes *hello* – **konnichiwa**. Read out aloud the words in the **Tango-hyō** below. If you have the cassette, listen to one word at a time, pause the cassette, say the word out aloud, then go on to the next word.

When you have completed this, you can test your pronunciation by winding back to the beginning of the **Tango-hyō** (set the counter on your cassette player if you have one), this time saying the word and then playing it on the cassette.

Follow this routine each time you are introduced to new vocabulary on the cassette, to develop a really authentic accent and a feel for the pronunciation of Japanese words. If you don't have a cassette, there are some pronunciation tips after the new words.

 ## Tango-hyō *Vocabulary*

Greetings

ohayō gozaimas(u)	good morning
konnichiwa	hello; good afternoon (late morning onwards)
konbanwa	good evening
oyasumi nasai	good night
sayōnara	goodbye (Lit. *If it must be so* – a fairly formal expression)
bai bai	goodbye (from the English *bye bye* – can sound childish)
ja mata ne!	see you! (casual)
mata ash(i)ta	see you tomorrow

Introductions

hajimemash(i)te	how do you do?
dōzo yorosh(i)ku	pleased to meet you
kochira wa ...	this person is ...
san	Mr/Mrs/Miss/Ms (addressing someone else)
dōmo arigatō (gozaimas(u))	thank you (very much)
arigatō	thanks
sumimasen	excuse me; sorry
hai	yes
Iie	no
desu	am, is, are

❇ Hinto   *Hints: Pronunciation tips*

- The **u** in **gozaimasu** and **desu** is usually not voiced (see the *Pronunciation guide* on page 8) or appears only as a whispered sound. This also applies to the second **i** in **hajimemashite** and **dōzo yoroshiku**.
- Give the vowels with a macron (**ohayō, sayōnara, dōzo, dōmo, arigatō**) an extra beat, but make it sound smooth (see the *Pronunciation guide* on page 8)
- Make sure the **n** syllable lasts for one beat. For example: **ko-n-ni-chi-wa, ko-n-ba-n-wa**.

Kaiwa   *Dialogue*

Reiko Yamaguchi and her son Takeshi are meeting Anne Jenkins at Narita International airport near Tokyo. Reiko sees an English girl standing on her own. If you have the cassette, switch it on and listen to the whole conversation once or twice. Then play it back line by line, pause the cassette, and say the conversation out aloud.

If you don't have the cassette, read through the dialogue below once or twice, then practise saying it out aloud, remembering what you learnt in the **Tango-hyō** section.

Reiko	**Ano** ... An Jenkins(u)-san desu **ka**.
Girl	Iie ...
Reiko (*embarrassed*)	A! Sumimasen.
Takeshi (*also embarrassed*) **Okaasan!**	

Anne is waiting nearby and sees Reiko's sign with her name on it.

Anne	Sumimasen, Yamaguchi-san desu ka.
Reiko	Hai, **sō desu**!
Anne	Hajimemashite, An Jenkinsu desu. Dōzo yoroshiku (*she bows*)
Reiko (*bowing*)	Hajimemashite, Yamaguchi Reiko desu. Dōzo yoroshiku.

Reiko then introduces her son to Anne.

Reiko	Takeshi desu. **Musuko** desu.
Takeshi (*bowing*)	Dōzo yoroshiku.
Anne (*bowing*)	Dōzo yoroshiku.

On the journey back to the Yamaguchi home everyone is quiet: Anne is tired and only knows a few phrases in Japanese; Takeshi is a little shy about practising his English; Reiko is rather hoping that Anne will teach her some English during her stay.

On the train Takeshi bumps into a schoolfriend, Jun, and although Anne doesn't understand a lot of what they say, she's pleased to catch at least one expression that she knows.

Takeshi	Konnichiwa!
Friend	Konnichiwa!

Takeshi introduces Anne to his friend.

Takeshi	Kochira wa An Jenkinsu-san desu.
Friend	Hajimemashite. Suzuki Jun desu. Dōzo yoroshiku (*bows*)

Later as they arrive at their station:

Takeshi	Ja mata ne!
Jun	Mata ashita!

ano ...	a hesitation word, like *er, erm*
ka	indicates a question
okaasan	mother
sō desu	that's right
musuko	(my) son

Nihon ni tsuite   *About Japan*

Bowing

Bowing is an integral part of everyday life in Japan. People bow when they meet each other; schoolchildren bow at the beginning and end of each lesson; shop assistants bow as you enter a store or elevator; roadwork signs have a picture of a workman bowing in apology for the delay; you will see mothers teaching young children to bow by pushing their heads gently forward; and you even see people bowing while on the phone!

The depth of the bow indicates the status of the person you are greeting – a shallower bow to a friend, a deep bow to someone important. Some companies now even run etiquette courses for new recruits because of concern that young people do not know how to use respectful language and customs such as bowing correctly.

As a foreigner you may find that Japanese people will follow the western custom and shake hands with you, but it shows a positive outlook and a knowledge of Japanese customs if you bow. If you are a man put your hands by your sides. If you are a woman cross your hands in front of you just above the knee (see the illustrations below). Bow from the waist – not too shallow, not too deep.

Take your lead from the other person.

 —— **Setsumei** *Explanations* ——

1 An Jenkinsu-san desu ka: *Are you Miss Anne Jenkins?*

The Japanese use **san** when they address other people. The nearest equivalent in English is the use of *Mr / Mrs / Miss / Ms*. However, there are some important differences. **San** is attached to the end of the name and can be used either with the surname or the first name. (In general, though, Japanese adults tend to use surnames rather than first names unless they know someone very well.)

It is very important to use **san** – it would sound impolite if you addressed a Japanese person only by their name. There are more polite and more casual forms of **san**:

sama is used when addressing letters and in more formal situations;

kun is used for young boys and men who know each other well;

chan may be used between children or by adults when addressing children.

teachers and professors have **sensei** attached to their name.

2 Hajimemashite, Yamaguchi Reiko desu: *How do you do? I am Reiko Yamaguchi*

A second important point to know about **san** is that you only use it to address other people and *never* when talking about yourself (or members of your family). Look back at the dialogue – there are a number of examples of this. For example, when Jun introduces himself to Anne:

Hajimemashite. Suzuki Jun desu. *How do you do? I am Jun Suzuki.*

And when Reiko introduces her son Takeshi:

Takeshi desu.   *He is Takeshi.*

3 Have you noticed from the examples in point 2 above that the name order is different in Japanese? The Japanese say their family name first followed by their first name:

Yamaguchi Takeshi

However, most Japanese will expect non-Japanese people to use the western convention (first name followed by surname) so you don't need to reverse the order when saying your name. This is why Anne said her name in the western order:

An Jenkinsu   *Anne Jenkins*

In a business situation you will probably only use your surname anyway.

4 Hajimemashite, An Jenkinsu desu. Dōzo yoroshiku: *How do you do? I am Anne Jenkins. I'm pleased to meet you.*

When you first meet someone you use the formal phrases, **hajimemashite** (*how do you do*) and **dōzo yoroshiku** (*pleased to* *meet you*, or *pleased to make your acquaintance*). After your name you say **desu** (*I am*). The same word (**desu**) is used for *you / we / they are* and *it / she / he is*. The important thing to remember is that **desu** comes at the end of the sentence. For example:

An Jenkinsu desu.	*I am Anne Jenkins.*
Musuko desu.	*He is my son.*

5 Yamaguchi-san desu ka: *Are you Mrs Yamaguchi?*

To make a question in Japanese you say **ka** at the end of the sentence. You can think of **ka** as being like a spoken question mark. When **ka** is written at the end of a sentence, there is no need to write a question mark as well. For example:

Yamaguchi-san desu *ka*	*Are you Mrs Yamaguchi?*
Tōkyō desu *ka*	*Is it Tokyo?*

6 Kochira wa An Jenkinsu-san desu: *This is Miss Anne Jenkins.*

To introduce someone else you use **kochira wa** (*this is ...*). For example:

Kochira wa An Jenkinsu-san desu.	*This is Miss Anne Jenkins.*
Kochira wa Yamaguchi Takeshi-san desu.	*This is Takeshi Yamaguchi.*
Kochira wa Suzuki-san desu.	*This is Mr (Mrs / Miss) Suzuki.*

However, you don't use **kochira** when introducing members of your own family. In the dialogue, Reiko simply says about Takeshi:

Takeshi desu.	*He is Takeshi.*

7 *Formal and informal greetings*

Throughout the book you will learn a number of set phrases used by the Japanese in formal situations: meeting someone for the first time, visiting someone's home, apologising or saying thank you.

The words you use when greeting someone depend on the time of the day to some extent. **Konnichiwa** is often translated as *hello*, but first thing in the morning you would say **ohayō gozaimasu** (*good morning*) or **ohayō** to a friend or within the family. In the evening you would use **konbanwa** (*good evening*). **Konnichiwa** is used later in the morning through to early evening.

In the same way there are different phrases for saying *goodbye*, just as there are in English.

Sayōnara is translated as *goodbye* but traditionally is used more formally with people you don't know well or with people you don't normally see every day.

Oyasumi nasai (*good night*) is a useful farewell phrase to remember when it is later in the evening, or **oyasumi** to a friend or member of your family. There is also the more casual **ja mata ne** (*see you*).

Simply using **arigatō gozaimasu** (*thank you*) is quite appropriate if you are leaving someone's house or if they have done something for you.

✳ Hinto   *Hints*

Before you begin this section, go back to the conversation and listen to it or read it again. This should help to clarify all the new language you have learnt. If there is something you are still not sure about, look it up in the **Setsumei** section before proceeding to the **Renshū** section. Make this a habit for all the units – it will increase your confidence and improve your performance in the activities.

✔ ———— Renshū   *Practice* ————

In this section you have the opportunity to practise what you have learnt. This will involve a building-up process – later units will draw on material from earlier units so that each activity will be reinforcing what you have learnt so far as well as practising the new language items. It is therefore important to feel confident when you progress to this section that you have understood the new material. It doesn't matter if you haven't quite mastered it yet – these exercises will give you the opportunity for practice, repetition and self-testing in an enjoyable format.

1 Look at the pictures below of people greeting each other at different times of the day. Say out aloud the greeting you think they are saying to each other. Then check the answers at the back of the book to see if you were right.

Now play the greetings from the **Tango-hyō** section on the cassette once more, pause the tape after each one, and say it out aloud. (Alternatively, read the correct greetings out aloud.)

 2 Introduce these people to each other as in the example. (The Japanese names have been written in Japanese order, with the surnames first.)

Rei (*example*): Yamada Takeshi/Bill Smith
Kochira wa Yamada Takeshi-san desu. Kochira wa Bill Smith-san desu.

Now listen to the cassette and practise the pronunciation of the Japanese names.

3 Using the same people as in Exercise 2 practise saying how they would introduce themselves to each other as in the example:

Rei: Hajimemashite, Yamada Takeshi desu. Dōzo yoroshiku.
         Hajimemashite, Bill Smith desu. Dōzo yoroshiku.

Remember that people don't use **san** when talking about themselves.

4 Now the cassette will present you with several of the characters from this book, in turn. Each time, pause the tape after a character has spoken and introduce yourself to that person, saying: **Hajimemashite,** *(your name)* **desu. Dōzo yoroshiku**.

You can still introduce yourself if you don't have the cassette – speak out aloud and aim to say your introduction from memory.

5 On the cassette you are going to hear snippets of conversation. Note down which of the expressions below you hear and how many times. (If you don't have the cassette, see if you can say these words in Japanese from memory. Speak out aloud.)

(a) Good morning
(b) Good night

(c) Thank you
(d) Good afternoon
(e) Goodbye
(f) See you
(g) Good evening
(h) Excuse me
(i) How do you do?

6   Try to decide whether **san** should be used in the sentences below. Write **san** in the gap if you think it should be, and X if not.

(a) Hajimemashite, An Jenkinsu _____ desu.
(b) Kochira wa Yamaguchi Reiko _____ desu.
(c) Kochira wa Suzuki _____ desu ka.
(d) Sumimasen, Yamaguchi _____ desu ka.

☑ Tesuto   *Test*

1   What do you say to somebody

(a) first thing in the morning?
(b) when you meet them for the first time?
(c) last thing at night?
(d) if you want to catch their attention?

2   How would you introduce yourself to a Japanese person? (Make sure you say your name slowly and clearly.)

3   How would you introduce Anne Jenkins to somebody else?

2

IGIRISUJIN DESU
I'm British

In this unit you will learn

- how to count from 1–12
- the names of countries, languages and nationalities
- the names of the months of the year
- the names of some useful objects and loanwords
- how to ask for a word in Japanese

Hajime ni

In this unit you will be introduced to two main topics:

- Numbers and ways they are used
- Making a simple sentence – *I am, it/she/he is, they/we/you are* – using **desu**. You have already met **desu** in Unit 1.)

There are a number of new vocabulary items but you will notice that some of them sound very similar to English, for example **tēpu** is the word for cassette tape. This is because these are loanwords which the Japanese have 'borrowed' from other languages, and in particular from English. These loanwords are written in their own special script – you will learn more about this in Unit 13.

———————— # Hanashimashō ————————

1 Read out these Japanese loanwords and see if you can work out what they mean. You may need to read them out a few times.

(a) uisukii
(b) kēki
(c) aisukuriimu
(d) tēpu rekōdā
(e) sutereo
(f) kompyūtā
(g) basu

(h) takushii
(i) pantsu
(j) kōto
(k) beddo
(l) resutoran
(m) pen

Now, if you have the cassette, listen to the pronunciation on the tape and practise saying the words. This will help you to check that your answers are right. If you are still not sure about the meaning of some of the words, the answers are at the back of the book.

Nihon ni tsuite

Loanwords

The Japanese language and culture have been influenced and added to over the centuries by other countries. China was the major outside influence in the pre-modern era, but from the 1850s American and European influences became predominant. The British and American influence is seen in particular in the large number of English loanwords which have become a part of the Japanese language. Many of these words reflect the types of items which have been introduced from Europe and America and were not traditional to Japan.

For example, the Japanese traditionally slept on futon (a mattress laid out on the floor) but the western-style bed has become popular with young people and is called **beddo**. In the area of modern technology the Japanese usually have adopted western words, for example **kompyūtā** (*computer*) and **shii dii pureyā** (*CD player*), but the sound is changed to suit Japanese pronunciation and sometimes the word is shortened, for example, **terebi** (*television* – remember that there is no **v** sound in Japanese and it is pronounced b instead); **wā puro** (*word processor*). There is sometimes a Japanese and a loanword for the same item: chicken cooked in a Japanese style is called **toriniku**, but cooked in a western style is called **chikin**.

Tango-hyō

If you have the cassette, switch it on. Listen to one item of vocabulary at a time, pause the cassette and say the word out aloud, then move on to the next word.

If you don't have the cassette, read the hints below this vocabulary list and make sure you speak out aloud when practising your pronunciation of these new words.

Countries	Languages	Nationalities
Igirisu (England)	**Eigo** (English)	**Igirisu-jin** (English person)
Amerika (America/USA)	**Eigo**	**Amerika-jin**
Furansu (France)	**Furansu-go**	**Furansu-jin**
Doitsu (Germany)	**Doitsu-go**	**Doitsu-jin**
Itaria (Italy)	**Itaria-go**	**Itaria-jin**
Indo (India)	**Indo-go**	**Indo-jin**
Nihon (Japan)	**Nihon-go**	**Nihon-jin**
Chūgoku (China)	**Chūgoku-go**	**Chūgoku-jin**

Useful items

tokei	watch or clock
hon	book
empitsu	pencil
pen	pen

Useful phrases

... wa Nihon-go de nan desu ka	what is ... in Japanese?
nan desu ka	what is it?
shitsurei shimasu	pardon me for interrupting

Hinto: *Pronouncing loanwords*

- there is no l sound in Japanese, and the r sound is somewhere between an l and an r. If you can't understand a word with an r sound, say it with an l sound instead. For example:

    Hoteru   Hotelu   = hotel

- Often the **u** and **i** sounds are hardly voiced, as in the example of **hotel(u)** above.

- A **b** sound is used instead of a **v** sound:

terebi = *televi(sion)*
bideo = *video*

The *Pronunciation guide* in the *Introduction* to this book explains these and other pronunciation tips.

Kaiwa

Anne has settled into her new life with the Yamaguchi family and today is her first day at the Japanese language school. Her teacher, **Satō-sensei**, is getting the new students to introduce themselves to the whole class.

Satō-sensei	**Mina-san**, ohayō gozaimasu.
Class	Sensei, ohayō gozaimasu.
Satō-sensei	Hajimemashite, Satō desu. **Watashi wa** Nihon-jin desu. Dōzo yoroshiku. (*she points to Anne*) **Hai, dōzo**.
Anne	An desu. Watashi wa Igirisu-jin desu. Dōzo yoroshiku.
Next student	Tani desu. Furansu-jin desu. Dōzo yoroshiku.
Student 2	Ano ... Haidi desu. Doitsu **kara** desu. Dōzo yoroshiku.
Student 3	Sukotto desu. **Ē to**, ē to ... *America* wa Nihongo de nan desu ka.
Satō-sensei	*America* wa Nihongo de A-me-ri-ka desu.
Scott (*amidst laughter*)	Aa! so desu ka. Ja, Amerika kara desu. Dōzo yoroshiku.

A new student arrives late and Satō-sensei uses this opportunity to get the class to practise their Japanese with one another.

New student (*entering room*)	Shitsurei shimasu. (*he bows*)
Scott	**O-namae wa?**
New student	Han desu. Chūgoku-jin desu.
Anne (*looks puzzled*)	Chūgoku wa eigo de nan desu ka.
Han	*China* desu.

Satō-sensei now goes on to check how many everyday objects the students know.

Satō-sensei*(points to her watch)* **Kore wa** Nihongo de nan desu ka.
Han Tokei desu.
Scott (*looking at watch*) Nihon no tokei desu.
Satō-sensei Sō desu. (*picks up Anne's coat*) Kore wa nan desu ka.
Tani Kōto desu.
Scott (*showing off a bit*) Igirisu no kōto desu.
Anne Iie, **Sukottorando** no kōto desu **yo**.

mina-san	everybody
watashi wa	I
hai, dōzo	go ahead; there you are
kara	from
ē to	another hesitation word (*er, erm*)
o-namae wa?	what's your name?
kore wa	this
Sukottorando	Scotland
yo	I tell you, actually

Setsumei

1 Watashi wa Nihon-jin desu: *I am Japanese.*

Watashi means *I* and **anata** means *you*. There are other words for *he*, *we*, etc, but the Japanese tend not to use them unless it needs to be made clear who is being talked about.

When addressing other people it is more polite to use their name rather than **anata**, and unless you need to emphasise *I* you don't need to say **watashi**.

Wa is used after a word to show that that word is the 'topic' of whatever is being talked about. It can sometimes be translated as *as for* in English:

Watashi wa Amerika-jin desu. *I* (the topic) *am American.*
                                 (*As for me, I am American.*)
Haidi-san wa Doitsu   *Heidi* (the topic) *is from Germany.*
  kara desu.   (*As for Heidi, she comes
                                 from Germany.*)

Don't worry too much about understanding this just yet – you will
have the chance to learn and practise many more examples throughout the units, and the main thing now is to remember and use the
phrases.

2 O-namae wa?   *Your name?*

In point 1 above you learnt that when addressing people it is more
polite to use their name rather than **anata** (*you*). The Japanese language has other ways of avoiding the use of **anata**. One of these is the
use of **o** in front of certain words to make them sound more polite or
formal when you are addressing other people (you don't use it to talk
about yourself or members of your family). Here are some examples:

o-namae	*your name*
namae	*(my) name*
o-shigoto	*your job*
shigoto	*(my) job*

Remember: you can only use **o** in front of certain words. You will meet
more of these in future units.

3 Doitsu kara desu: *I'm from Germany.*

Kara means *from* and follows the word, unlike English where we say
from first. For example:

Tōkyō *kara*	**From** *Tokyo*
Furansu *kara*	**From** *France*
(Watashi wa) Igirisu *kara* desu.	*I'm **from** England.*
Uisukii wa Sukottorando	
** *kara* desu.**	*Whisky is **from** Scotland.*

4 **Nihon no tokei desu:** *It's a Japanese watch.*

No inserted between two words works something like **'s** in English:

| **An-san no kōto** | *Anne's coat* |
| **sensei no tēpu** | *the teacher's tape* |

It also gives the meaning of my, your, etc. For example:

| **watashi no tokei** | *my watch* |
| **anata no hon** | *your book* |

It connects an item with its owner, origin or language:

| **Igirisu no kōto** | *an English coat (a coat of / from England)* |
| **Doitsu-go no hon** | *a German (language) book* |

5 **Nihon-go de nan desu ka:** *What is it in Japanese?*

This is a useful phrase if you want to build up your vocabulary in Japanese and you are able to speak to a willing Japanese speaker. Also, if you don't understand a Japanese word you can say:

| **Eigo de nan desu ka.** | *What is it in English?* |

If you want to specify a word you put it at the beginning of the phrase followed by wa (you learnt something about **wa** in point 1 above). For example:

| **Book wa Nihon-go de nan desu ka.** | *What is **book** in Japanese? (As for **book**, what is it in Japanese?)* |

| **Tokei wa Eigo de nan desu ka.** | *What is **tokei** in English?* |

6 **Igirisu:** *England/Britain*

The Japanese use the word **Igirisu** to refer to Britain, although it does come from the word *England*. If you want to express Scotland, Wales or Ireland you can say **Sukottorando**, **Wēruzu**, **Airurando.**

7 Sūji: *Numbers (1–12)*

If you have the cassette, switch it on and listen to the pronunciation
of the numbers 1–12.

1	ichi	7	shichi (nana)
2	ni	8	hachi
3	san	9	ku (kyū)
4	shi (yon)	10	jū
5	go	11	jū-ichi
6	roku	12	jū-ni

 ### Hinto: *Remembering numbers*

You can use sound association for remembering new Japanese words.
Look at the suggestions below and then see if you can think of some
associations.

1	ichi	sounds like 'itchy'
2	ni	sounds like 'knee'
3	san	as in **san** – *Mr/Mrs*
4	shi	in 'she' (her)
5	go	go-ing somewhere
6	roku	a large rock(-u)

You will see that there are two ways of saying 4, 7 and 9. Learn **shi**,
shichi and **ku** first, but you will begin to see as we progress through the
book that there are times in each case when the alternative word is used.

The months of the year

Numbers are very useful in Japanese and are used in many ways.
The first use we are going to learn is in saying the months. The
Japanese call *January* 'one (first) month', *February* 'two (second)
month', and so on. Study the list below and practise saying the
months out loud.

ichi-gatsu (*January*)	shichi-gatsu (*July*)
ni-gatsu (*February*)	hachi-gatsu (*August*)
san-gatsu (*March*)	ku-gatsu (*September*)
shi-gatsu (*April*)	jū-gatsu (*October*)
go-gatsu (*May*)	jū-ichi-gatsu (*November*)
roku-gatsu (*June*)	jūni-gatsu (*December*)

✳ Hinto: Learning tip

You may have noticed that a dash (-) is used between the number and the word for month (**gatsu**) for example **ichi-gatsu**.

In the same way, a dash was placed between country and person (**Amerika-jin**), country and language (**Furansu-go**) and in counting numbers, between 10s and units (11 = **jū-ichi**). This is to help you at first to see how the new word is made up of two words. For example, **Doitsu-go** (*German*) is made from **Doitsu** (*Germany*) and **go** (*language*).

Once this idea has been introduced to you, the dash will no longer be used, as you will see in the **Renshū** below. If later you are unsure of any words, look the word up in the index at the back. It will tell you on which page the word was first introduced so you can refer back to it and see which two words it is derived from.

Denwa-bangō *Phone numbers*

Phone numbers are said using the individual digits **ichi**, **ni**, **san** ... **ku**. A dash between groups of numbers is usually spoken using **no**. 0 is pronounced as **zero** or **rei** (the **ze** of **zero** rhymes with the **he** of the name 'Helen'). For example:

> 0181-776-7333 = zero-ichi-hachi-ichi **no** nana-nana-roku **no** shichi-san-san-san

You usually use **nana** (not **shichi**) for 7, **yon** (not **shi**) for 4 and **kyū** (not **ku**) for 9, when saying phone numbers.

You should note that you have learnt two words for the word *number* in this unit: **sūji** is used to describe numbers that you count – 1, 2, 3, etc. **Bangō** is used to describe items or information that you number, such as phone, bus and room numbers.

 ───────── **Renshū** ─────────

1   Practise *saying out aloud* these Tokyo phone numbers, then check you have said them correctly against the answers in the back of the book. (Use **yon** (4), **nana** (7) and **kyū** (9).)

(a) 03-3276-5453   (c) 03-7762-1234
(b) 03-8893-3221   (d) 03-8283-4455

2 Kiku-renshū (*Listening practice*)

Satō-sensei finished off the first Japanese lesson by practising numbers. First of all, each of the students wrote down their Japanese family's phone number on the board, then Satō-sensei read them out but not always correctly. The students marked down whether they thought the numbers were read correctly or incorrectly. (She didn't say '03' because this is not needed when dialling within Tokyo.) Look at the table below, listen to the cassette and see if you can do the same exercise (or simply read the numbers out loud).

Student	Phone number	True/false
Anne	(03) 1353-0154	
Scott	(03) 9745-6622	
Tani	(03) 1898-1234	
Heidi	(03) 4222-6789	
Han	(03) 6969-5656	

Months

3 Kiku-renshū

Anne has been finding out the birthdays (**tanjōbi**) of her host family. Listen to the cassette and write down in English the birthday month of each member of the family.

Name	Month
(a) Reiko Yamaguchi	
(b) Mr Yamaguchi	
(c) Emi	
(d) Takeshi	

4 Match the Japanese months on the left with their English equivalent by drawing lines from one to the other.

sangatsu	*January*
shichigatsu	*February*
kugatsu	*March*
shigatsu	*April*
jūichigatsu	*May*
ichigatsu	*June*
gogatsu	*July*
jūnigatsu	*August*
rokugatsu	*September*
nigatsu	*October*
hachigatsu	*November*
jūgatsu	*December*

Now check your answers with the list on page 31.

 5 Kiku-renshū

Listen to the tape and write in English in the right hand column (Country/Nationality) which country each item/person comes from.

Item/Person	Country/Nationality
(a) Camera	
(b) Watch	
(c) Whiskey	
(d) Coat	
(e) Jean-san	
(f) Maria-san	

Hinto: Listening for specific information

Many of the listening activities contain extra vocabulary which you haven't learnt. Do not worry about understanding every word: the aim of the activities is to help you develop the important skill of scanning information and selecting the parts that you need.

Tesuto

1   How would you say these phrases in Japanese?

(a)   What is 'hat' in Japanese?

(b)   Pardon me for interrupting (when entering a room).

(c) I am English.

(d) It's a Japanese (language) book.

2 Crossword

How many words and phrases do you remember from the first two units? The clues are in English and you write the answers in Japanese. Try to do as many as possible from memory. **Gambatte!** (*good luck!*)

Yoko (*across*)

1 A greeting in the evening (8)

3 A Japanese person (8)

5 The word for *pencil* (7)

6 India (4)

9 Scott comes from this country (7)

11 The number 7 (6)

14 A farewell phrase (8)

15 Han comes from this country (7)

16 The word for *book* (3)

17 The number 12 (4)

19 A watch or clock (5)

20 See you! (2, 4, 2)

Tate (*down*)

1 September (7)

2 A casual thanks (7)

4 Britain or England (7)

7 Pleased to meet you:
   Dōzo _____ (9)

8 To catch someone's attention/
   say sorry (9)

10 *Hello* or *good afternoon* (10)

12 The Italian language (8)

13 A casual *goodnight* to friends/
   family (7)

18 *No* (3)

3 Write the answers to these sums in Japanese and English.

    (a)   ichi + san =

    (b)   go + ni =

    (c)   kyū – roku =

    (d)   jū – san =

3

O-SHIGOTO WA
NAN DESU KA
What is your occupation?

In this unit you will learn

- how to say what your job is
- how to talk about your interests
- how to say *I am not ...*
- how to count from 13–20
- different ways to count in Japanese

Hajime ni

In this unit you will be introduced to a common sentence pattern – a 'person/item' is 'something'. For example:

An-san *wa* Igirisujin *desu*.   *Anne is English.*
Kore *wa* tokei *desu*.   *This is a watch.*

The pattern in Japanese is: noun **wa** noun **desu**.

—————— Hanashimashō ——————

1 Using the pattern 'noun **wa** noun **desu**' can you make statements about these people's nationalities? Say them aloud. (The first one has been done for you in **Hajime ni**.)

Person	Nationality
Anne	English → An-san **wa** Igirisujin **desu**.
Scott	American
Han	Chinese
Takeshi	Japanese
Tani	French
Heidi	German

Tango-hyō

If you have the cassette, switch it on for practice of the new words and phrases. Try recording yourself and comparing your pronunciation with the cassette! This should help you to remember the new words too.

Next, read each word from the **Tango-hyō** out aloud, remembering all you have learnt from the *Pronunciation guide* and other tips. (Have a look back at the *guide* every now and again to refresh your memory). If you have a Japanese friend, ask him or her to say the words for you. If you can, record them so that you can listen to them and repeat back. It's good practice to get used to different voices speaking Japanese.

Occupations

shigoto	work
sensei	teacher, professor
kaisha-in	company worker/ employee
gakusei	student
seito	pupil
shufu	housewife
isha	doctor
haisha	dentist
ten'in	shop assistant
hisho	secretary

Interests

shumi	hobby
supōtsu	sports
sakkā	football
sukii	skiing
gorufu	golf
dokusho	reading
suiei	swimming
jōba	horse riding
dansu	dancing
engei	gardening
ikebana	flower arranging

Kazoku *Own family*

haha	mother
chichi	father
ani	older brother
otōto	younger brother

Counting people

nan-nin	how many people?
hitori	one person, alone
futari	two people
san-nin	three people
yo-nin	four people
nan (sometimes **nani**)	what?

Useful phrases

Mōichido itte kudasai.	Please say it again.
Yukkuri itte kudasai.	Please say it more slowly.

Kaiwa

Anne and her fellow classmates have brought in photos of their home-stay and real families to show to the class. Anne is talking about the Yamaguchi family.

Anne	Kochira wa Yamaguchi Masaki-san desu. Yamaguchi san wa kaisha-in desu. Shumi wa sukii **to** gorufu desu.
Tani (*pointing to photo*)	Kochira wa **donata** desu ka.
Anne	Ano, Takeshi-kun desu. Takeshi-kun wa gakusei desu. Shumi wa suiei desu.
Heidi	**Go-kazoku** wa **zembu de** nan-nin desu ka.
Anne	Zembu de yo-nin desu.
Scott	Sumimasen, mōichido itte kudasai. Nan-nin desu ka.
Anne	Yo-nin desu.

Next Tani passes round photos of her own family and holds up one to discuss.

Tani	**Kono hito** wa haha desu. Haha wa isha desu. Shumi wa dokusho desu. Kono hito wa Henri desu. Henri wa ani desu. Shumi wa jōba desu.
Han (*points to photo*)	Kochira **mo** Henri-san desu ka.
Tani (*blushing*)	Iie, Henri **ja arimasen**. Watashi no **bōi-furendo** desu.
Scott	Nani...? Yukkuri itte kudasai.

to	and
donata	who
go-kazoku	someone else's family
zembu de	altogether
kono hito	this person

mo	also, too
ja arimasen	is not
bōifurendo	boyfriend

Now go over the dialogue once more, play the cassette or read the dialogue line by line and say it out aloud. Pay particular attention to how you say the words with double consonants, that is **yukkuri** (*slowly*) and **itte** (*say*). You pause slightly before the **kk** and before the **tt** (as you would when saying the English word *headdress* – see *Pronunciation guide*, page 11).

 ───────────── **Setsumei** ─────────────

1 Takeshi-kun wa gakusei desu: *Takeshi is a (school) student.*

We have already talked about and practised the pattern 'noun **wa** noun **desu**', and in the dialogue you have come across more ways of using it when talking about jobs and hobbies. For example:

Kono hito wa haha desu.	*This (person) is my mother.*
Haha wa isha desu.	*My mother is a doctor.*
Shumi wa dokusho desu.	*(Her) hobby is reading.*

Remember that you learnt in Unit 2 (setsumei 1, page 28) that **wa** highlights the word that is the topic. It can sometimes be translated as *as for*. For example:

Shumi wa dokusho desu.	*As for her hobby, it is reading.*
Shigoto wa isha desu.	*As for her job, she is a doctor.*

2 Kochira wa donata desu ka: *Who is this?*

Donata means *who* and is a more polite version of the question word **dare** which also means *who*. **Donata** would be used on more formal occasions. In English this phrase might translate as: *Might I ask who this is?*

3 Kochira mo Henri-san desu ka: *Is this also Henri? (Is this Henri as well?)*

Mo means *also* and is used as follows.

(a) Tani Watashi wa gakusei desu.   *I am a student.*
     Anne Watashi **mo** gakusei desu.   *I am **also** a student.*
     (*I am a student **too**.*)

(b) **Satō-sensei wa Nihonjin desu.**   *Mrs Sato is Japanese.*
     Takeshi-kun *mo* Nihonjin desu. *Takeshi is Japanese as well.*

(c) **Ani wa kaisha-in desu.**   *My older brother is a*
                                       company worker.

   Otōto *mo* kaisha-in desu.   *My younger brother is a*
                                       company worker too.

You can also use **mo** in this way:

   An-san *mo* Tani-san *mo*   *Both Anne and Tani are students.*
     gakusei desu.
   Takeshi-kun *mo* Satō-sensei   *Both Takeshi and Mrs Sato*
     ***mo* Nihonjin desu.**   *are Japanese.*

4 Kono hito wa haha desu: *This person is my mother.*

Japanese people show respect for other people outside their family by using polite words and phrases. For example, you learnt in Unit 1 that **san** is attached to a name when you address someone else. And you learnt in Unit 2 that **o** is sometimes attached to certain words when talking to other people (**o-namae** – *your name*).

In contrast, Japanese people use words which are more 'humble' (or modest) to talk about themselves and their families. Therefore, Tani doesn't say **kochira wa** ... (*this person*) when talking about her mother. Instead she says **kono hito** which is a more everyday word for *this person*.

5 Iie, Henri ja arimasen: *No, he's not Henri.*

To say *is not, am not, are not*, etc., in Japanese you use **ja arimasen** or the more polite version, **dewa arimasen**. For example:

Tokei ja arimasen.	*It is not a watch.*
Ichigatsu ja arimasen.	*It's not January. It's February.*
Nigatsu desu.	

To say *was* or *were* in Japanese you change **desu** to **deshita**. For example:

Chichi wa haisha deshita.	*My father was a dentist.*
Sensei wa Furansujin deshita.	*My teacher was French.*

And to say *wasn't* or *weren't* you use **ja arimasen deshita** (or **dewa arimasen deshita**). Here is a list of these expressions which you can refer back to.

am / is / are	*was / were*	*am not / is not / are not*	*was not / were not*
desu	**deshita**	**ja/dewa arimasen**	**ja/dewa arimasen deshita**

6 Haha mo chichi mo isha desu. *Both my mother and father are doctors.*

There is an important difference here between Japanese and English. In English we say *one doctor* but *two doctors*, in other words we have a singular and a plural, but generally in Japanese there is no difference between one or more than one of something, and as you saw in **setsumei** 5 above **desu** covers all the different words we use in English (*is*, *are*, *am*). This of course is good news for Japanese language learners because it means you have fewer words and changes to remember.

7 Nan-nin desu ka. Yo-nin desu: *How many people are there? There are four.*

Counting people

When you learnt the months of the year in Unit 2 you learnt that you simply add the numbers **ichi**, **ni**, **san** ... to the word **gatsu** (*month*). For example: **ichigatsu** ('first month' which is *January*). Japanese uses a similar method when counting people: **nin** means *person / people* (remember, there is no plural) and **san-nin** means *three people*.

However, when saying one person you use **hitori**, and for *two people* you use **futari**. Also, the word for *four* (**yon**) is shortened to **yo**.

To ask *how many people?* you say **nan-nin desu ka**. (**Nan** means *what* but translates better as *how many* in this case.)

8 Mōichido itte kudasai: *Please say it again.*

When you haven't understood all that is being said to you, this is a polite way of asking the speaker to repeat the information. **Yukkuri itte kudasai** is a way of getting the person to speak a little slower. You can say **sumimasen** first to be more polite. For example:

Sumimasen, mōichido itte kudasai. *Excuse me but would you mind saying that again please.*

9 Shumi wa suiei desu: *His hobby is swimming.*

This is another example of the pattern you were introduced to in **Hajime ni**. A word for *his*, *her*, *my*, etc. is not needed when it is understood who is being talked about. Here are some more examples:

Shumi wa engei desu. *(His) hobby is gardening.*
Shumi wa dansu desu. *(Her) hobby is dancing.*
Shumi wa ... desu. *My hobby is ... (say your hobby)*

10 Sūji: *Numbers (13–20)*

❇ Hinto

Once you have mastered the numbers 1–10 you can count to 99 using combinations of the first 10 numbers. You have already learnt that 11 is **jū-ichi**, i.e. 10 + 1, and 12 is **jū-ni**, i.e. 10 + 2. Try and work out and say out aloud how to count from 13–19, then look at the list below.

13	jū-san	17	jū-shichi (jū-nana)
14	jū-shi (jū-yon)	18	jū-hachi
15	jū-go	19	jū-kyū (jū-ku)
16	jū-roku	20	ni-jū

The number for 20 (**ni-jū**) is the reverse of 12 (**jū-ni**). A rule to help you to remember which is which is to think of the order like this:

10 + 2 = 12 (**jū-ni**), and 2 x 10 = 20 (**ni-jū**).

In the same way you can work out 30, 40, 50 ...

3 x 10 = 30 = **san-jū**; 4 x 10 = 40 = **yon-jū** (**yon** is always used for 40, not **shi**)

Work out 50–90, say them out aloud and write them down. This will prepare you for Unit 4.

Renshū

1 **Kiku-renshū**

On the tape you are going to hear some Japanese people talk about their families, their work and their interests. As you listen to the tape, write down in English the information required on the table below.

Name	Number in family	Occupation	Interests
(a)			
(b)			
(c)			
(d)			

2 Imagine you have joined a Japanese class and have been asked to introduce all the members to each other. Look at the pictures of the class members below and read the information about them, then introduce each of them out aloud. The first one has been done for you.

Rei: (Steven Richards, student, likes sport)

Kochira wa Steven Richards-san desu. Steven-san wa gakusei desu. Shumi wa supōtsu desu.

Susan Bond, housewife, hobby is dancing

Rei: (a) (b) Andrew Wal shop assistai football

(c) Peter O'Connor doctor, golf

(d) John Rogers, company employee

3 Tani's Japanese homework is to write out the Japanese occupations next to their English equivalent. However, she's got them confused. Imagine you are talking to her and help her to correct her work, following the example. Remember to speak out aloud.

Rei: *Secretary* = kaishain   Iie, kaishain ja arimasen. Hisho desu.

(a) Doctor   = gakusei
(b) Housewife   = haisha
(c) Shop assistant = seito
(d) Student   = isha

4 Kiku-renshū – Sūji

Listen to the cassette and write down in numbers the answers to the questions below:

(a) Takeshi's age _____
(b) Heidi's age _____
(c) The bus number _____
(d) Anne's home phone number _____
(e) Mr Yamaguchi's work phone number _____

(f) The number of people in Han's family _____
(g) Reiko's birthday month _____

5 Make the pairs of sentences below into one sentence using **mo ... mo** (*both ... and*), as in the example. Speak out aloud.

Rei: Takeshi-kun wa seito desu. Jun-kun wa seito desu.
= Takeshi-kun mo Jun-kun mo seito desu.

(a) An-san wa gakusei desu. Haidi-san wa gakusei desu.
(b) Tani-san wa Furansujin desu. Henri-san wa Furansujin desu.
(c) Haha wa haisha desu. Chichi wa haisha desu.

☑ *Tesuto*

1 Read out aloud the sequence of numbers below.

7, 17, 12, 20, 14, 2, 9, 13, 16, 40, 50, 60

2 How would you ask someone

(a) to repeat something?
(b) to speak more slowly?

3 **Chichi wa isha desu** means:

(a) My father is a secretary.
(b) My hobby is reading.
(c) My father is a doctor.

4 How would you say in Japanese: *I am not a teacher. I am a student*?

5 Count numbers of people backwards in sequence, beginning with **gonin**.

6 Imagine you are introducing yourself to a Japanese person. Give as much information as you can (name, occupation, interests). Speak out aloud.

✳ Hinto: *Remembering new words*

You have already been introduced to a number of new words in the first three units. You may find it very useful at this stage to start organising your own 'dictionary'. You could buy a small exercise book or even arrange vocabulary alphabetically in an address book-style notebook. If you have a PC, why not set up a list of vocabulary on this?

Include in your dictionary the 'tango-hyō' and 'tango' sections from units 1–3 and the loanwords in Unit 2; then as you work through the book, continue to add new words at the end of each unit. Different people learn in different ways, but you may want to try grouping items of vocabulary by theme (family, occupations, food, etc.) or alphabetically, to help you remember them.

You may also find it useful to start your own English–Japanese glossary. Arrange the English meanings of new words alphabetically in a notebook (or on your PC) and write the Japanese next to them. This will enable you to quickly look up words for completing activities and texts and, in general, will help you in expressing yourself in Japanese.

4

KAZOKU WA GONIN DESU
— *There are five people* —
in my family

In this unit you will learn

- how to talk about dates and birthdays
- how to say how old you are
- how to talk about your family
- how to count from 21–99

Hajime ni

You have already met some words for family members in Units 1 and 3. You will have noticed in Unit 3 that there are different words for *older* and *younger* brother. There are also different words for *older* and *younger* sister, and for when you talk about your own family or someone else's. This may seem like a lot of extra vocabulary, but take it step by step, starting with the words that are relevant to your own family.

———— Hanashimashō ————

1 Using the title of this unit, how would you say *there are 6 people in my family*?

2 How would you say how many people there actually are in your family?
3 Look back on Units 1 and 3 and find out:

 (a) how Takeshi says *mother* (Unit 1, page 15)
 (b) how Tani talks about her mother and older brother (Unit 3, page 39)
 (c) the word for *younger brother* (Unit 3, page 38)
 (d) how Heidi says *your family* to Anne (Unit 3, page 39).

Nihon ni tsuite

The in-group versus outsiders

The Japanese distinguish between the group they belong to, the 'in-group' (family, company, etc.), and the 'out-group' (other families, companies, foreigners, etc.). When referring to the in-group, they use language which expresses humility, and when referring to the out-group they use language which expresses politeness and deference.

This is illustrated well in the words used for family members. For example, when you talk to someone outside your family about your mother you use the humble word **haha**, whereas when you talk about someone else's mother you use the polite word **okaasan**. And when you talk of your own family you say **kazoku**, but for someone else's family you add the respect word **go** and say **go-kazoku**.

However, when Japanese people talk directly to their family they use the polite rather than the humble words. For example, Takeshi in Unit 1 calls his mother **Okaasan**.

Tango-hyō

If you have the cassette, use it as you did in Units 1–3 to listen to and practise saying out aloud the new words, then read through the complete list.

If you don't have the cassette, say each new word out aloud and read through the pronunciation tips at the end of the **Tango-hyō**.

Own family		Someone else's family
kazoku	family	go-kazoku
shujin	husband	go-shujin

kanai	wife	**okusan**
musume	daughter	**musume-san**
musuko	son	**musuko-san**
haha	mother	**okaasan**
chichi	father	**otōsan**
ani	older brother	**oniisan**
ane	older sister	**oneesan**
imōto	younger sister	**imōto-san**
otōto	younger brother	**otōto-san**
nan sai desu ka	how old are you?	
sai	age	
gojū sai	50 years old	
tanjōbi	birthday	

✳ Hinto:

Pay attention to the long sounds and make sure they last twice as long as single syllables. Here are some examples to help you. Each sound should smoothly run into the next; they shouldn't sound disjointed. Speak them out aloud.

otōto (*younger brother*)	o-to-u-to
imōto (*younger sister*)	i-mo-u-to
okaasan (*mother*)	o-ka-a-sa-n (pronounce **ka-a** like *car* with a long *a*)
o-nee-e-sa-n (*older sister*)	o-ne-e-sa-n (pronounce **ne-e** like *ney*)
ane (*older sister*)	a-ne
okusan (*wife*)	o-k(u)-sa-n (**u** is almost unvoiced; sounds like **oxan**)

Kaiwa

Anne is telling the Yamaguchi's about her family and showing them some photos.

Reiko (*studying a photo*) Otōsan desu ka.
Anne   Ē, sō desu.
Reiko   **Wakai** desu ne.
Anne   Sō desu ka. Chichi wa gojū-sai desu.
Emi   Kochira wa donata desu ka.

Anne	Imōto desu. Imōto wa gakusei desu.
Emi	**Kawaii** desu ne. Imōto-san wa nansai desu ka.
Anne	Jūroku-sai desu. **Are**, tanjōbi wa shichigatsu deshita. Ja, jūnana-sai desu.
Takeshi	Kochira wa okaasan desu ka.
Anne	Ē, so desu. Haha wa nijūni-sai desu.
Takeshi	Are! Okaasan wa nansai desu ka. Mōichido itte kudasai.
Anne	Nijūni-sai desu.
Takeshi	**Demo** ... An-san mo nijūni-sai desu ne?
Emi (*admist laughter*)	Takeshi-kun! **Jōdan** desu yo.

ē	yes (softer than **hai**)
wakai	(looks) young
kawaii	pretty, cute
are	(expression of surprise)
demo	but
jōdan	joke

Sūji   *Numbers 21–99*

In Unit 3 you learnt how to say 20, 30, etc. by remembering this rule:

$2 \times 10 = 20 = $ ni-jū

30	sanjū		70	nanajū
40	yonjū		80	hachijū
50	gojū		90	kyūjū
60	rokujū			

To say 21, 22, etc. you simply add **ichi**, **ni**, etc. after **nijū**:

21	nijūichi	22	nijūni	23	nijūsan
24	nijūyon (shi)	25	nijūgo	26	nijūroku
27	nijūnana (shichi)	28	nijūhachi	29	nijūkyū (ku)

Now you can count from 0–99. Practise in short spurts – try 20–30, then 30–40, etc. The main thing is to keep counting until you begin to feel more confident. There will be lots of opportunities throughout the units to keep practising and testing yourself on the numbers.

Setsumei

1 Imōto-san wa nansai desu ka: *How old is your younger sister?*

In Unit 2 you learnt **nan desu ka** (*what is it?*). **Nan** means *what*, and if you attach **sai** to it you form the question word **nansai** – *what age?* or *how old? In the same way, you can ask *what month is it?* (**nangatsu desu ka**) and *how many people?* (**nannin desu ka**). You will add to these question words as you progress through the units.

To answer, you simply attach the number to **sai**: *I am 14* = **Watashi wa jūyon-sai desu**. Be careful with ages which end in 1, 8 or 10, for example, 11, 18, 30. The numbers are shortened to:

11 = **jūissai**
18 = **jūhassai**
28 = **nijū hassai**
10 = **jussai**
30 = **sanjussai**, etc.

Also, the age of 20 (when Japanese people come of age) has its own special word: **hatachi**.

Jane-san wa hatachi desu. *Jane is 20.*

Practise saying these ages before you move on to point 2 below. Cover up the Japanese, then check if you are right.

(a)	15 years old (**jūgo-sai desu**)	(b)	25 years old (**nijūgo-sai desu**)
(c)	44 years old (**yonjūyon-sai desu**)	(d)	18 years old (**jūhassai desu**)

2 Go-kazoku wa nannin desu ka: *How many people are in your family?*

(a) You've been introduced to a lot of words for family members and you're not expected to learn them all in one go! Start by learning to describe your own family using Anne's family as a model.

Anne *Kazoku wa gonin desu. Haha, chichi, ane, imōto **to watashi** desu.*

(**to watashi** = *and me*; say *and me* last.) Now work out how to describe your own family.

(b) If you have two brothers use **futari no**:
futari no ani (*two older brothers*);
futari no musuko (*two sons*).
Three is **sannin no**: **sannin no ane** (*three older sisters*).

(c) You can then expand this by giving information on their age:

Ane wa nijūgo-sai desu.   My older sister is 25.
Watashi wa yonjūgo-sai desu.   I am 45.

3 Watashi no tanjōbi wa nigatsu jūhachi-nichi desu: *My birthday is February 18th*

You learnt how to say the months in Japanese in Unit 2. Now you are going to learn the dates. This is done by adding **nichi** (*day*) to the number. Say the dates in the table on the next page out aloud to familiarise yourself with them.

11th jūichi-nichi	18th jūhachi-nichi	25th nijūgo-nichi
12th jūni-nichi	19th jūku-nichi	26th nijūroku-nichi
13th jūsan-nichi	20th **hatsuka**	27th nijūshichi-nichi
14th jū**yokka**	21st nijūichi-nichi	28th nijūhachi-nichi
15th jūgo-nichi	22nd nijūni-nichi	29th nijūku-nichi
16th jūroku-nichi	23rd nijūsan-nichi	30th sanjū-nichi
17th jūshichi-nichi	24th nijū**yokka**	31st sanjūichi-nichi

Notice that 14th, 20th and 24th differ, in the same way that in English we say 1st, 2nd and 3rd rather than 1th, 2th, 3th.

You are probably wondering where 1st–10th are. You will learn these in Unit 9 because they follow a different rule to the one above. If your own birthday is between 1st and the 10th, however, look at page 118.

When you say a date in Japanese you always say the month first and then the date. For example:

13th May = Gogatsu, jūsan-nichi

In English we have the choice between 13th May and May 13th, but there is no such choice in Japanese.

 ——————————— **Renshū** ———————————

 1 Kiku-renshū
The odd one out. Look at the sequence of numbers below as you listen to the tape and circle the number which is *not* said on the tape.

(a) 3, 5, 9, 2, 8, 10
(b) 11, 17, 15, 17, 19, 14
(c) 21, 31, 41, 51, 61, 91
(d) 98, 89, 56, 65, 88
(e) 1, 11, 20, 12, 21, 2
(f) 6, 9, 66, 99, 81, 88

 2 Kiku-renshū
Dates. Look at the groups of dates below as you listen to the tape and circle the one(s) you hear.

(a) 18th, 28th, 11th
(b) 16th, 20th, 23rd
(c) 14th, 24th
(d) 21st, 31st, 27th, 17th

3 Below are the birthday dates of some of the characters you have met so far. Say out aloud the dates as in the example. (The dates with * are ones which are said differently – be careful!).

Rei: Anne, February 18th = An-san no tanjōbi wa nigatsu jūhachi-nichi desu.

(a) Scott, May 11th
(b) Tani, August 21st
(c) Heidi, November 20th*
(d) Han, September 25th
(e) Takeshi, January 14th*
(f) Emi, April 30th

Now say your own birthday out aloud: **watashi no ...**

4 Family trees
Below are the family trees of Scott, Tani, Mr Yamaguchi and Satō-sensei. Take the place of each of these people and describe 'your' family tree as in the example ('you' are underlined).

Rei: Mother, father (50), older sister (25), younger sister (17), <u>Anne</u> (22) = Kazoku wa gonin desu. Haha, chichi, ane, imōto to watashi desu.

○ = male   △ = female

5   Using the family trees in Exercise 4, give the ages of each member (where you have the information), once more pretending each is your own family. Don't forget to include 'yourself'.

Rei: (Anne's family) Chichi wa gojū-sai desu. Ane wa nijūgo-sai desu ...

6   Try Exercise 5 again, but this time you are yourself and so you must use the words for other people's family:

Rei: (Anne's family) Otōsan wa gojū-sai desu ...

7   **Kiku-renshū**
Families. Below are some pictures of families labelled (a)–(e). You will hear four descriptions of families on the tape (1–4). As you listen, look at the pictures, decide in each case which is being described and write the appropriate number underneath. The speaker is marked **watashi**.

8   Practise saying and write out a brief introduction to your family including their ages, interests, birthdays and occupations where possible.

☑ Tesuto

1   Read the months and dates below out aloud:

(a) March 29th
(b) August 11th
(c) December 25th
(d) 13th January*
(e) 31st May*
(*Be careful! – Remember the Japanese order.)

2   Draw lines connecting the words below to their English equivalent.

haha	*three sons*
ane	*someone else's mother*
okaasan	*someone else's father*
kazoku	*own mother*
futari no imōto	*own older sister*
sannin no musuko	*own family*
otōsan	*two younger sisters*

3   Say out aloud this sequence of numbers.

99, 98, 97, 96, 95, 94, 93, 92, 91 ...

Can you count backwards to 1?!

5

IMA NANJI DESU KA
What time is it?

In this unit you will learn

- how to tell the time
- some useful shopping phrases
- saying *this* and *that*
- opening and closing times

Hajime ni

You learnt in the last unit that **nan** (*what*) is attached to words to make questions, for example, **nansai desu ka** (*how old (what age) are you?*). When you attach **nan** to **ji** you form the question **nanji desu ka** (*what time is it?*). To answer, you replace nan with a number, for example, **goji desu** means *it is 5 o'clock*.

You are also going to use a new word, **kudasai** – *may I (have)*, for example, **hon o kudasai** (*may I have the book*), **biiru o kudasai** (*may I have a beer* or simply *a beer please*).

Hanashimashō

1 Look at the clock times below and work out how to say the time for each one.

Rei: Ni-ji

2 Ask if you may have the objects below using the phrase **... o kudasai**. The first one is done for you.

Rei: (a) Shimbun o kudasai.

Tango-hyō

Read through the new words below, saying each one out aloud. There are some pronunciation tips after the **Tango-hyō** to help you.

Shopping phrases

... o kudasai	may I have ... (or '... please')
... o misete kudasai	please may I see ...
kore	this one

---

kono	this
sore	that one
sono	that
are	that one over there
ano	that over there
dore	which one
dono	which
ōkii	big
chiisai	small
chōdo ii	just right
chotto	a little, a bit
motto	more
motto chiisai	smaller
irasshaimase	welcome! (said by shop assistants and traders)
shōshō omachi kudasai	please wait a moment (very formal)
dewa (sometimes shortened to ja)	right! (when you've made up your mind)
kara	from
made	until
depāto	department store
sūpā	supermarket
kanjō	bill (in a restaurant, etc)

✳ Hinto:

Say the sounds smoothly; each sound should run into the next:

misete (*show me*)	mi-se-te
kore (*this*)	ko-re (remember that the **r** is soft; it comes between **l** and **r** in sound)
are (*that over there*)	a-re
irasshaimase (*welcome*)	i-ra- (slight pause) sha-i-ma-se
shōshō (*a little*)	sho-u-sho-u
made (*until*)	ma-de

Kaiwa

Reiko has taken Anne and Emi shopping in a Tokyo department store. Anne needs a new watch.

Assistant Irasshaimase!

Anne (*points to display in front of assistant*) Sono tokei o misete kudasai.

Assistant	Hai, dōzo.
Anne (*tries on watch*)	Chotto ōkii desu. (*Points to the window display*) Ano tokei mo misete kudasai.
Assistant	Shōshō omachi kudasai. (*returns with watch*) Dōzo. (*Anne tries on watch*)
Emi	Sore wa chiisai desu ka.
Anne	Iie, chōdo ii desu.
Emi	Sono tokei wa **suteki** desu ne.
Anne	Sō desu ne. Dewa, kore o kudasai.
Assistant	Hai, arigatō gozaimasu.

Later they are having lunch in a coffee shop.

Reiko	An-san, Nihongo no kurasu wa nanji kara desu ka.
Anne	Ni-ji kara desu.
Emi	Ima nanji desu ka.
Anne (*looks proudly at watch*)	Ichi-ji han desu... Are! Kurasu wa **mō sugu** desu.
Reiko	An-san! **Hayaku!** (*to the waitress*) O-kanjō o onegaishimasu.

suteki	smart, fashionable
mō sugu	soon
hayaku	quick, hurry up
onegaishimasu	please

Nihon ni tsuite

Gift-wrapping

When you buy a gift in Japan the shop assistant will gift-wrap it for you as a free part of the service. Gift-wrapping is quite an art and the assistant with a few deft folds will produce a beautifully wrapped article, complete with a ribbon tied around it and a gift card.

———————— **Setsumei** ————————

1 Irasshaimase: *Welcome (May I help you?)*

Japanese shop assistants may use very formal Japanese phrases when dealing with customers. We have met two such phrases in the passage – **irasshaimase** and **shōshō omachi kudasai**. You don't have to use these phrases, but be aware that you may hear them if you go to Japan.

2 Sono tokei: *That watch*

You will notice two main points about saying *this* and *that* in Japanese from the **Tango-hyō**. Firstly, there are two sets of words. For example, both **kore** and **kono** mean *this*. Think of **kore** as meaning *this one*. Anne says **Dewa, kore o kudasai** (*Right! I'll have this (one) please*). **Kono**, on the other hand, is followed directly by the item it describes: **kono tokei o kudasai** means *may I have **this** watch* please. Similarly, **sore** means *that (one)* and **sono** means *that*. Here are some examples:

Sore o misete kudasai. *Please show me that (one).*
Sono hon o misete kudasai. *Please show me that book.*

Also note:

Are o kudasai. *I'll have that (one) over there.*
Ano tokei o kudasai. *I'll have that watch over there.*

This last example takes us on to the second point. Whereas in English we have two words, *this* and *that*, in Japanese there is a third – **are** (or **ano**), meaing *that one over there*. The item in this case is at a distance from the person speaking and the person being spoken to.

The two pictures below will help you to understand how this works; they also illustrate how **kore**, **sore** and **are** (**kono**, **sono** and **ano**) are used from the *speaker's* point of view. The first picture shows Anne's point of view, and the second picture shows the shopkeeper's.

1 (a) Kore/ Kono tokei (b) Sore/ Sono tokei (c) Are/ ano tokei

2 (b) Sore/ Sono tokei (a) Kore/ Kono tokei (c) Are/ ano tokei

To ask *which one?* (*which watch?*) you say **dore (dono tokei?)** and this is the same for all three positions (a, b and c in the pictures).

Now read through the **Kaiwa** again with this in mind.

3 ... o kudasai/... o misete kudasai: *May I have/may I see ...*

These are two useful and easy-to-use phrases for shopping (and for other situations too). You simply put the object at the beginning of the phrase:

Kōhii o kudasai.	*May I have some coffee?*
Eigo no shimbun o kudasai.	*May I have an English newspaper?*
***Shashin* o misete kudasai.**	*May I see the **photo** please?*

4 Ima nanji desu ka: *What time is it (now)?*

In **Hanashimashō** in this unit you were introduced to telling the time. Let's practise now, using the clocks below as prompts. Put your hands over the times, say each time out aloud, then check to see if you are right by looking at the times below each clock.

Ichiji Niji Sanji Yoji*

Shichiji** Kuji† Jūichiji Jūniji

*For 4 o'clock you say **yoji** (not **yon** or **shi**).
Use **shichi not **nana**.
†For 9 o'clock use **ku** (not **kyū**).

5 Ichiji han desu: *It's half-past one.*

Saying *half-past* is straightforward too; just add **han** (*half-past*) after **ji**.

(a) Niji han desu. (b) Yoji han desu. (c) Kuji han desu. (d) Jūichiji han desu.

❋ Hinto

By practising saying the time you are revising two things: the numbers 1–12 and times. Practise saying the times first in numerical order – 1 o'clock, half-past one, 2 o'clock, etc. Then make your practice real – get into the habit of saying the time in Japanese whenever you notice that the real time is on the hour or half-past. Finding opportunities to use Japanese in real situations is one of the best ways to remember it and to feel that you are making real progress.

6 Niji kara desu: *(It's) from 2 o'clock.*

Kara means *from* (you first met this in Unit 2, setsumei 3, (page 29) and **made** means *to/until*. They can take on the meaning of *starts/opens at* and *finishes/closes at*. For example:

Nihongo no kurasu wa niji kara goji made desu.
The Japanese class is from 2 o'clock until 5 o'clock.

Depāto wa kuji kara rokuji made desu.
The department store opens at 9 and closes at 6.

Notice that **kara** and **made** are placed *after* the time:

kuji *kara*   *from 9*
rokuji *made*   *until 6*

Kara and **made** are not just used with the time of day. For example, you can say:

nigatsu kara rokugatsu made   *From February to June (time of year)*
Igirisu kara Nihon made   *From England to Japan (place)*

7 Gozen/gogo

If you want to distinguish between *a.m.* and *p.m.* when saying the time, use **gozen** (*a.m.*) and **gogo** (*p.m.*). These are spoken before the time:

Ima gozen hachiji desu.   *It's now 8 a.m.*
Shigoto wa gogo goji han made desu.   *My work finishes at 5.30 p.m.*

Gogo also means *afternoon (after midday)*:

Nihongo no kurasu wa gogo desu.   *The Japanese class is in the afternoon.*

Renshū

 1 **Kiku-renshū**

Furansu wa ima nan ji desu ka: *What time is it in France now?*
Takeshi is doing his geography homework. He has to work out the
time differences between Japan and a number of other countries.
Listen to the tape and write down the times next to the countries.

(a) Japan
(b) England
(c) France
(d) Germany
(e) New York
(f) San Francisco

 2 **Kiku-renshū**

In the left-hand column below there is a list of places/events, and
in the right-hand column there is a list of times/dates. Listen to
the tape and match the places and events with the information on
the right.

(a) Department store	(i)	11th–27th
(b) Work	(ii)	8.30–4.30
(c) Supermarket	(iii)	8.30–6 p.m.
(d) School (**gakkō**)	(iv)	9 a.m.–8 p.m.
(e) Holiday (**yasumi**)	(v)	11th–14th
(f) Ski tour (**sukii tsuā**)	(vi)	9 a.m.–12.30

3 On the next page you have some information in Japanese about
Japanese classes run by volunteers for non-Japanese people living
in Tama city in Japan. You won't be able to read most of the
information but you will be able to pick out the starting and fin-
ishing times of the three different classes.

Say out aloud these times using **kara** and **made**, as well as the
words for *a.m.* and *p.m.* The name of the class is provided for you
in Japanese.

(a) Getsuyō kurasu (*Monday class*) = Getsuyō kurasu wa...
(b) Kinyō kurasu (*Friday class*)
(c) Doyō kurasu (*Saturday class*)

(d) クラス：月曜クラス　（1 0：0 0 a m〜1 2：0 0 a m）多摩センター地区市民ホール

(e) 　　　金曜クラス　（ 7：0 0 p m〜 9：0 0 p m）多摩市役所第二庁舎 (ボランティアセンター) 2 F

(f) 　　　土曜クラス　（ 2：0 0 p m〜 4：0 0 p m）多摩市役所第二庁舎 (ボランティアセンター) 2 F

4   Scott is trying to increase his Japanese vocabulary by asking you the name of things around the room. Answer his questions using the information given below – make sure you use **kore**, **sore** and **are** correctly.

Rei:

Scott　Kore wa Nihongo de nan desu ka.
You　　Sore wa Eigo no hon desu.

(a)

　　　Scott　　Are wa Nihongo de nan desu ka.
　　　You　　　...

(b)

　　　Scott　　Sore wa Nihongo de nan desu ka.
　　　You　　　...

(c)

　　　　　　　　　　　Scott　　Kore wa Nihongo de
　　　　　　　　　　　　　　　nan desu ka.
　　　　　　　　　　　You　　　...

(d)

> Scott   Sore wa Nihongo de nan desu ka.
> You   ...

5   Read out aloud the items on the menu below and see if you can work out what they are in English (answers are at the back of the book).

Nomimono (drinks)
Kōhii
Miruku
Biiru
Aisukōhii
Jūsu

***

Tabemono (food)
Sandoitchi*
Supagetti
Piza
Aisukuriimu
Kēki

---

*Pronunciation tip: **sa-n-do-i** (slight pause) **chi**

Now imagine that you are at a restaurant with Anne. Can you fill in your part of the dialogue?

Waiter	Irasshaimase.
You	*Ask to see the menu –* **menyū**
Anne	Kōhii to sandoitchi o kudasai.
You	*Order a food and a drink item from the menu.*

6 Underline the correct word in the sentences below.

Rei: <u>Kono</u>/kore hon wa watashi no hon desu.

(a) Sore/sono o misete kudasai.
(b) Ja, kore/kono o kudasai.
(c) Are/ano shimbun wa eigo no shimbun desu ka.
(d) Sore/sono wa nan desu ka.
(e) Dore/dono hon desu ka.

7 Kaiwa

Can you say out aloud in Japanese the conversations between the shopkeeper (**ten'in**) and the customer (**o-kyakusan**) in each of these two dialogues?

(a) O-kyakusan   *Please may I see that book?* (near to the **ten'in**)
    Ten'in   *Which one?*
    O-kyakusan (*pointing*) *That one.*

(b) Ten'in   *Welcome.*
    O-kyakusan   *Could I see that watch (over there) please?*
    Ten'in   *Which watch?*
    O-kyakusan (*pointing*) *That one over there.*
    Ten'in   *Yes, there you are.*
    O-kyakusan   *Thank you.*

✅ Tesuto

1 Can you say these times out aloud?

(a) 6 p.m.   (d) 11 o'clock
(b) 8 a.m.   (e) 7.30
(c) 10 a.m.   (f) 4.30

2 Look at the timetable below and say what time each class starts and finishes.

Rei: Rekishi wa kuji kara jūji made desu.

Jikan-hyō (timetable)

9–10	10–11	11.30–12.30	1.30–2.30	3–4
History*	Japanese	French	English	Tennis club
(**rekishi**)				(**tenisu kurabu**)

---

3 How would you say in Japanese?
  (a) May I see the menu please?
  (b) May I have this please?
  (c) Please show me that watch.
  (d) May I see that watch over there?
  (e) Which one?

6

IKURA DESU KA
How much is it?

In this unit you will learn

- how to count in units of 100 and 1000
- how to ask about and say prices of things
- ways of counting objects
- how to ask for something in a shop
- shop names

Hajime ni

Before you begin this unit look over the numbers 1–99. Vary the ways you practise counting – try counting in fives and tens, for example, or try counting backwards. You will increase your confidence about counting by regularly reviewing numbers, and if you vary the way that you do this, it will make the review more interesting and challenging.

In this unit you will learn to count in 100s (**hyaku**) and 1000s (**sen**). If you go to Japan you will find most prices are counted in these amounts – you could pay between 300 and 600 yen for a cup of coffee, for example, and around 5000 yen for a **yukata** (*cotton kimono*).

Hanashimashō

1 Try saying the numbers below by adding the numbers 1–9 to the words **hyaku** (100) and **sen** (1000). For example, 400 is **yonhyaku** and 5000 is **gosen**. (Check your answers with the **tango-hyō** below.)

   (a) 200
   (b) 500
   (c) 900
   (d) 2000
   (e) 6000
   (f) 9000

2 Now try saying these numbers as in the example. (Answers at the back of the book.)

Rei: 250 = **nihyaku gojū**

   (a) 450
   (b) 950
   (c) 550
   (d) 2200
   (e) 2500
   (f) 2250

Tango-hyō

Read through the new words, saying each word out aloud. When you feel familiar with them, test yourself by seeing if you can count in 100s and 1000s starting from 100:

Sūji *Numbers*					
100	hyaku	400	yonhyaku	700	nanahyaku
200	nihyaku	500	gohyaku	800	happyaku
300	sambyaku	600	roppyaku	900	kyūhyaku
1000	sen	4000	yonsen	7000	nanasen
2000	nisen	5000	gosen	8000	hassen
3000	sanzen	6000	rokusen	9000	kyūsen

en	yen (Japanese currency)
ikura desu ka	how much is it?
... arimasu ka	do you have ...?
hon ga arimasu ka	do you have a book?

✳ Hinto

You may have noticed that the numbers 300, 600, 800, 900, 3000 and 8000 are said in a slightly different way from the pattern you learnt in **Hanashimashō**. There are some tips for remembering these in **setsumei** 1.

kyokuin	postmaster/assistant
hagaki	postcard
kitte	stamp(s)
tegami	letter
mai	counter for flat items
hon (pon/bon)	counter for cylindrical items
jū-mai	10 (stamps, tickets, etc.)
ni-hon	2 (bottles, pens, etc.)
koko	here (this place)
soko	there (that place)
asoko	over there (that place over there)
kippu	ticket

Kaiwa

Anne has gone to the local post office (**yūbinkyoku**) to post some letters home.

Anne	Sumimasen, kono tegami wa Igirisu made ikura desu ka.
Kyokuin (*weighs the letter*)	Nihyaku jū-en desu.
Anne	Ano ... hagaki wa Igirisu made ikura desu ka.
Kyokuin	Nanajū go-en desu.
Anne	Ja, nanajū go-en no kitte o jū-mai kudasai.
Kyokuin	Hai, dozo. **Kore de yoroshii** desu ka.
Anne	Ē to, hagaki ga arimasu ka.
Kyokuin	Ē, asoko desu ... Ichi-mai hyaku-en desu.
Anne	Hai, kono hagaki o jū-mai kudasai.
Kyokuin	Arigatō gozaimasu. Zembu de ... (*he works it out on his abacus*) sen kyūhyaku rokujū-en desu.

yūbinkyoku	post office
kore de yoroshii desu ka	is that all?

Nihon ni tsuite

The soroban or abacus

Despite the image of Japan as a technically advanced country, it is not unusual to see a **soroban** (Japanese-style abacus) instead of a calculator being used in places such as larger department stores and post offices. It is considered that a **soroban** is quicker than a calculator for addition and subtraction (but not for multiplication and division). Also, the Japanese tend to be proud of their traditions and are keen to preserve them. Children can learn the **soroban** by attending special schools in the evenings. However, in recent years the numbers attending such schools have fallen.

 ——————— **Setsumei** ———————

1 Counting above 100

You practised counting in 100s and 1000s in the **Hanashimashō** section of this unit. The **Tango-hyō** section gives you the numbers between 100 and 9000. You may have noticed that these numbers change when combined with **hyaku** (100):

   300 (**sambyaku**)   600 (**roppyaku**)   800 (**happyaku**)

These numbers change when combined with **sen** (1000).

   3000 (**san zen**)   8000 (**hassen**)

(Also **issen** = 1000/**sen** = a 1000 – you can use either.)

The best way to remember these changes is to keep practising them, first by themselves and then in sequence with the other 100s/1000s. You should find that gradually the pattern will fix itself in your memory.

There is a further category of number once you reach 10,000. Whereas in English we count in 1000s until we reach 1 million, the Japanese have another unit called **man** used for countings in 10,000s. You add the numbers **ichi, ni, san** ... to the word **man**. For example: **ichiman** = 10,000 (1 × 10,000) and **niman** = 20,000 (2 × 10,000).

You may find yourself using this unit of currency when buying long-distance train tickets, for example, or when paying for a hotel room or an expensive meal. Here are some more examples. Cover up the answers and try saying the amounts, then check to see if you are right. (The **Hinto** below will help you.)

(a) 10,000
     (**ichiman**)
(b) 30,000
     (**sanman**)
(c) 45,000
     (**yonman, gosen**)

(d) 56,500
     (**goman, rokusen, gohyaku**)
(e) 82,450
     (**hachiman, nisen,
     yonhyaku, gojū**)

✱ Hinto

Count four digits back from the end and draw a line (real or imaginary) between the fourth digit and the digits to its left. The digits on the left are the amount in **man**, the others will break down into 1000s, 100s and 10s.

Rei: 45,200 = 4|5, 200 = yon man, go sen, ni hyaku

2 O-kane: *Money*

The yen is the Japanese unit of currency. Here is the range of coins and notes:

ichi-en (*1 yen* coin)   go-en (*5 yen* coin)   jū-en (*10 yen coin*)
gojū-en (*50 yen coin*) hyaku-en (*100 yen coin*) gohyaku-en (*500 yen coin*)
sen-en (*1000 yen*)   gosen-en (*5000 yen*)   ichiman-en (*10,000 yen*)

If you know someone who has been to Japan or if you have a Japanese friend, have a look at some Japanese coins and notes. You will see that the amounts are written both in our arabic numbers and in the Japanese number script.

The person pictured on the 1000 yen note is Natsume Sōseki, a famous Japanese novelist (1867–1916). The person on the 5000 yen note is Nitobe Inazu, a key figure in education (1862–1933). On the 10000 yen note is Fukuzawa Yukichi, a famous scholar and founder of one of Japan's top universities (1835–1901).

3 Hagaki wa Igirisu made ikura desu ka: *How much is a postcard to England?*

You ask how much something is using the phrase **... wa ikura desu ka**. For example:

Kitte wa ikura desu ka.	*How much is a stamp?*
Kippu wa ikura desu ka.	*How much is a ticket?*

If you want to state the destination put **made** (*to*) (you met this in the last unit) after the name of the city or country. For example:

Kono tegami wa Amerika made ikura desu ka.	*How much is this letter to the USA?*
Kippu wa Kyōto made ikura desu ka.	*How much is a ticket to Kyoto?*

4 Hagaki ga arimasu ka: *Do you have any postcards?*

If you want to enquire whether a shop or person has the thing you are looking for, use the phrase **... ga arimasu ka**. For example:

Eigo no shimbun ga arimasu ka.	*Do you have any English newspapers?*
Kitte ga arimasu ka.	*Do you have any stamps?*

If you want to say that you have or possess something, use **... ga arimasu**. For example:

Uchi ga arimasu.	*I own a house.*
O-kane ga arimasu.	*I have money.*
Shimbun ga arimasu.	*I've got a newspaper.*

5 More about numbers

In the following examples you will notice that two different words are used to say *one*, and also that it is not enough in Japanese simply to say **ichi** when talking about numbers of items.

Ichi-mai **hyaku-en desu**.	*One (postcard) is 100 yen.*
Hitotsu **sambyaku-en desu**.	*One (coffee, etc.) is 300 yen.*

There are actually two different way in Japanese of counting from 1–10 (called system A and system B in this book).

System A

You have already learnt to count using **ichi**, **ni**, **san** .... When you talk about numbers of items you need to attach a special word – called a counter – after the number. We sometimes use counters in English, for example, *a **loaf** of bread, two **slices** of toast, three **bottles** of beer*.

The Japanese use counters to a much greater extent. In this unit you will learn two counters which are used with **ichi**, **ni**, **san** .... Now look at these examples below.

(a) **Mai** is a counter for flat objects – stamps, tickets, paper, cards, etc.

    1 = ichi-mai
    2 = ni-mai
    3 = san-mai, etc.

(b) **Hon (pon, bon)** is a counter for long or cylindrical objects – bottles, pens, etc.

1 = ippon
2 = nihon
3 = sambon

There are many more special counters in Japanese for counting different groups of items, for example, birds, animals, books, machines. However, the two examples above are enough for you to get by at this stage.

System B

The second set of numbers 1–10 is used for the many items which don't have a special counter. You could use this system for counting any object, in which case you don't need to add a special counter (see the examples in setsumei 6 below). Although in some cases you might sound a little childish to a Japanese listener, you will be able to make yourself understood.

This list may look daunting to begin with, but pace yourself. Learn perhaps three at a time and keep re-testing yourself. Remember 'a little, often' is the best way to learn.

1 = hitotsu	6 = muttsu
2 = futatsu	7 = nanatsu
3 = mittsu	8 = yattsu
4 = yottsu	9 = kokonotsu
5 = itsutsu	10 = tō

hitotsu	futatsu	mittsu

After **tō** (10) you use **jūichi** (11); **jūni** (12), etc., just as you learnt to count in Units 3 and 4.

� Hinto: *Tips for remembering this counting system*

- 1–9 ends in **tsu** – **hitotsu**, **futatsu**, etc.
- You learnt to count people in Unit 3. You should note that *one person* (**hitori**) and *two people* (**futari**) are similar to **hitotsu** and **futatsu**, but **tsu** is substituted for **ri** at the end of the word.
- The word *four* (**yottsu**) begins with **yo** (you already known **yon**); *seven* (**nanatsu**) is **nana** plus **tsu**.
- *Ten* (**tō**) sounds a bit like the English word *toe* – and there are ten toes on your feet!

See if you can think of some more words and sounds that will help you to remember these numbers.

6 Kitte o jūmai kudasai. *May I have 10 stamps please?*

We learnt **... o kudasai** (*may I have ...*) in the last unit. When you want to say an amount you put the number (plus counter if necessary) between **o** and **kudasai**. For example:

Kōhii o futatsu kudasai.	*May I have two coffees please.* (system B)
Biiru o ippon kudasai.	*May I have a (bottle of) beer please.* (system A)
Biiru o hitotsu kudasai.	*May I have a (glass) of) beer please.* (system B)
Kitte o gomai kudasai.	*May I have 5 stamps please.* (system A)

You could also say:

Kitte o itsutsu kudasai.	*May I have five stamps please.* (system B)

But **gomai** sounds more sophisticated, as explained in explanation 5.

7 Nanajūgo-en no kitte o jūmai kudasai. *May I have 10 × 75 yen stamps please?*

You can add information about the price, using '**no**'. You were introduced to '**no**' in unit 2 (setsumei 4, page 30). It is used to show a relationship between two items/people. For example, **Sensei no hon** means *the teacher's book*. In the examples below, you could think of '**no**' as meaning literally 'priced', for example:

Hyaku-en *no* kitte o ichimai kudasai.	*May I have 1 × 100 yen **priced** stamp, please?*
Nihyaku-en *no* pen o nihon kudasai.	*May I have 2 × 200 yen **priced** pens, please?*
Sambyaku-en *no* aisukuriimu o mittsu kudasai.	*May I have 3 × 300 yen **priced** ice-creams, please?*

8 Asoko desu: *It's over there.*

In Unit 5 you learnt the words **kore**, **sore** and **are** for *this one, that one* and *that one over there* (also **kono**, **sono** and **ano**). *Here/this place*, *there/that place* and *over there/that place over there* follow a similar pattern using the words **koko**, **soko** and **asoko**. For example:

Koko wa Tōkyō desu.   *This place is Tokyo.*
Hagaki wa asoko desu.   *The postcards are over there.*

The question word is **doko** (*where*) and you will meet this in Unit 7.

9 Shop names

Ya in Japanese means *shop/store*, and you add this to the end of words to make shop names. For example:

hana (flower) + ya = hanaya (*florist's*)

What shop names do you get when you add **ya** to the following words?

sakana (*fish*)
denki (*electric*)
pan (*bread*)
niku (*meat*)
kusuri (*medicine*)

Some words do change, however. For example:

yasai (*vegetables*) becomes **yaoya** (*greengrocer's*)
sake (*alcohol*) becomes **sakaya** (*wine shop/off-licence*).

It is worth mentioning, though, that, as in this country, *supermarkets* (**sūpā**) in Japan have taken over the role of the individual shop to a certain extent.

Hinto: *How to remember groups of vocabulary*

Try drawing pictures/symbols to prompt your memory rather than writing down the English word. For example, how many shop names can you say by looking at the pictures below?

Renshū

1 Kiku-renshū

Below are different amounts of money. Listen to the tape and in each case circle the amount that you don't hear on the tape.

(a)	200 yen	300 yen	400 yen
(b)	800 yen	600 yen	500 yen
(c)	450 yen	750 yen	950 yen
(d)	1000 yen	2000 yen	3000 yen
(e)	1500 yen	1050 yen	8050 yen
(f)	10,000 yen	40,000 yen	4000 yen
(g)	25,000 yen	20,500 yen	20,050 yen

2 Kiku-renshū

You will hear people asking for amounts of the items listed below. How many do they ask for?

Item	How many?
(a) Apples (**ringo**)	
(b) Stamps	
(c) Tickets	
(d) Bottles of beer	
(e) Bottles of sake	
(f) Postcards	
(g) Rolls of film (**firumu**)	
(h) Video tapes	

3 Below are some examples of Tokyo underground tickets with the amounts written in yen (the half-price amounts are child fares).

(a) Practise saying the adult fares in Japanese.

(b) Practise asking how much it is to the destination printed on the ticket.

Rei: Shinjuku made ikura desu ka.

Rei: *destination* Shinjuku

(i) *destination* Shimbashi

(ii) *destination* Zushi

(iii) *destination* Ōme

(iv) *destination* Kōenji

4 Below are some examples of Japanese stamps.

(a) Practise asking for each stamp as in the example below.
Rei: Nanajū-en no kitte o kudasai.

(b) Now practise asking for three of stamp (*i*), ten of stamp (*ii*), five of stamp (*iii*), one of stamp (*iv*), four of stamp (*v*) and 20 of stamp (*vi*).

Rei (two stamps): Nanajū-en no kitte o nimai kudasai.

5 Below are some examples of the prices of journeys from Tokyo by Japan Railways (JR). Say the destination and prices out aloud. Some are over 10,000 yen. The first one has been done for you.

Rei: Tōkyō kara Yokohama made yonhyaku yonjū-en desu.

	Place	Fare
(a)	Yokohama	440
(b)	Narita	2890
(c)	Kyoto	12,970
(d)	Shin-Osaka	13,480

(e)	Hiroshima	17,700
(f)	Nagasaki	23,510
(g)	Sapporo	21,380

6 Ask for the items below as in the example. The counter system to use is in brackets.

Rei: Two cups of coffee = kōhii o futatsu kudasai

(a) Three postcards (**mai**)
(b) One bottle of beer (**hon**)
(c) Two glasses of milk (system B)
(d) Six pens (**hon**)
(e) Three × 200 yen cakes (system B)
(f) Two × 1000 yen tickets (**mai**)

7 Practise saying these years as in the example.

Rei: 1995 = sen kyūhyaku kyūjū go-nen (**nen** = *year*)

(a) 1996
(b) 1066
(c) 1963
(d) 1980
(e) 1945

Now try saying the year of your birth.

8 In which specialist shops would you buy the following items? Answer in Japanese.

(a) Kitte
(b) Ringo
(c) Sake
(d) Biiru
(e) Sakana
(f) Pan

———— Fukushū *Review* ————

You have now completed six units of Japanese – **omedetō**! (*Congratulations*). You have been introduced to a number of basic structures and some different ways of using numbers. You are also beginning to build up your vocabulary. Instead of a test for this unit, look back over the dialogues in the first six units. Listen to them on the tape and/or read through them and check how much you now understand. Use this opportunity to give yourself a vocabulary test on all the new words from the *tango-hyō* and *tango* sections. If you have been building up your own 'dictionary' (see Unit 3, page 46) use this to test yourself.

In the next six units you will be learning new sentence structures and new vocabulary, but it is important to keep looking back and practising what you have already learnt. Go over the **Renshū** activities at the end of each unit and speak Japanese out aloud – this will give you the confidence to really use it. Practise talking about yourself – there are now lots of things you can say. You could even record yourself and then listen to it. If you have a Japanese friend, ask him or her to listen to you and comment on your pronunciation. The main point is – keep practising what you have learnt!

7

YŪBINKYOKU WA DOKU DESU KA

Where is the post office?

In this unit you will learn

- how to ask for directions
- how to give directions
- how to say exactly where places are

Hajime ni

In Unit 5 you learnt that **kudasai** meant *please* or *may I have*. This word is also used when giving directions: *(please) go straight ahead, (please) turn left*.

In Units 4 and 5 we also talked about question words (**nan/i**, *what?*; **nanji**, *what time?* **nansai**, *how old?* etc.).

In this unit you are going to learn a new question word **doko** (*where?*) to ask where something is (see also Unit 6 (setsumei 8, page 81). For example, **yūbinkyoku wa doko desu ka** (*where is the post office?*). Notice the sentence order: *place* **wa doko desu ka**.

As well as asking for directions you also need to be able to understand the answer you are given. Remember that it is not important to understand every word. Learning to pick out the necessary information such as **massugu itte**, **migi ni magatte** is a very valuable skill. You may also find yourself in a situation in your own country where you need to help a Japanese person who is lost.

As a check, repeat the directions as they are given to you. You don't need to repeat **kudasai**. And don't be afraid of asking people to speak more slowly or to say something again. (See unit 3, page 43).

——————— Hanashimashō ———————

1 Imagine you need to stop someone to ask them for directions. How do you:

    (a) catch their attention? (*excuse me*)
    (b) ask where a bank (**ginkō**) is?
    (c) ask them to repeat something?
    (d) say thank you?

 Tango hyō

To go straight on

... itte kudasai	(please) go ...
massugu	straight on
chotto	a little way
massugu itte kudasai	please go straight on
chotto itte kudasai	please go a little way

To turn

... magatte kudasai	(please) turn ...
migi	right
hidari	left
migi *ni* magatte kudasai	please turn *(to the)* right
hidari *ni* magatte kudasai	please turn *(to the)* left

Orientation points

shingō	traffic lights
kōsaten	crossroads
kado	corner
michi	road
tsugi no ...	the next ...
tsugi no shingō	the next traffic lights
nibanme no ...	the second ...
nibanme no kōsaten	the second crossroads

Giving directions

shingō o* massugu itte kudasai	go straight at the traffic lights

---

kōsaten o* migi ni magatte kudasai turn right at the crossroads
tsugi no kado o* hidari ni
magatte kudasai   turn left at the next corner

*Think of **o** in this case as acting like *at*. Note that it comes after the word: **shingō o** (*at the traffic lights*). You will learn more about **o** in Unit 8.

Some useful places

ginkō	bank
eki	station
eigakan	cinema

Exact location

tonari	next to
chikaku	near to
ichiban chikai	the nearest
mukaigawa	opposite (side)
mae	in front of
hidarigawa	left-hand side
migigawa	right-hand side
... no tonari	next to the ...
ginkō no tonari	next to the bank
yūbinkyoku wa ginkō no tonari desu	the post office is next to the bank

✳ Hinto

You've now met two meanings for the word **itte**.

(a) *say* as in **mōichido itte kudasai** (*please say it again*):
(b) *go* as in **massugu itte kudasai** (*please go straight on*).

You will always know the meaning from the situation, so you don't need to worry about this. (There are lots of words in English with more than one meaning too, for example, bank; light; post.)

———————— Kaiwa ————————

Scott is going to visit Anne's host family and he is looking for Shibuya train station. (While you listen to the cassette or read the **Kaiwa** look at the map below and see if you can follow the directions to the station.)

Scott   Sumimasen, Shibuya eki wa doko desu ka.

Passer-by   **Aaa**, sumimasen, watashi wa eigo ga **dekimasen**. (*The passer-by rushes off*)

Scott   **Ē!** (*sees another passer-by*) Sumimasen, Shibuya eki wa doko desu ka.

Passer-by   Shibuya eki desu ka. Ēto, kono michi o massugu itte, tsugi no shingō o hidari ni … Aa, sumimasen, tsugi no shingō o migi ni magatte kudasai. **Sorekara**, nibanme no kōsaten o hidari ni magatte kudasai. Shibuya eki wa Tōkyō ginkō no mukaigawa desu.

Scott   Sumimasen, kono michi o massugu itte … sorekara? Mō ichido itte kudasai.

Passer-by   Sorekara, tsugi no shingō o migi ni magatte kudasai.

Scott   **Wakarimashita**. **Soshite**, nibanme no kōsaten o hidari ni magatte …

Passer-by   Hai, sō desu. Nihongo ga **jōzu** desu ne!

Scott   **Iie, mada dame** desu. Dōmo arigato gozaimasu.

aa! ē!	(expressions of surprise)
dekimasen	can't (the passer-by is saying he can't speak English. Scott has spoken in Japanese but some Japanese people aren't used to this and feel they should be able to speak English)
sorekara } **soshite** }	and, and then
wakarimashita	I understand (Lit. I've understood)
jōzu	good at
iie, mada dame desu	no, I'm no good yet*

*Japanese people are pleased if foreigners try to speak in Japanese and will praise your attempts. The way to reply to this is in a modest fashion – even if you think you are doing quite well!

Setsumei

1 ... wa, doko desu ka: *Where is ...*

(a) The pattern here is fairly straightforward. You put the name of the place you want to go to at the beginning of the phrase. **Place wa doko desu ka** means *Where is place?* To be more polite, say *excuse me* (**sumimasen**) before you ask. For example:

Sumimasen, ginkō wa doko   *Excuse me, where is the bank?*
desu ka.

(b) You might want to specify which bank (supermarket, etc.). In this case, put the name first. For example:

Sumimasen, Jusco sūpā wa   *Excuse me, where is Jusco*
doko desu ka.   *supermarket?*

(c) If you want to ask where the nearest one is, put **ichiban chikai** before the place. For example:

Sumimasen, ichiban chikai   *Excuse me, where is the nearest*
depāto wa doko desu ka.   *department store?*

2 Understanding and giving directions

(a) In this unit you've been introduced to two important phrases for giving directions: **... itte kudasai** means *please go ...*, and **... magatte kudasai** means *please turn ...*.

Once you have mastered some of the vocabulary in this unit you can gradually build up from fairly simple directions to more complex ones. Practise saying the build-up phrases on the next page. Some of these are recorded on the cassette. When you feel confident, try covering up the Japanese side and see if you can remember how to give directions using the English as a prompt.

Massugu itte kudasai.	*Please go straight ahead.*
Kōsaten o massugu itte kudasai.	*Please go straight on at the crossroads.*
Tsugi no kōsaten o massugu itte kudasai.	*Please go straight on at the next crossroads.*
Nibanme no kōsaten o massugu itte kudasai.	*Please go straight on at the second crossroads.*
Hidari ni magatte kudasai.	*Please turn left.*
Migi ni magatte kudasai.	*Please turn right.*
Shingō o hidari ni magatte kudasai.	*Please turn left at the traffic lights.*
Shingō o migi ni magatte kudasai.	*Please turn right at the traffic lights.*
Tsugi no shingō o migi ni magatte kudasai.	*Please turn right at the next traffic lights.*
Nibanme no shingō o hidari ni magatte kudasai.	*Please turn left at the second set of traffic lights.*

(b) You can link two directions simply by leaving out the first **kudasai**. Thus, **massugu itte kudasai** + **shingō o migi ni magatte kudasai** becomes:

Massugu itte, shingō o migi ni magatte kudasai.	*Go straight on **and** turn right at the traffic lights.*

✴ Hinto

When you are learning phrases or sentence patterns, try writing down just the first letter of each word in the phrase: so **Shingō O Hidari Ni Magatte Kudasai** (*turn left at the traffic lights*) would become: **S O H N M K**. This will help prompt your memory and also will help you to say the phrase in the correct order.

Remember that when you pronounce double consonants (**massugu, magatte, itte**) you pause slightly before you say the sound (as in the English word *headdress*). Look at the **Pronunciation guide** for more practice of this.

3 Giving the exact location

(a) **Ginkō no mukaigawa desu** means *(it's) opposite the bank*. The word order is important here. In English, the word *opposite* comes before the location; in Japanese *opposite* comes after the location, with **no** in between. You could think of it as meaning *the bank's opposite*. (See Unit 2 for more information on **no**).

Yūbinkyoku no chikaku desu.	*(It's) near the post office.*
eki no mae desu	*(It's) in front of the station*
Migigawa desu.	*(It's) on the right-hand side.*

(b) If you want to specify the place, you put it at the beginning of the sentence followed by the particle **wa**. (Look back to Unit 3 for notes on **wa** and **desu**.)

Depāto wa ginkō no mukaigawa desu.	*The department store is opposite the bank.*
Sūpā wa eki no tonari desu.	*The supermarket is next to the station.*
Eigakan wa hidarigawa desu.	*The cinema is on the left-hand side.*

❇ Hinto: *Developing listening skills*

As stated earlier in this unit, it is useful to develop the skill of listening for essential information, without trying to understand every word. Keep listening to the dialogues on the cassette to improve your understanding and build up your vocabulary.

Renshū

1   Consider how you would ask a passer-by the way to each of the places below.

(a) Yūbinkyoku   (b Hana-ya   (c) Ginkō   (d) Eki   (e) Sūpā

Now try covering up the Japanese words and use the pictures as prompts to ask the way.

Finally, how would you ask where the nearest of each of the above places was?

2   Kiku-renshū

As the passer-by gives you the directions to each of the places, look at the map below, read the directions and match the numbers (1) to (5) with the appropriate place names.

Directions

(a)   Yūbinkyoku desu ka? Chotto itte, kado o migi ni magatte kudasai. Yūbinkyoku wa hidarigawa desu.

(b)   Kono michi o massugu itte, tsugi no shingō o hidari ni magatte kudasai. Hanaya wa depāto no tonari desu.

(c) Ēto, tsugi no shingō o migi ni magatte, chotto itte kudasai. Ginkō wa eigakan no mukaigawa desu.

(d) Sō desu ne. Massugu itte, tsugi no shingō o migi ni magatte kudasai. Eki wa eigakan no tonari desu.

(e) Sūpā desu ka. Shingō o hidari ni magatte, tsugi no kōsaten o migi ni magatte kudasai. Sūpā wa kōsaten no chikaku desu.

3 (a) The diagrams below represent different directions (*go straight on, turn right*, etc.). How many can you say? Speak out aloud, then check your answers in the back of the book.

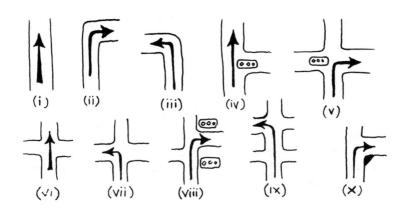

(b) Now try linking these directions together: i + ii; i + iii; iv + vii; iv + x; viii + i; vi + x.

4 **Kiku-renshū**

True or false? Listen to the directions on the cassette and decide whether they correctly describe the maps (a)–(f) below. As in the Japanese style, you can use a *circle* (**maru**) if it's true or a *cross* (**batsu**) if it's false. Put the circle or cross in the box below the map.

5   Mr Suzuki is writing a pamphlet for his local tourist information
    office about the facilities in his town. However, he has made some
    errors. Can you correct them by looking at the map and changing
    the underlined parts of the text if necessary? (Be careful – some
    are correct.)

(a)   Eigakan wa Mitsukoshi depāto no <u>chikaku</u> desu.
(b)   Jusco sūpā wa hanaya no <u>mae</u> desu.

(c) Yūbinkyoku wa ginkō no <u>mukaigawa</u> desu.
(d) Mitsukoshi depāto wa <u>eki</u> no tonari desu.
(e) Ginkō wa eki no <u>mukaigawa</u> desu.
(f) Eki wa <u>eigakan</u> no chikaku desu.

6 Using the same map as in Exercise 5, imagine you are at the *hotel* (**hoteru**) and give the directions and exact location for the places listed below. Try and link your directions and give as much information as possible. For example, in (a) you could say *Go on a little way and turn left at the next traffic lights. The bakery is in front of Jusco supermarket.*

(a) The bakery
(b) The station
(c) The bank
(d) The fishmonger's

7 (a) Hidden in the wordsearch below are ten places you'd expect to find in a medium-sized city in Japan. Can you find them? You can read horizontally, vertically or diagonally, and either forwards or backwards.

A	Y	A	N	A	K	A	A
O	A	Y	H	A	U	Y	O
G	O	N	O	S	S	Z	D
A	Y	A	E	I	U	M	E
A	A	P	S	K	R	P	P
N	A	K	A	G	I	E	A
D	E	N	K	I	Y	A	T
H	A	N	A	Y	A	U	O

Clues: (*i*) Where would you find the following items: sakana; tēpu rekōdā; ringo (apple); hana; pan; kusuri; eiga (film/movie); densha (train); yōfuku (clothes)?
(ii) What type of shop is 'Jusco?'

(b) The remaining letters make up a greeting word you learnt in Unit 1. Can you work out what it is?

☑ Tesuto

1 Count up in units of 100 (100, 200, etc.). Then count down in units of 1000 from 10,000.

2 Which phrase would you choose to ask someone where the post office is?

(a) Kōhii o futatsu kudasai.
(b) Yūbinkyoku wa doko desu ka.
(c) Yūbinkyoku no mae desu.

3 How would you say the following?

(a) Good morning.
(b) Go straight on and turn right at the crossroads.
(c) The greengrocer's is opposite the bank.
(d) May I have a coffee and some cake?
(e) Where is the nearest bakery?

8

NICHIYŌBI NI NANI
O SHIMASU KA
What do you do on Sundays?

In this unit you will learn

- ten useful doing words for describing your day
- how to say when you do something
- how to ask about someone's future schedule
- the days of the week
- some useful question words

Hajime ni

In this unit you are going to learn how to talk about your daily routines and how to talk about future plans. You will find this very useful if you want to describe your day or ask somebody about their day. You will learn ten new doing or action words, (for example, *I/he/they ... eat, drink, watch TV.*) You will find that these are very simple to use once you know the new vocabulary.

———— Hanashimashō ————

1 **Ima nanji desu ka**
How well can you remember telling the time? Refresh your memory by saying these times.

(a) 6 o'clock
(b) 4.30
(c) 9 p.m.
(d) 7.30 a.m.
(e) 12 o'clock
(f) 11.30 a.m.

2 Say the times that these places open and close (start and finish) as in the example.

Rei: Wine shop, 10–8 Sakaya wa jūji kara hachiji made desu.

(a) Bank, 9–3
(b) Supermarket, 8–8
(c) Post office, 9–6
(d) Bakery 8–6

 Tango-hyō

Action words	
okimasu	wake up (get up)
tabemasu	eat
yomimasu	read
shimasu	do, make, play
nemasu	go to bed
nomimasu	drink
mimasu	see, watch, look
benkyō shimasu	study
gorufu o shimasu	play golf
kaimono o shimasu	do the shopping

❋ Hinto: *Pronunciation tip*

The final **u** of these action words is very soft and hardly spoken.

Time expressions	
nanji ni	*at* what time
nanyōbi ni	*on* what day
asa	morning
hiru	midday
yoru	evening
asagohan	breakfast
hirugohan	lunch
yorugohan/bangohan	evening meal

Food and drink

tabemono	food
tōsuto	toast
pan	bread
tamago	eggs
niku	meat
yasai	vegetables
ringo	apples
gohan	rice
nomimono	a drink
ocha	green tea
kōcha	black tea
jūsu	juice
miruku	milk
kōra	cola
mizu	water

Useful objects

zasshi	magazine
manga	comic book
terebi	television
eiga	movie
soshite/sorekara/sore ni	and (then)
goro	about (used when saying times)
daitai	more or less, generally
tokidoki	sometimes

Kaiwa

Scott has come round to the Yamaguchi home to interview Mr Yamaguchi about his typical day, as part of a Japanese homework project.

Scott Asa, nanji ni okimasu ka.

Mr Yamaguchi Daitai, rokuji han goro okimasu.

Scott **Hayai** desu ne! Sorekara, asagohan ni nani o tabemasu ka.

Mr Yamaguchi Sō desu ne. Tōsuto o tabemasu. Sore ni kōhii o nomimasu.

Anne Shigoto wa nanji kara desu ka.

Mr Yamaguchi Daitai, hachiji han kara rokuji made desu.

	Hirugohan wa ichi ji kara desu.
Scott	Yoru nani o shimasu ka.
Mr Yamaguchi	Bangohan o tabemasu. Soshite terebi o mimasu. Jūichiji han goro nemasu.
Scott	Nichiyōbi ni nani o shimasu ka.
Mr Yamaguchi	Sō desu ne. **Rirakkusu** shimasu ne. Zasshi o yomimasu. Tokidoki gorufu o shimasu …
Anne (*laughing*)	Ē? Daitai **ichinichi jū** nemasu yo.

hayai	early
rirakkusu	relax
ē?	what?
ichinichi jū	all day

Nihon ni tsuite

The working week

The traditional image of the Japanese 'salaryman' or employee is of someone who works six days a week and stays at work until late in the evenings with colleagues and bosses either in the office or at local bars. Even on Sunday he may be expected to play a round of golf with his boss or with clients. There are increasing reports of changes to this typical image.

Some larger companies have reduced the hours of a working week; some have even introduced a 5-day week. Younger men are said to want to spend more time with their family and are less willing to work long hours. It remains to be seen how this will affect Japanese working life in the future.

Setsumei

1 Action words (masu words)

(a) Japanese doing words are very simple to use – you will notice that they all end in **masu**. This gives the meaning *I do* or *I will do something*. For example, the question **nichiyōbi ni nani o shimasu ka** could have the meaning *what do you do on Sundays?* or *what are you going to do on Sunday?* The context will tell you which one is intended.

Also, the **masu** ending does not change whether you say *I/you/he/she/it/we/they do something*. For example:

Nichiyōbi ni Sukotto-san wa terebi o mimasu.	*Scott watches TV on Sundays.*
Nichiyōbi ni terebi o mimasu.	*I watch TV on Sundays.*

And you don't need to use the words *you/I/he*, etc. unless it's not clear who is being spoken about. It is then better to use a person's name rather than *you*. For example:

Nichiyōbi ni nani o shimasu ka.	*What do (you) do on Sundays?*
Yamaguchi-san, nichiyōbi ni nani o shimasu ka.	*Mr Yamaguchi, what do you do on Sundays?*

(b) **Tokidoki gorufu o shimasu:** *I sometimes plays golf.*

Shimasu is a useful word meaning *do, make* or *play*. Here are some examples of its use:

Tenisu o shimasu.	*I play tennis.*
Sakkā o shimasu.	*I play football.*
Kaimono o shimasu.	*I do the shopping.*
Denwa o shimasu.	*I make a phone call.*
Kuji kara jūji made eigo o benkyō shimasu.	*I study English from 9 until 4.*

When you add **tokidoki** you are talking about what you do sometimes. For example:

Tokidoki denwa o shimasu.	*I sometimes make phone calls.*
Tokidoki tenisu o shimasu.	*I sometimes play tennis.*

When you add **daitai** you are saying *generally* .... For example:

Daitai rokuji ni okimasu.	*I generally get up at 6.*

2 Tōsuto o tabemasu: *I eat some toast.*

There is no equivalent in English of the word **o**, but in Japanese you say it after the item you eat, drink read, etc. Here are some examples with the item in italics.

Gohan o tabemasu.	*I eat **rice**.*
Kōcha o nomimasu.	*I drink **black tea**.*
Kaimono o shimasu.	*I do **the shopping**.*

You should note that the **masu** word always comes at the end of the sentence.

3 Yamaguchi-san wa kōhii o nomimasu: *Mr Yamaguchi drinks coffee.*

When you mention the person who eats, drinks, etc., this word is followed by **wa**. (Remember that **wa** acts like a highlighter and can be translated as *as for* …. See Unit 2, setsumei 1 (page 28). Here are some examples with the subject in italics.

An-san wa nihongo no hon o yomimasu.	*Anne reads a Japanese book.*
Watashi wa Nihongo o benkyō shimasu.	*I study Japanese.*
Sukotto-san wa kaimono o shimasu.	*Scott is going to do the shopping.*

You should note the order which you say these sentences.

(a) You say the person who does the action, followed by **wa**.
(b) You say the item (or person) which has the action done to it, followed by **o**.
(c) You say the action word – the **masu** word.

An-san wa	hon o	yomimasu
1	2	3

4 Nichi yōbi ni nani o shimasu ka: *What do you do on Sundays?*

When you say the day or time that you do something, it is followed by **ni** meaning *on* or *at*. For example:

Nichiyōbi ni terebi o mimasu.	*I watch TV on Sundays.*
Hachiji ni okimasu.	*I get up at 8 o'clock.*

You can replace **ni** with **goro** (*about*) if you want to give an approximate time. For example:

Hachiji goro okimasu.   *I get up at about 8 o'clock.*

The important point to remember is that **ni** and **goro** are said *after* the time/day.

The time expression is usually said at this point in a sentence:

An-san wa *hachiji kara*   *Anne watches TV from 8 o'clock.*
  terebi o mimasu.
***Hachiji ni* asagohan o tabemasu.** *I eat breakfast at 8 o'clock.*
***Rokuji ni* okimasu.**   *I get up at 6 o'clock.*

5 To ask when somebody does something you can use nanji ni (at what time):

Nanji ni okimasu ka.   *(At) what time do you get up?*

Or **nanyōbi ni** (*on what day*):

Nanyōbi ni gorufu o shimasu ka. *(On) what day/s do you play golf?*

Or **nannichi ni** (*on what date/days of the month?*):

Nannichi ni sakkā o   *On what date are you going to*
  shimasu ka.   *play football?*

Or the more general question **itsu** (*when*):

Itsu kaimono o shimasu ka.   *When do you do the shopping?*

You do not need to say **ni** after **itsu** because you are not saying *in*, *on* or *at*:

Itsu sakkā o shimasu ka.   *When are you going to play*
                                   football? (not: on when are you
                                   going to play football?)

See setsumei 7 for more information about this.

6 Bangohan o tabemasu: I eat dinner.

The words for the three main meals in Japanese are interesting. They are made up of the word for *rice* (**gohan**) and the words for *morning* (**asa**), *midday* (**hiru**) and *evening* (**ban** – as in **konbanwa**, *good evening*; also **yoru**). Therefore, **asagohan** (*breakfast*) literally means *morning rice*, **hirugohan** (*lunch*) is *midday rice*, and **bangohan** (*dinner/evening meal*, also **yorugohan**) is *evening rice*. You've probably worked out the reason for this – traditionally in Japan every meal is accompanied by a bowl of rice. (See Unit 15 for more information on meals.)

7 Asa nanji ni okimasu ka: *What time do you get up in the morning?*

In Unit 5 we learnt **gozen** (*a.m.*) and **gogo** (*p.m./afternoon*). A more informal way of saying this is to use **asa** (*morning*) and **yoru** (*evening*). For example:

Asa shichiji ni okimasu.   *I get up at 8 o'clock in the morning.*
Yoru terebi o mimasu.   *I watch TV in the evenings.*

You should note that you don't need **ni** after **asa** and **yoru**. **Ni** is only used with *exact* times, days and dates. (You will learn more about this in Unit 9.)

8 Asagohan ni nani o tabemasu ka: *What do you eat for breakfast?*

To ask what someone eats at mealtimes, use **ni** (in this case meaning *for*) after the meal word. For example:

Bangohan ni nani o   *What do you eat for dinner?*
tabemasu ka.

To answer, just say the food that you eat.

Tamago o tabemasu.   *I eat eggs.*

If you want to include what you drink, use one of the *and* words (**sore ni**, **soshite**, **sorekara**). You say these at the beginning of a new sentence. For example;

Tamago o tabemasu. Sore ni   *I eat eggs. And I drink coffee.*
kōhii o nomimasu.

To make a statement about what you have for breakfast (etc.), start with: **asagohan ni ...**. For example:

Asagohan ni tamago   *I eat eggs for breakfast.*
o tabemasu.

9 The days of the week

Practise saying the days of the week. Speak out aloud.

Hinto

All the days of the week end in **yōbi,** meaning *day*.

Nichiyōbi	*Sunday*
Getsuyōbi	*Monday*
Kayōbi	*Tuesday*
Suiyōbi	*Wednesday*
Mokuyōbi	*Thursday*
Kinyōbi	*Friday*
Doyōbi	*Saturday*

There is more information about how to *read* the days of the week in Unit 13.

Hinto

In this unit you have been introduced to whole new groups of vocabulary, for example, food and drink items, verbs and days of the week. You could make the learning process more interesting by writing out in English the days of the week, and by each day write down one or two things which you might do (it doesn't have to be true!). Then practise saying them in Japanese. For example: *Monday, eat toast for breakfast. Then study Japanese.*

Renshū

1 **Kiku-renshū**

Below are some sequences using days of the week. You have a choice of two sequences (i and ii) for each question. Listen to the tape and underline the sequence you hear.

Rei: (i) <u>Monday</u>, <u>Wednesday</u>, <u>Friday</u>
(ii) Monday, Friday, Wednesday

(a) (i) Tuesday, Friday, Saturday
(ii) Friday, Tuesday, Thursday

(b) (i) Sunday, Monday

      (ii) Monday, Sunday
(c)   (i) Wednesday, Thursday, Saturday
      (ii) Thursday, Saturday, Wednesday

2 Kiku-renshū

Takeshi has recorded his weekly schedule for Anne and she has written out the information that she has understood. Can you fill in the gaps for her as you listen to the tape?

Day	Time/part of day	Activity
(a) Wednesday	Morning ?	? Plays football
(b) ?	?	Watches TV
(c) Saturday	? ?	Studies English Watches a film
(d) Sunday	? In the evening	Reads comics ?
(e) ?	12.00	?

3 Nanyōbi desu ka

In the left column of the table below are the days of the week in English; in the right column are the days in Japanese. Can you match them up by drawing lines from one to the other? There is one extra day in the Japanese list. Which one is it (in English)?

(a) Monday   (i)   Suiyōbi
(b) Thursday   (ii) Nichiyōbi
(c) Wednesday   (iii) Kayōbi
(d) Saturday   (iv) Mokuyōbi
(e) Sunday   (v) Kinyōbi
(f) Tuesday   (vi) Nichiyōbi
(g) Friday   (vii) Getsuyōbi
(h) _____   (viii) Doyōbi

4 Say what each of the characters below have for their breakfast, as in the example:

Rei: Yamaguchi-san wa asagohan ni tōsuto o tabemasu. Sore ni kōhii o nomimasu.

5 Describe Anne's day using the chart below. Use **sorekara**, **soshite** and **sore ni** as indicated. Use **daitai** (*generally / usually*) and **tokidoki** (*sometimes*).

An-san no ichinichi

Gets up at about 7.30.
Usually has eggs and black tea (**soshite**) for breakfast.
Then (**sorekara**) studies Japanese from 9 until 4.
Generally has lunch at 12.30.

Plays tennis on Saturdays.
Sometimes watches *TV in the evening* (say **yoru** before **tokidoki**).
And finally (**sore ni**) goes to bed at about 11 p.m.

6 Anne has been writing up her interview with Emi. These are the answers to her questions. Can you write out the questions in full, in Japanese?

(a) Q: What time?   A: Hachiji ni okimasu.
(b) Q: What?   A: Asagohan ni tōsuto to tamago o tabemasu.
(c) Q: What day?   A: Doyōbi ni kaimono o shimasu.
(d) What?   A: Yoru tokidoki eiga o mimasu.
(e) When?   A: Getsuyōbi kara kinyōbi made benkyō shimasu.

☑ Tesuto

1 Can you say these days in Japanese?

(a) Friday
(b) Tuesday
(c) Monday
(d) Thursday

2 Can you fill in the missing parts of Mr Yamaguchi's schedule? (You may wish to re-read the dialogue at the beginning of the unit first.)

Asa rokuji han goro _____. Sorekara _____ ni tōsuto o_____. Sore ni kōhii _____ _____. Shigoto wa hachiji han _____roku _____ _____ desu. _____ wa ichiji kara desu. Yoru _____ _____ tabemasu. Soshite terebi o _____. Jūichi _____ han goro _____. Nichiyōbi_____ zasshi o _____.

3 Answer these questions to describe your own typical day.

(a) Nanji ni okimasu ka.
(b) Asagohan ni nani o tabemasu ka.
(c) Shigoto wa nanji kara nanji made desu ka.
(d) Itsu kaimono o shimasu ka.
(e) Nanyōbi ni Nihongo o benkyō shimasu ka.
(f) Nanji ni hirugohan o tabemasu ka.
(g) Yoru nani o shimasu ka.
(h) Nanji goro nemasu ka.

9

PĀTII O SHIMASHŌ
Let's have a party!

In this unit you will learn

- how to say you are going or returning from somewhere
- how to invite someone
- how to make suggestions and accept or refuse
- the dates 1st–10th
- some useful time expressions

Hajime ni

In the last unit you learnt some useful action words for talking about daily activities. In this unit you are going to add three more important words to these: *go*, *come* and *return*.

You will also learn how to use the action words in a new way: to invite someone to do something or to suggest doing something as in the title of this unit: **pātii o shimashō** (*let's have a party!*).

─── Hanashimashō ───

To suggest doing something you change the **masu** ending of the doing word to **mashō** (*let's*). Can you change the following sentences into suggestions, as in the example?

Rei: Kōhii o nomi**masu**   Kōhii o nomi**mashō**.
    (*drink coffee*)   (*Let's drink some coffee.*)

1   Tenisu o shimasu (*play tennis*)
2   Kaimono o shimasu (*do some shopping*)
3   Sushi o tabemasu (*eat sushi*)
4   Ocha o nomimasu (*drink green tea*)
5   Eiga o mimasu (*watch a film*)
6   Nihongo o benkyō shimasu (*study Japanese*)

Tango-hyō

Say these words out aloud a few times, then test yourself by covering the Japanese words and seeing if you can say them from memory.

ikimasu	go
kaerimasu	return, go back (used to express 'going back to where you live')
kimasu	come
Time expressions	
mainichi	every day
kyō	today
ashita	tomorrow
maishū	every week
maitsuki	every month
konshū	this week
kongetsu	this month
konban	this evening
raishū	next week
raigetsu	next month
... dō desu ka	how about ...?
ii desu ne	that sounds nice
yorokonde	I'd love to
zannen desu	it's a shame/pity

Kaiwa

Tani's stay in Japan is coming to an end.

Anne	Itsu Furansu ni kaerimasu ka.
Tani	Raishū no doyōbi ni kaerimasu.
Scott	Zannen desu ne. Ja, pātii o shimashō!
Tani	Ii desu ne.
Anne	Konshū no doyōbi wa dō desu ka.
Tani	Doyōbi wa **chotto** ... **Tomodachi** to resutoran ni ikimasu.
Scott	Ja ... Nichiyōbi wa?
Tani	Nichiyōbi wa ii desu yo.
Satō-sensei	Mina-san, watashi no **uchi ni kimasen ka**.
Everyone	Ii desu ne!
Tani	A! Yorokonde!

chotto	a bit (in this case 'a bit inconvenient')
tomodachi	friend
uchi ni kimasen ka	would you like to come to my house?

Setsumei

1 Ikimasu, *go*; kimasu, *come*; kaerimasu, *return*

(a) You were introduced to **masu** words in the previous unit. These three can be learnt together as a group. For example:

Tani san wa resutoran ni ikimasu.	*Tani is going to a restaurant.*
Ashita Furansu ni kaerimasu.	*I'm going back to France tomorrow.*
An-san wa watashi no uchi ni kimasu.	*Anne is coming to my house.*

Look at the sentence order. The person doing the action is followed by **wa**. **Ni** means *to* and comes after the place you are going to. For example:

Furansi **ni** *to France*   resutoran **ni** *to a restaurant*

As you saw in Unit 8, the action word (or verb) always comes at the end of a Japanese sentence. (Unit 8, **setsumei** 4 and **setsumei** 3 in this unit practise the other meaning of **ni** that you have learnt.)

(b) **Kaerimasu** is used when you return or go back to the place you come from, either your home, your town or your country. For example:

Watashi wa uchi ni kaerimasu. *I return home / shall return home*
Yamaguchi-san wa ashita *Mr Yamaguchi will return to*
  Tōkyō ni kaerimasu. *Tokyo tomorrow.*

2 Ashita doko ni ikimasu ka: *Where are you going tomorrow?*

In Unit 7 you learnt the question word **doko** (*where*). You can now use it with these three new verbs. For example:

Ashita doko ni ikimasu ka. *Where are you going tomorrow?*

You answer by replacing **doko** with the place, keeping the same sentence order. For example:

Ashita Tōkyō ni ikimasu. *I'm going to Tokyo tomorrow.*
Yamaguchi-san wa mainichi *Where does Mr Yamaguchi*
  doko **ni ikimasu ka.** *go every day?*
Yamaguchi-san wa mainichi *Mr Yamaguchi goes to work*
  shigoto **ni ikimasu.** *every day.*

Or more simply:

Shigoto **ni ikimasu.** *He goes to work.*

3 Hachigatsu ni Igirisu ni kaerimasu: *I'm returning to England in August.*

In Unit 8, setsumei 4, (page 104) you learnt that **ni** is used after a day or time to mean *on* or *at*. In the same way, it is used when saying months or dates. For example:

Jūichi-nichi *ni* **on** *the 11th*
Rokugatsu *ni* **in** *June*

And you can make these question words using **nan** (*what?*):

Nannichi ni *On what date?*
Nangatsu ni *In which month?*

And don't forget the general question word **itsu** (*when?*).

When you use general time expressions such as **ashita** (*tomorrow*), **raishū** (*next week*) and **mainichi** (*every day*), you don't need **ni**. (In the same way, you don't say *on tomorrow* or *in next week* in English.) You have already learnt this with the words **asa** (*morning*) and **yoru** (*evening*) in Unit 8, setsumei 7. For example:

Raishū Kyōto ni ikimasu.   *I'm going to Kyoto next week.*
Emi-san wa mainichi daigaku *Emi goes to university every day.*
 ni ikimasu.

You should note that you say the time expression before the place and the action word. (Also look back at Unit 8, setsumei 4 to remind yourself of sentence order.)

4 Raishū no doyōbi ni kaerimasu: *I am going back next Saturday.*

You can combine time expressions with **no** to make the following:

raishū no doyōbi	*next Saturday*
ashita no ban	*tomorrow evening*
kongetsu no hatsuka	*the 20th of this month*

Hinto

You'll meet a few of these time expressions in each unit from now on, so that you can gradually build up your vocabulary. Try making sentences about your daily activities using these expressions and the new verbs you have learnt. This will help you to remember new words because you are putting them in meaningful situations (*I'm going to the cinema tonight, I'm going to the supermarket tomorrow*, etc.).

5 Pātii o shimashō: *Let's have a party!*

You have already practised making suggestions in the **Hana-shimashō** section of this unit. Here are some more examples:

Doyōbi ni eigakan ni ikimashō. *Let's go to the cinema on Saturday.*
Ashita kaimono ni ikimashō. *Let's go shopping tomorrow.*

If you want to ask somebody to do something with you, turn the phrase into a question by adding **ka**. For example:

Doyōbi ni eigakan ni ikimashō ka.	*Shall we go to the cinema on Saturday?*
Raishū no nichiyōbi ni *doraibu* ni ikimashō ka.	*Shall we go for a **drive** next Sunday?*

To answer you can say:

Ii desu ne. Sō shimashō.   *That sounds nice. Let's do that!*

Or:

Yorokonde.   *I'd love to.*

(To *refuse*, see **setsumei** 7 below.)

6 Watashi no uchi ni kimasen ka: *Would you like to come to my house?*

This phrase literally means *won't you come to my house?* To express *I don't ...* (the negative) in Japanese you change **masu** to **masen**. For example:

Kōhii o nomi*masen*.	*I **don't** drink coffee.*
Asagohan o tabe*masen*.	*I **don't** eat breakfast.*
Ashita shigoto ni iki*masen*.	*I'm **not** going to work tomorrow.*

You can politely invite someone to do something by adding **ka** to the negative. For example:

Kōhii o nomimasen ka.	*Would you like to (lit. won't you) drink some coffee?*
Eigakan ni ikimasen ka.	*Would you like to go to the cinema?*
Watashi no uchi ni kimasen ka.	*Would you like to come to my house?*

(You will learn more about the negative in Unit 12).

7 Konshū no doyōbi wa dō desu ka: *How about this Saturday?*

When suggesting dates or times to do an activity, you can use the phrase **... wa dō desu ka** (*how about ...?*). For example:

Kayōbi wa dō desu ka.   *How about Tuesday?*

Rokuji wa dō desu ka.	*How about 6 o'clock?*
Ashita wa dō desu ka.	*How about tomorrow?*

To say *yes*, use **... wa ii desu** (*it's fine*). For example:

Kayōbi wa ii desu.	*Tuesday is fine.*
Rokuji wa ii desu.	*6 o'clock is fine.*

(For other ways to accept see **setsumei** 5 above.)

To refuse politely use **... wa chotto ...** (*It's a bit ...*). For example:

Ashita wa chotto ...	*Tomorrow's a bit ...*
	(implying 'inconvenient')

You can precede this with **zannen desu ga ...** (*it's a pity but ...*). For example:

Zannen desu ga ashita	*It's a shame but tomorrow*
wa chotto ...	*is a bit ...*

When you trail your sentence off at the end like this, the listener will understand that it's inconvenient without you having to say so.

8 Tomodachi to resutoran ni ikimasu: *I'm going with a friend to a restaurant.*

In Unit 3 you learnt that **to** means *and* when you link two objects. For example:

Kōhii to jūsu o kudasai.	*May I have a coffee and some juice?*
Yamaguchi-san wa gorufu to	*Mr Yamaguchi plays golf*
tenisu o shimasu.	*and tennis.*

To can also have the meaning *with*. For example:

tomodachi to	*with my friend*
An-san to	*with Anne*

You should note that **to** comes after the person you do something with. For example:

***An-san to* benkyō shimasu.**	*I study **with Anne**.*

You say **tomodachi to** (etc.) after any time expression and before the place/item. For example:

Ashita *tomodachi to* Rondon ni ikimasu.	*I am going to London with a friend tomorrow.*
Sukotto-san wa *An-san to* eiga o mimasu.	*Scott is going to watch a film with Anne.*

9 The dates 1st–10th

You learnt to say the dates from the 11th to 31st in Unit 4 by adding **nichi** to the appropriate number: 11th = **jūichi-nichi**. The exceptions to this rule were **jūyokka** (14th), **nijūyokka** (24th) and **hatsuka** (20th). The 1st–10th are also slightly different:

tsuitachi	1st	muika	6th
futsuka	2nd	nanoka	7th
mikka	3rd	yōka	8th
yokka	4th	kokonoka	9th
itsuka	5th	tōka	10th

✳ Hinto

Try to find some word associations to help you remember these new numbers. You may already find these dates familiar. If you look back to Unit 6 (setsumei 5, page 79), you will see that the system B method of counting (**hitotsu**, **futatsu**, **mittsu** ...) is similar to these dates, apart from **tsuitachi** (*1st*). The main difference is that the dates end in **ka**, whereas the numbers end in **tsu**.

Perhaps some of the same word associations will help you to remember these dates. **Tōka** (*10th*) sounds like the English word **toe**, and you have ten toes on your feet! **Nanoka** (*7th*) sounds very close to **nana** (7). **Itsuka** (*5th*) is like **itsu** (*when*). **Kokonoka** (*9th*) sound like the English word *coconut*! The **yō** of **yōka** (8th) rhymes with *yolk*.

These are a few ideas to help you, but don't feel you have to be able to remember every item of vocabulary in one go! It takes time and practice to master vocabulary and new phrases. You will remember some words quicker than others, especially those more relevant to your life. For example, if your birthday is on the 10th you will probably remember **tōka** more easily. And of course, if you have a chance to speak with a Japanese person, these personal details will be very useful and relevant.

Renshū

1   Kiku-renshū

In the left-hand column below are the names of some Japanese festivals and special days. In the right-hand column are the dates of the festivals. Listen to the cassette and match each festival with its correct date by writing the letters a–h, as appropriate, in the brackets after the dates.

(a)	Girls' Day (**Hina Matsuri**)	3rd November ( )
(b)	Boys' Day (**Kodomo ni hi**)	7th July ( )
(c)	Star Festival (**Tanabata**)	15th November ( )
(d)	7–5–3 Festival (**Shichi go san**)	3rd March ( )
(e)	Bean throwing Festival (**Setsubun**)	4th Feburary ( )
(f)	Culture Day (**Bunka no hi**)	10th October ( )
(g)	Change of clothing day (**Koromogae**)	5th May ( )
(h)	Sports Day (**Taiiku no hi**)	1st October ( )

2 (a) Using the information below make sentences saying where you are going and when.

> **Rei:** Next week, cinema = (Watashi wa) raishū eigakan ni ikimasu.

(i)   Tomorrow, London
(ii) This evening, concert (**konsāto**)
(iii) Today, France
(iv) Every day, home (go back)

Remember: you don't need to say **watashi wa** (*I*) unless you need to put emphasis on it – (see Unit 2, setsumei 1).

(b) Now make sentences about Tani using the same information.

> **Rei:** Next week, cinema = Tani-san wa raishū eigakan ni ikimasu.

(c) Finally, can you change these sentences into questions using **doko** (*where?*)?

> **Rei:** Next week, where? = Raishū doko ni ikimasu ka.

3 The sentences below have gaps, and you have to decide whether or not to write **ni** (meaning *on, in* or *at*). Write a **batsu** sign (×) if **ni** is not needed.

Look back at setsumei 3 if you need to remind yourself of the rules.

(a) An-san wa jūji _____ Nihongo no kurasu ni ikimasu.
(b) Sukotto-san wa ashita _____ tenisu o shimasu.
(c) Tani-san wa raishū _____ Furansu ni kaerimasu.
(d) Mina-san wa konshū no doyōbi _____ watashi no uchi ni kimasu.
(e) Yamaguchi-san wa mainichi _____ kaisha ni ikimasu.
(f) Takeshi-san wa shichigatsu _____ Kyōto ni ikimasu.

4   Make sentences using the information in the chart below.

Time/day	Activity	Type of suggestion
(a) Tomorrow	watch a film	Shall we?
(b) Next week	go for a drive	Let's!
(c)	read this magazine	Would you like to?
(d) Today	have lunch	Shall we?
(e) This evening	come to my house	Would you like to?
(f) Next Saturday	go shopping	Let's!
(g)	drink some coffee	Would you like to?
(h) Tomorrow evening	go to a restaurant	Shall we?

5   Imagine you are inviting your Japanese friend out. Can you fill in your part of the dialogue using the information in English?

You   *Say 'Hello'.*
Friend   Konnichi wa!
You   *Ask if they'd like to come to your house next week.*
Friend   Ii desu ne! Yorokonde ikimasu.
You   *Ask 'how about Wednesday?'*
Friend   Suiyōbi desu ka. Suiyōbi wa chotto …
You   *'How about Thursday then?'*
Friend   Zannen desu ga mokuyōbi ni Rondon ni ikimasu. Doyōbi wa dō desu ka.
You   *Say 'Saturday will be fine. How about 4 o'clock?'*
Friend   Hai, wakarimashita. Arigatō gozaimasu.
You   *Say 'See you' and 'goodbye'.*

6 Tani is being invited out to a disco by Scott but she doesn't really want to go! Can you help her make excuses? Use **zannen desu ga ...** and **chotto**, but try to think of some reasons why she can't go – playing tennis with a friend, going to a restaurant with Anne, etc.

Scott   Konshū no doyōbi ni disuko ni ikimashō ka.
Tani   ...
Scott   Ja, kinyōbi wa dō desu ka.
Tani   ...
Scott   Aa, sō desu ka. mokuyōbi wa dō desu ka.
Tani   ...
Scott   Ēto, raishū no getsuyōbi wa?
Tani   ...
Scott   Sō desu ka. Zannen desu ne. (*sees Anne*) An-san! doyōbi ni disuko ni ikimashō ka!

☑ Tesuto

1 Which phrase would you choose to ask your friend where they are going tomorrow?

(a) Raishū doko ni ikimasu ka.
(b) Yūbinkyoko wa doko desu ka.
(c) Ashita doko ni ikimasu ka.

2 Change these sentences into suggestions or invitations according to the information in brackets.

(a) Ashita resutoran ni ikimasu. (*shall we?*)
(b) Raishū watashi no uchi ni kimasu. (*would you like to?*)
(c) Konban eiga o mimasu. (*let's*)
(d) Ja, sushi o tabemasu. (*shall we?*)
(e) Mokuyōbi ni doraibu ni ikimasu. (*shall we?*)
(f) Terebi o mimasu (*would you like to?*)

3 How do you say these sentences in Japanese?

(a) I'm going to London with a friend tomorrow.
(b) It's a shame but Sunday is a bit ...
(c) Would you like to drink a beer?
(d) How about Thursday?
(e) Saturday is fine. I'd love to.
(f) My birthday is August 8th.
(g) Where shall we go?

10

SENSHŪ KYŌTO NI IKIMASHITA

Last week I went to Kyoto

In this unit you will learn

- how to talk about past events (the past tense)
- how to say where an activity took place
- about types of transport
- more time expressions
- how to say you want to do something

Hajime ni

In Units 8 and 9 you learnt how to talk about daily and future activities. In this unit you will learn how to talk about past events and activities. This is a simple process: you change the **masu** ending to **mashita**, as in the title of this unit:

Kyōto ni iki*mashita*. *I went to Kyoto.*

Hinto *Pronunciation tip*

The **i** sound in **mashita** is almost unspoken – **ma-sh-ta**.

Hanashimashō

Talk about activities that you did by changing these sentences into the past tense as in the example:

Rei: Asagohan o tabe**masu**. Asagohan o tabe**mashita**. (*I ate breakfast.*)

1 Kōhii o nomi**masu**. _____ (*I drank some coffee.*)
2 Kaimono o shi**masu.** _____ (*I did the shopping.*)
3 Terebi o mi**masu**. _____ (*I watched TV.*)
4 Shimbun o yomi**masu**. _____ (*I read the newspaper.*)
5 Resutoran ni iki**masu**. _____ (*I went to a restaurant.*)
6 Uchi ni kaeri**masu**. _____ (*I went home.*)

 Tango-hyō

Transport

aruite	on foot
chikatetsu	underground
basu	bus
densha	train
fune	boat
jitensha	bicycle
shinkansen	bullet train
hikōki	plane
kuruma	car
takushii	taxi
nan de	how?

Time expressions

senshū	last week
kinō	yesterday
kesa	this morning
sengetsu	last month
kinō no ban	last night
gogo	afternoon
kotoshi	this year
kyonen	last year
rainen	next year
kakarimasu	it takes
jikan	hour
gofun	five minutes
juppun	10 minutes
gurai	about
ryokō shimasu	travel
dono gurai	how long?

Kaiwa

Anne is talking to Takeshi about a recent school trip.

Takeshi   Senshū Kyōto ni ikimashita. **Shūgaku ryokō** deshita.
Anne   Ii desu ne! Nan de ikimashita ka.
Takeshi   Tōkyō eki kara shinkansen de ikimashita. Kyōto made go jikan gurai kakarimashita.
Anne   **He! Hayai** desu ne! Kyōto de nani o shimashita ka.
Takeshi   Kayōbi ni **o-tera** o **takusan** mimashita. Sorekara **gekijō** ni ikimashita. Kyōto no **odori** o mimashita.
Anne   Sō desu ka. Watashi wa odori o **mitai** desu. Suiyōbi ni nani o shimashita ka.
Takeshi   **Mata** o-tera o mimashita. Soshite Tōkyō ni kaerimashita.
Anne   Kyōto no **ryōri** wa dō deshita ka.
Takeshi   Wakarimasen. Mainichi **kappu nudoru** o tabemashita.
Anne   Takeshi-kun! **Yokunai** desu yo!

shūgaku ryokō	school trip
he!	hey, really!
hayai	quick, fast
o-tera	temples
takusan	many
gekijō	theatre
odori	dancing
mitai	want to see
mata	again
ryōri	cookery
kappu nudoru	cup noodles
yokunai	no good

Nihon ni tsuite

Kyōto

Kyoto is the old capital of Japan and today is often referred to as the religious centre of Japan. This is because there are many Buddhist temples (**o-tera**) and Shinto shrines (**jinja**) here. During the Second World War, Kyoto was one of the few cities not significantly damaged by bombing, and so many of the old buildings still stand today. Kyoto is a very popular tourist attraction both with the Japanese and with foreigners, but is is also a very peaceful place, especially if you explore places away from the main attractions.

Setsumei

1 Senshū Kyōto ni ikimashita: *Last week I went to Kyoto.*

You have already practised talking about past activites in the *Hanashimashō* section of this unit. You have also been introduced to some more time expressions. Here are some more examples of sentences describing past activities. Practise them by covering the Japanese and using the English as a prompt to say the sentences:

An-san wa kinō Nihongo o benkyō shimashita.	*Yesterday Anne studied Japanese.*
Tani-san wa senshū no doyōbi ni Furansu ni kaerimashita.	*Tani went back to France last Saturday.*
Scott-san wa kyonen Nihon ni kimashita.	*Scott came to Japan last year.*
Emi-san wa sengetsu tomodachi to ryokō o shimashita.	*Emi did some travelling last month with a friend.*

2 Kyōto de nani o shimashita ka: *What did you do in Kyoto?*

To say where an activity happens or happened you use **de**, meaning *in* or *at*. You say **de** after the place. For example:

Kyōto de	*in Kyoto*
uchi de	*at home*
resutoran de	*at a restaurant*
gekijō de	*at the theatre*
Takeshi-kun wa *gekijō de* odori o mimashita.	*Takeshi watched dancing at the theatre.*
Yamaguchi-san wa *uchi de* shimbun o yomimashita.	*Mr Yamaguchi read a newspaper at home.*

Reiko-san wa mainichi *sūpā de* *Reiko does the shopping every*
kaimono o shimasu. *day **at the supermarket**.*

Notice the sentence order:

(a) the person who does the action;
(b) the time expression;
(c) the place;
(d) the item followed by **o**;
(e) the action word. (See also Unit 8, setsumei 1, page 102 and Unit 9, setsumei 1, page 113)

3 Nan de ikimashita ka: *How did you get there?*

This is the other use of **de** that you will learn in this unit. When used with transport, **de** takes the meaning of *by*. For example:

densha de	*by train*
hikōki de	*by plane*
Takeshi-kun wa basu de gakkō ni ikimasu.	*Takeshi goes by bus to school.*
Reiko-san wa kuruma de sūpā ni ikimasu.	*Reiko goes to the supermarket by car.*
Shinjuki kara Shibuya made chikatetsu de ikimashita.	*I went from Shinjuku to Shibuya by underground.*

However, you don't need to use **de** when saying **aruite** (*on foot*):

Aruite tomadachi no uchi *I went to my friend's house*
ni ikimashita. *on foot.*

The question word is **nan de** (*how?*):

Nan de kaisha ni ikimasu ka. *How do you get to work?*

Answer by replacing **nan** with the mode of transport:

Jitensha de ikimasu. *I go by bicycle.*

4 Kyōto made gojikan gurai kakarimasu: *It takes about five hours to Kyoto.*

To say how long a journey takes, you use **kakarimasu**. Lengths of time are expressed by adding **kan** to **ji** (*o'clock*), **nichi/ka** (*day*), **shū** (*week*), etc. For example:

ich**iji**kan	*one* **hour**
futsuka**kan**	*two* **days**
ni**shū**kan	*two* **weeks**
go**fun** (**kan**)	*five* **minutes**

You can omit **kan** when saying minutes and days as long as the meaning is clear. For example:

yonjuppun	*40 minutes*
mikka	*three days* (or *the third day*)

One day in Japanese is **ichinichi**.

Gurai means *about*, for example, **gofun gurai** (*about five minutes*). You have already learnt **goro** meaning *about*, but this is only used when actually saying the time, not a length of time. For example:

Hachiji *goro* **okimasu.**	*I get up at* **about** *8 o'clock.*
Hachijikan *gurai* **kakarimasu.**	*It takes* **about** *8 hours.*

To ask *how long does it take?*, you say: **dono gurai kakarimasu ka**. For example:

Rondon kara Tōkyō made dono gurai kakarimasu ka.	*How long does it take from London to Tokyo?*
Hikōki de jūnijikan gurai kakarimasu.	*By plane it takes about twelve hours.*
Yūbinkyoku made dono gurai kakarimasu ka.	*How far is it to the post office?*
Aruite juppun gurai kakarimasu.	*On foot it's about ten minutes.*

5 Watashi wa odori o mitai desu: *I want to see some dancing.*

To say that you want to do something, you replace **masu** with **tai desu**. For example:

yomi**masu**	*I read*	yomi**tai desu**	*I want to read*
nomi**masu**	*I drink*	nomi**tai desu**	*I want to drink*
tabe**masu**	*I eat*	tabe**tai desu**	*I want to eat*

Here are some examples:

Eigo no shimbun o yomitai desu.	*I want to read an English newspaper.*
Biiru o nomitai desu.	*I want to drink a beer.*
Tōkyō ni ikitai desu.	*I want to go to Tokyo.*
Uchi ni kaeritai desu.	*I want to go home.*

5 *More about time expressions*

In the last three units you have been learning a number of time expressions. In this unit the focus has been on past time expressions as well as *year* expressions (*this/last/next year*). Below are some examples of how these phrases are used.

You may wish to practise these phrases in the following way. First familiarise yourself with the time expressions in the **Tango-hyō** section of this unit (for example, say them out aloud; cover the English side, then the Japanese side; get someone to test you). Then cover up the Japanese side of the phrases below and see if you can say these time expressions:

senshū no doyōbi	*last Saturday*
kesa (no) hachi ji ni	*this morning at 8 o'clock*
kinō no gogo	*yesterday afternoon*
kyonen no hachigatsu	*last August*
rainen no sangatsu	*next March*
kotoshi no shigatsu	*this April*
sengetsu no kokonoka	*the 9th of last month*

 ———————— **Renshū** ————————

 1 **Kiku-renshū**

The pictures (a)–(h) below show different forms of transport. On the cassette you will hear people saying how they get to different places (i)–(viii). Match up the modes of transport and the destinations.

(i)	France	(iv)	Korea (**Kankoku**)
(ii)	Shinjuku Station	(v)	School
(iii)	Shibuya Station	(vi)	Company
		(vii)	Bank

2 Anne is talking about some of the activities she did at the weekend. Listen to the cassette and link each activity with where it took place. Listen carefully – the activites are not said in the order (a)–(e)!

(a) Had a meal with a friend   (i) in Tokyo
(b) Watched a film   (ii) at home
(c) Did Japanese homework
    (*shukudai*)   (iii) at a restaurant
(d) Went shopping   (iv) at a friend's house
(e) Bought some postcards   (v) at a department store

3 Say out aloud the approximate times from the fourth column of the chart below. The first one has been done for you.

Rei: (a) Jūnijikan gurai kakarimasu.

From	To	Transport	Approx. time
(a) London	Tokyo	aeroplane	12 hours
(b) Tokyo	Kyoto	bullet train	5 hours
(c) Derby	Sheffield	train	40 minutes
(d) Anne's house	Scott's house	underground	1 hour
(e) Anne's house	supermarket	on foot	5 minutes

Now, again using the chart, say out aloud how long the journeys take. The first one has been done for you, but try saying it yourself first, then check that you were correct. Keep the information in the same order as it is presented in the chart.

Rei: (a) Rondon kara Tōkyō made hikōki de jūnijikan gurai kakarimasu.

4 Link the time expressions in the left-hand column below with their Japanese equivalent on the right.

(a) Yesterday evening   (i) Senshū no kinyōbi
(b) Tomorrow night   (ii) Kotoshi no rokugatsu
(c) Next Thursday   (iii) Raishū no mokuyōbi
(d) Last February   (iv) Kinō no ban
(e) This June   (v) Sengetsu no tōka
(f) Last Friday   (vi) Kyonen no nigatsu
(g) The 10th of last month   (vii) Ashita no ban

5 Using the pictures and information below, make sentences about some of Reiko's past and future activities:

(a) Shopping in the Ginza last Saturday
(b) At home, last Wednesday
(c) At a restaurant with a friend, tomorrow
(d) Last year, in Kyoto
(e) Yesterday evening
(f) Last month on the 10th, at a Tokyo theatre

6 Below is a Japanese **pazuru** (*puzzle*) which has been partially completed. To fill in the spaces you need to work out how to say the English sentences below in Japanese. You then have to work out which sentence fits which line of spaces (a)–(g) in the **pazuru!** Put one letter in each square. **Gambatte ne!** (*good luck!*)

(a) _ _ _ made _ _ _ _ _ _ _ _ _ _ gofun _ _ _ _ _ _ _ _ _ _

(b) _ _ _ _ _ _ _ _ _ _ _ _ _ shitai _ _ _ _

(c) _ _ _ _ _ _ _ _ _ _ _ _ _ _ kaisha _ _ _ _ _ _ _ _

(d) _ _ _ _ no _ _ _ _ _ _ _ _ _ _ no tōsuto _ _ _ _ _ _ _ _ _ _ _

(e) Kotoshi _ _ _ _ _ _ _ _ _ _ _ _ _ _ _ _ _ _

(f) _ _ _ _ _ _ _ _ kugatsu _ _ _ _ _ _ _ _ ikimasu

(g) _ _ _ _ _ _ _ _ ban gekijō _ _ _ _ _ _ _ _ _ _ _

- Next September I am going to Japan.
- Tomorrow I want to do some shopping.
- This morning I had toast for breakfast.
- Shall we go to the theatre on Tuesday evening?
- This year I want to go to France.
- It takes five minutes to the station by bicycle.
- My father goes to work (company) by car.

☑ Tesuto

This test takes the form of **Fukushū** (*revision*) of all the units you have learnt so far. Each question refers you back to the relevant units.

1 How do you say these phrases in Japanese? (Unit 1)

(a) Good morning
(b) How do you do?
(c) Good night
(d) Excuse me
(e) Thank you very much
(f) See you!

2 A Japanese visitor is visiting your area and you have been asked by the local newspaper to interview him or her, and write a short article.

 (a) Think of five questions you could ask (hint: name, age, birthday, family size, nationality, job, hobbies, etc.).

 (b) Now imagine you are the person being interviewed and answer your questions. (Units 2–4)

3 Choose the correct English meaning for each of these phrases. (Units 5–7)

 (a) Sono kamera o kudasai.
  (i) May I have this camera please?
  (ii) May I see that camera please?
  (iii) May I have that camera please?

 (b) Yūbinkyoku wa kuji kara goji han made desu.
  (i) The supermarket is open from 9–5.30.
  (ii) The post office is open from 9–5.30.
  (iii) The supermarket is open from 9–5.

 (c) Tsugi no shingō o hidari ni magatte kudasai.
  (i) Turn left at the next crossroads.
  (ii) Turn right at the next traffic lights.
  (iii) Turn left at the next traffic lights.

4 Fill in the missing parts of these sentences. (Units 8–10)

 (a) Kinō kaimono o _____ .

 (b) Raishū _____ doyōbi _____ pātii o _____ mashō!

 (c) Mainichi gakkō _____ Nihongo_____benkyō _____ .

 (d) Asagohan ni tamago _____ _____ .

 (e) Senshū Tani-san _____ Furansu ni _____ .

 (f) Sengetsu eiga _____ _____ .

 (g) Kinō _____ ban jū ji _____ ne _____ .

 (h) Uchi _____ eki _____ basu _____ _____ masu.

11

II O-TENKI DESU NE

It's nice weather, isn't it?

In this unit you will learn

- how to describe people, objects and places
- two types of describing words
- how to make a comment and agree with someone
- how to talk about the weather and the seasons

Hajime ni

You are going to be introduced to two types of describing words (or adjectives) in this unit. Examples of English adjectives are: *beautiful*, *small*, *expensive*. Such words are used to describe items and people (as well as feelings, emotions, etc.).

There are of course many adjectives in Japanese (as there are in English), but this unit will select just a few of the more useful ones which you can use in everyday life. Later units will introduce you to more, but in this unit you will have the chance simply to understand how adjectives work in Japanese.

Hinto

Don't worry at this stage if there are things you don't know how to say. Concentrate on what you can say – it is this gradual building-up of vocabulary with plenty of short-term goals which will ultimately improve your confidence and grasp of Japanese.

Hanashimashō

You have already come across some Japanese adjectives in previous units. Look back now at the dialogues of the following units and answer the questions below.

(a) How does Reiko say *He looks young, doesn't he?* (Unit 4, page 50)
(b) How does Emi say *She's pretty, isn't she?* (Unit 4, page 51)
(c) How does Emi say *That watch is smart, isn't it?* (Unit 5, page 61)
(d) How does the passer-by compliment Scott on his Japanese? (Unit 7, page 90)
(e) How does Scott comment on how early Mr Yamaguchi gets up? (Unit 8, page 101)
(f) How does Tani say *That will be nice?* (Unit 9, page 113)

These describing words have been included in the vocabulary list below.

 Tango-hyō

I *adjectives*

atsui (desu)	(it is) hot	**atsukatta desu**	it was hot
samui desu	it is cold	**samukatta desu**	it was cold
tanoshii desu	it is pleasant	**tanoshikatta desu**	it was pleasant
omoshiroi desu	it is interesting, funny	**omoshirokatta desu**	it was interesting
takai desu	it is expensive	**takakatta desu**	it was expensive
yasui desu	it is cheap	**yasukatta desu**	it was cheap
ōkii desu	it is big	**ōkikatta desu**	it was big
chiisai desu	it is small	**chiisakatta desu**	it was small
oishii desu	it is delicious	**oishikatta desu**	it was delicious
ii desu	it is good, nice	**yokatta desu**	it was good
warui desu	it is bad	**warukatta desu**	it was bad
kawaii desu	it is cute, pretty	**kawaikatta desu**	it was pretty
hayai desu	it is early/quick	**hayakatta desu**	it was early
wakai desu	he is young	**wakakatta desu**	he was young

Seasons

haru	spring
natsu	summer
aki	autumn
fuyu	winter

Na *adjectives*

(o)genki	well, healthy, lively
benri	convenient
shizuka	quiet
shinsetsu	kind
suteki	smart, fashionable
jōzu	good at
(o)hisashiburi	long time, no see
kissaten	coffee shop
hontō ni	really, in truth
	very

Kaiwa

Reiko is meeting up with a friend, Haruko, whom she hasn't seen for a while.

Haruko Aa! Reiko-san! O-genki desu ka.
Reiko Ee, **okagesama de**. Haruko-san, o-hisashiburi desu ne.
Haruko Sō desu ne. Ja, kono kissaten de kohii o nomimashō!

In the coffee shop:

Reiko Kyō wa ii o-tenki desu ne.
Haruko Sō desu ne. **Mō** haru desu.
Reiko Kyonen no natsu wa atsukatta desu ne.
Haruko Ee, kotoshi no natsu mo atsui **ka na?**

As they are getting ready to leave:

Haruko Kono kissaten no kēki wa oishii desu ne.
Reiko Ee, chotto takai desu **ga** totemo oishii desu.
Haruko Kyō wa hontō ni tanoshikatta desu. Arigatō gozaimashita.
Reiko Dewa, mata aimashō. **O-genki de!**
Haruko Sayōnara!

okagesama de	I'm fine, thanks (said in reply to **o-genki desu ka**. *Lit.* thanks to you)
mō	already
ka na?	I wonder (casual speech)
ga	but
o-genki de	take care

Nihon ni tsuite

Weather and seasons

The weather is a popular topic of conversation in Japan. When people meet up with each other they often comment on the weather – **ii o-tenki desu ne!** – rather than on a person's health (unless they haven't seen each other for a long time). Letters also often open with a comment on the weather.

Books about Japan often refer to 'four distinct seasons'. This needs some clarification. *Spring* (**haru**) is pleasantly warm and is the season of the famous cherry blossoms. The television news follows the spread of these blossoms from the south to the north of the country.

Between spring and *summer* (**natsu**) is the rainy season which lasts for about two weeks. Immediately after this, summer begins in earnest and the weather becomes very hot and increasingly humid.

Autumn (**aki**) begins in September and is sometimes preluded by another short rainy season with the occasional typhoon. The weather is fresh and fine, and the leaves on the trees change to stunning colours – this is known as the 'leaf viewing season' and it sweeps across the country from north to south, again followed avidly on the daily news.

Winter (**fuyu**) is cold and crisp with blue skies during the day, but also with plenty of snow, particularly in the northern and mountain areas.

 ——————— **Setsumei** ———————

1 O-genki desu ka: *Are you well?*

As you learnt in Unit 2 (setsumei 2, page 29) **o** is said in front of certain words to make them sound more polite or formal when addressing other people. It is sometimes translated as *honourable*, although this makes some words sound ridiculous in translation (for example, **o-tearai**, *the honourable toilet!*). Women in particular use **o** – it has the effect of making their speech sound more genteel. Here are some more examples of its use:

o-tenki   *the weather*

o-sushi	*sushi*
o-hisashiburi	*long time, no see*
o-hashi	*chopsticks*
o-tanjōbi	*birthday*
o-furo	*the bath*

2 Kyō wa ii o-tenki desu ne: *Today is nice weather, isn't it?*

There are two types of adjectives or describing words in Japanese. These are usually referred to as **i** adjectives and **na** adjectives. This unit will mostly use **i** adjectives.

(a) **I** adjectives. There are two basic ways to use adjectives in a sentence:

Oishii kēki desu ne. *It's a delicious cake, isn't it?*
Kono kēki wa oishii desu ne. *This cake is delicious, isn't it?*

You should note that the English and Japanese order is the same. There are some more examples below. Use these as an exercise by first looking at the **i** adjectives in the **Tango-hyō** section. When you feel familiar with the new words, try covering the Japanese phrases below and see if you can say them from memory, using the English translations as prompts.

Kyō wa atsui desu ne. *It's hot today, isn't it?*
Nihon no fuyu wa samui desu. *The Japanese winters are cold.*
Kono eiga wa omoshiroi desu ne. *This film is interesting, isn't it?*
Omoshiroi e desu ne. *It's an interesting picture, isn't it?*
Kono pātii wa tanoshii desu ne. *This party is enjoyable, isn't it?*
Sono sēta wa takai desu. *That jumper is expensive.*
Yasui kōhii desu ne. *It's cheap coffee, isn't it?*
Kono kēki wa oishii desu ne. *These cakes are delicious, aren't they?*
Natsu wa atsui desu. *The summer is hot.*
An-san wa kawaii desu ne. *Anne is pretty isn't she?*

(b) **Na** adjectives. It will soon become clear why these adjectives are called **na** adjectives:

Kono kissaten wa shizuka desu ne. *This coffee shop is quiet, isn't it?*

Shizuka*na* kissaten desu ne.　*It's a quiet coffee shop, isn't it?*

When the describing word is followed immediately by the item/person it is describing, you put **na** between the two words. It may help you to think of **na** in a similar way to *no*. For example:

watashi *no* tokei	*my watch*
Reiko-san *no* tomodachi	*Reiko's friend*
benri*na* sūpā	*a useful supermarket*

Here are some more examples of phrases using **na** adjectives: (Note that 'na' is not used if the adjective comes immediately before 'desu'.)

O-genki desu ka.	*Are you well?*
Genki*na* hito desu ne.	*She's a lively person, isn't she?*
Kono resutoran wa shizuka desu.	*This restaurant is quiet.*
Shizuka*na* tokoro desu ne.	*It's a quiet place, isn't it?*
Satō-sensei wa shinsetsu*na* hito desu.	*Mrs Sato, the teacher, is a kind person.*
Sore wa suteki*na* tokei desu.	*That's a smart watch.*

(c)　To agree with someone you can say **Sō desu ne** (*yes, it is*). For example:

Ii o-tenki desu ne. Sō desu ne.　*It's nice weather isn't it? Yes, it is.*

Haruko uses this reply twice in the dialogue. Look back and see where she uses it.

✳ Hinto

You have been introduced to a lot of new vocabulary in this unit, in the form of adjectives or describing words. You may find it helpful to make two lists of adjectives, one called **i** adjectives and the other called **na** adjectives. You can keep adding to these lists as you learn more of these words.

It is important to keep practising these new words in phrases that you can use every day. For example, make a comment to yourself about the weather every day: **Kyō wa atsui (samui/chotto atsui/chotto samui/ii o-tenki) desu ne**. And try describing items and people around you. Talk to yourself or impress your friends(!) and try to keep using the new vocabulary in meaningful situations.

3 Kyonen no natsu wa atsukatta desu ne: Last summer was hot, wasn't it?

(a) **I**-adjectives

In Japanese, the **i** adjectives have their own past tense. In English, we change *is* to *was*:

It is hot. → It was hot.

In Japanese, *hot* itself changes:

Atsu**i** desu. → Atsu**katta** desu.

To make this change, you drop the last **i** of the adjective and add **katta**. Now look back at the **Tango-hyō** section for more examples, then try covering up the two right-hand columns and saying the past of the adjective from looking at the present form. (Note that **ii** (*good*) changes to **yokatta**).

(b) **Na** adjectives

The past tense of these adjectives is formed in the same way as English adjectives:

Shizuka desu. → **Shizuka deshita.** *It is quiet.* → *It was quiet.*
Shizukana kissaten desu. → *It is a quiet coffee shop.* →
  Shizukana kissaten deshita. *It was a quiet coffee shop.*

4 Mō haru desu: It's spring already.

To say that something has already happened, you use **mō**. For example:

Mō asagohan o tabemashita. *I've already eaten breakfast.*
Mō aki desu. *It's autumn now.*

To say that something hasn't happened yet, you use **mada** (*not yet*). For example:

Mō haru desu ka. *Is is spring yet?*
Iie, mada desu. *No, not yet.*
Mō asagohan o tabemashita ka. *Have you eaten breakfast already?*
Iie, mada desu. *No, not yet.*

5 Chotto takai desu ga totemo oishii desu: *It's a bit expensive but very delicious.*

Here **ga** means *but* and can be used between two phrases as in these examples:

Kyō wa chotto atsui desu ga ii otenki desu.   *Today is a bit hot but it's nice weather.*

Asagohan o tabemashita ga hirugohan o tabemasen deshita.   *I ate breakfast but I didn't eat lunch.*

Kono sētā wa chotto takai desu ga suteki desu.   *This jumper is a bit expensive but it's smart.*

 ———————— **Renshū** ————————

1. Look at the pictures below and make a comment about each one using the new adjectives (describing words) you have learnt in this unit.

   Rei: Takai kuruma desu ne.

2. Now describe the pictures in the past tense without saying the item/person, as in the example.

   Rei: Takakatta desu ne.

3 Can you make the present tense from the past tense of these adjectives?

    (a) Atsukatta desu.
    (b) Shizukana gakkō deshita.
    (c) Tanoshikatta desu.
    (d) Sono eiga wa yokatta desu.
    (e) Kono sandoitchi wa oishikatta desu.
    (f) Reiko-san wa shinsetsu deshita.
    (g) Sutekina sētā deshita.
    (h) Ano hito wa kawaikatta desu.

4 Can you say these sentences in Japanese, linking them with **ga** (*but*)?

    (a) She was a quiet person but she was interesting.
    (b) This ice-cream is delicious but it is a bit expensive.
    (c) I want to go to Japan but it's expensive.
    (d) Last year's spring was a little cold but this year's spring is a little hot.
    (e) This jumper is a bit big but that jumper is a bit small.

5 Kiku-renshū

Listen to Anne and Scott chatting in Japanese talking on the cassette and circle the correct adjective to describe what they think about various things.

Rei: The film was ((interesting) /good/expensive)

    (a) The car was (big/small/fast).
    (b) Today's weather is (hot/cold/pleasant).
    (c) The supermarket is (convenient/cheap/hot).
    (d) The jumper is (smart/cute/nice).
    (e) Scott is (young/bad/kind).
    (f) Tokyo is (quiet/expensive/interesting).
    (g) The school was convenient/quiet/nice).

6 Kiku-renshū

You will hear a short weather report on the cassette. Write next to each of the five cities on the map of Japan below:

    (a) the temperature (this is given in centigrade);
    (b) a comment on the weather.

These words will help you:

ame *rain* (a-me)
hare *fine* (ha-re)
do *degrees* (**jūichido** = *11 degrees*)
nochi *later* (**hare nochi ame** = *fine **later** rain*)

☑ Tesuto

1 Underline the correct word in the brackets below.

   (a) An-san no otōsan wa (wakai/wakaina) desu.
   (b) Kinō no pātii wa (tanoshii/tanoshikatta) desu.
   (c) (Shizukana/shizuka) tokoro desu ne.
   (d) Kono sūpā wa (benri/benrina) desu ne.
   (e) Ano aisukuriimu wa oishikatta (desu/deshita).

2 Link the sentences on the left with the comments on the right. There may be more than one correct answer but they should all make sense!

(a) Kinō resutoran ni ikimashita.	(i) Ii desu ne.
(b) Mō bangohan o tabemashita ka.	(ii) Atsui desu ne.
(c) Mō natsu desu.	(iii) Benri desu ne.
(d) Eiga ni ikimasen ka.	(iv) Tanoshikatta desu.
(e) Eki wa uchi no chikaku desu.	(v) Hai, oishikatta desu.

3   Imagine you are talking with Anne and fill in your part of the conversation.

You   *Say you saw a Japanese language film last week.*
Anne   Dō deshita ka.
You   *Say that it was interesting.*
Anne   Watashi mo Nihongo no eiga o mitai desu.
You   *Suggest that you go to the cinema together tomorrow night.*
Anne   Kissaten ni mo ikimashō ka.
You   *Say you'd love to and suggest going to 'Luna' coffee shop.*
Anne   'Luna' kissaten wa dō desu ka.
You   *Say it is a bit expensive but the ice-cream is very delicious.*

12

SUPŌTSU WA TENISU
GA SUKI DESU
The sport I like is tennis

In this unit you will learn

- how to talk about things that you like
- how to say that you don't like something very much
- how to say what you or another person is good at
- the negative of **masu** words
- how to describe the location of a person or an object

Hajime ni

This is the last unit in which you will be introduced to new language and structures. Some of the unit will already be familiar to you.

In Unit 9 (**setsumei** 6) you were introduced briefly to how to say *I/you/they do not* (etc.). In other words, the *negative* of **masu** words. To do this, you learnt to change the **masu-** ending to **masen**.

In Unit 7 (**setsumei** 3) you learnt how to describe where places are. For example, **eki no mae** means *in front of the station*. You will learn more about this in this unit.

Hanashimashō

1 Change these doing words into the negative. The first one has been done for you. Can you remember what all these words mean?

Tabe**masu** (*I eat*)　　　　Tabe**masen** (*I don't eat* or
　　　　　　　　　　　　　　　　　　　I won't eat)

Nomi**masu**
Gorufu o shi**masu**
Oki**masu**
Ne**masu**
Yomi**masu**
Iki**masu**

2 How do you say these phrases in Japanese? (Look back to Unit 7, setsumei 3 (page 92) if you need to remind yourself.)

(a) The bank is next to the post office.
(b) The station is near to the cinema.
(c) The department store is opposite the bank.
(d) The flower shop is in front of the department store.

 Tango-hyō

suki	like
amari suki dewa/ja arimasen	don't like very much
jōzu	good at, skilful
tokui	good at
totemo	very (much)
amari	not very (much)
zenzen	never

Supōtsu *Sports*

hokkē	hockey
yakyū	baseball
kuriketto	cricket
hyaku mētoru	100 metres (sprint)
kyōsō	a race

Ongaku *Music*

rokku	rock music
jazu	jazz
kurashikku	classical music
poppusu	pop music

Terebi bangumi *TV programmes*

eiga	films
komedi	comedy
nyūsu	news
dorama	drama
hōmu dorama	soap opera
manga	cartoons
dokyumentarii	documentary
ryōri bangumi	cookery programme

Location

naka	inside
ue	above
ushiro	behind, at the back
soto	outside
shita	below
kono chikaku ni	near here

Dōshi *Verbs*

mottekimasu	bring, get
owarimasu	end, finish
demasu	take part in

Objects

tēburu	table
isu	chair
tsukue	desk
honbako	bookcase

Kaiwa

Emi and Anne are watching Takeshi's school sports day and are talking to his teacher.

Sensei An-san, supōtsu wa nani ga suki desu ka.

Anne Sō desu ne. **Gakusei no toki**, hokkē ga suki deshita ga **saikin** amari supōtsu o shimasen.

Sensei Tenisu wa dō desu ka.

Anne Watashi wa amari suki dewa arimasen ga Emi-san wa tenisu ga suki desu. Totemo jōzu desu.

Emi Iie, mada dame desu yo!

Anne	Takeshi-kun wa doko ni **imasu** ka.
Emi	**Kyōgijō** ni **imasen** ka.
Anne	A! Asoko desu. Takeshi!
Takeshi	An-san, konnichiwa. **Oneesan**, nomimono ga arimasu ka. **Nodo ga kawaiteimasu.**
Emi	Hai, jūsu o mottekimashita. Ano kaban no naka ni arimasu.
Takeshi	**Itadakimasu** ... Oishii!
Emi	Takeshi, kyō nan no kyōsō ni demasu ka.
Takeshi	Ano ... hyaku mētoru desu. Boku wa hyaku mētoru ga tokui desu.
Anne (*points over to sports field*)	Are wa hyaku mētoru dewa arimasen ka.
Takeshi	Are! Mō owarimashita. **Hidoi** desu.

Tango

gakusei no toki	when I was at school
saikin	recently
kyōgijō	playing field
oneesan	older sister (younger siblings use this)
nodo ga kawaiteimasu	I'm thirsty
hidoi	terrible
imasu/imasen	is/is not (see setsumei 3)

Nihon ni tsuite

Undōkai *(sports day)*

School sports days are normally held in October when the weather is fine and not too hot. Japan has a special day called **Taiiku no Hi** (*Physical Education Day*) which commemorates the opening of the Tokyo Olympics in 1964. Since then it has become a tradition to hold sports days around this date. School sports days are often held on Sundays, especially at primary schools, so that fathers can also attend. There are even special races for parents!

ⓞ ——————— **Setsumei** ———————

1 Supōtsu wa nani ga suki desu ka: *What sports do you like?*

(a) When you want to ask somebody what they like, you use the word **suki** (*like*) in this pattern: category **wa nani ga suki desu ka**. For example:

Supōtsu wa nani ga suki   *What sports do you like?*
  desu ka

(The **u** of **suki** is hardly spoken – **s(u)-ki**.)

You can talk about other categories such as *food* (**tabemono**), *drink* (**nomimono**), *music* (**ongaku**) and *TV programmes* (**terebi bangumi**) in the same way. For example:

Tabemono wa nani ga suki   *What food do you like?*
  desu ka.
Nomimono wa nani ga suki   *What drink do you like?*
  desu ka.
Ongaku wa nani ga suki desu ka.   *What music do you like?*

(b) **Emi-san wa tenisu ga suki desu:**   *Emi likes tennis.*

To answer the question you replace **nani** (*what?*) with the item that you like. For example:

Watashi wa tōsuto ga suki desu.   *I like toast.*
Reiko-san wa kōhii ga suki desu.   *Reiko likes coffee.*
Emi-san wa kurashikku ongaku   *Emi likes classical music.*
  ga suki desu.

You can also answer in this way (look also at the title of this unit):

Supōtsu wa tenisu ga suki desu. *The sport I like is tennis.*
                    (Or simply *I like tennis.*)
Tabemono wa sushi ga suki desu.*The food I like is sushi.*
                    (*I like sushi.*)
Ongaku wa jazu ga suki desu.   *The music I like is jazz.*
                    (*I like jazz music.*)

(c) If you really like or love something, you add the word **totemo**:

Takeshi-kun wa hyaku mētoru   *Takeshi loves the 100 metres.*
ga totemo suki desu.
Terebi bangumi wa komedi   *I really like TV comedies.*
ga totemo suki desu.
Yamaguchi-san wa biiru ga   *Mr Yamaguchi loves beer.*
totemo suki desu.

(d) If you don't really like something, use **amari suki dewa/ja arimasen** (*don't like very much*):

Watashi wa niku ga amari   *I don't like meat very much.*
suki ja arimasen.
Sukotto-san wa kuriketto ga   *Scott doesn't really like cricket.*
amari suki dewa arimasen.

2 Emi-san wa tenisu ga jōzu desu: *Emi is good at tennis.*

(a) **Jōzu** means *good at,* and you use the same pattern that you learnt with **suki** to compliment other people on their skills. For example: Person **wa** skill **ga jōzu desu.** (*Someone is good at something.*)

An-san wa Nihongo ga jōzu desu. *Anne is good at Japanese.*
Takeshi-kun wa hyaku mētoru *Takeshi is good at the 100 metres.*
ga jōzu desu.
Reiko-san wa ryōri ga jōzu desu. *Reiko is good at cooking.*

Add **totemo** for *very*:

Emi-san wa tenisu ga totemo   *Emi is very good at tennis.*
jōzu desu.

When you talk about your own skills, use **tokui** rather than **jōzu**. This word gives the idea of your strengths rather than your skills and so sounds less big-headed! (The Japanese, like the British, tend to be very modest about themselves.) For example:

Watashi wa supōtsu ga   *I'm good at (my strong point is)*
tokui desu.   *sports.*

(b) On the same theme of modesty, if someone compliments you, a usual reply is to deny this (just as Anne did in the **Kaiwa** section of Unit 7):

Nihongo ga jōzu desu ne.   *You're good at Japanese,*
                                 aren't you?

Iie, mada dame desu.   *No, I'm no good yet.*

Alternatively, to say that you're not very good at something, you can use a similar pattern to the one you learnt for *don't like very much*:

Watashi wa tenisu ga amari   *I'm not very good at tennis.*
jōzu ja arimasen.

3 Takeshi-kun wa doko ni imasu ka: *Where is Takeshi?*

Imasu and **arimasu** are used to talk about where an object or person is located. **Imasu** is used to talk about people and animals (i.e. animate objects), and **arimasu** is used for inanimate objects. For example:

Takeshi-kun wa kyōgijō   *Takeshi is on the sports field.*
ni imasu.

Uchi ni imasen.   *He's not in the house.*

Jūsu wa kaban no naka   *The juice is in the bag.*
ni arimasu.

(Note that you say **ni** after the location and before **imasu/arimasu**. This is a special use of **ni** with the words **arimasu** and **imasu**.)

You can often replace **arimasu/imasu** with **desu**, as you learnt in Unit 7:

Yūbinkyoku wa doko desu ka. *Where is the post office?*

Using **imasu/arimasu** puts more emphasis on the location:

Yūbinkyoku wa doko ni   *Where is the post office located?*
arimasu ka.

But look at the difference in meaning in these two sentences:

Uchi ni imasu.   *He's at home.*
Uchi desu.   *It's a house.*

You have already learnt a different meaning of **arimasu** in Unit 6 – **... ga arimasu ka** (*do you have any ...?*):

Hagaki ga arimasu ka.   *Do you have any postcards?*

4 Nomimono wa kaban no naka ni arimasu: *The drinks are in the bag.*

In this unit you are going to add a few more 'position words' to those you learnt in Unit 7. The list below includes all the ones you have been introduced to so far:

ue	*above, on top*	shita	*below, underneath*
mae	*in front*	ushiro	*behind, at the back*
naka	*inside*	soto	*outside*
tonari	*next to*	chikaku	*near*
mukaigawa	*opposite*	kono chikaku ni	*near here*

Here are some examples of their use with **imasu/arimasu**. Try covering the Japanese words and work out how to say the phrases yourself.

Tokei wa honbako no ue ni arimasu.	*The clock is (located) on top of the bookcase.*
Inu wa beddo no shita ni imasu.	*The dog is under the bed.*
Posuto wa depāto no mae ni arimasu.	*The postbox is in front of the department store.*
An-san wa sūpā no mukaigawa ni imasu.	*Anne is opposite the supermarket.*
Furansa wa Igirisu no chikaku ni arimasu.	*France is near to England.*
Suzuki-san wa tonari no uchi ni imasu.	*Mr Suzuki is next door.*
Emi-san wa ginkō no soto ni imasu.	*Emi is outside the bank.*
Yūbinkyoku wa kono chikaku ni arimasu.	*The post office is near here.*

5 Saikin amari supōtsu o shimasen: *Recently I haven't played sports very much.*

(a) You've already practised saying the negative in the **Hanashimashō** section of this unit. To say *I/you/he* (etc.) *didn't* (the past negative), you add **deshita** to the negative. For example:

Takeshi-kun wa kyōsō ni demasen deshita.	*Takeshi didn't take part in the race.*

Yamaguchi-san wa undokai ni ikimasen deshita.
Mr Yamaguchi didn't go to the sports day.

An-san wa asagohan o tabemasen deshita.
Anne didn't eat any breakfast.

(b) **Amari** (*not very much / not often*) and **zenzen** (*never*) are used only with the negative of the action words. For example:

Watashi wa *zenzen* kōhii o nomimasen.
*I **never** drink coffee.*

Reiko-san wa *amari* terebi o mimasen.
*Reiko doesn't watch TV **much**.*

Gakusei no toki *amari* shukudai o shimasen deshita.
*When I was at school I **didn't often** do homework.*

You say **amari** and **zenzen** before the item and action word.

Renshū

1 Kiku-renshū

You will hear people on the cassette describing the location of people/items. As you listen, decide whether the pictures (a–f) match the descriptions on the cassette. If you think the description is correct, draw a circle (**maru**) under the picture; or draw a cross (**batsu**) if you think it is not correct.

If you don't have the cassette, you can read the dialogues for this and the next activity in the answers section.

2 Kiku-renshū

You are going to hear characters from this book talking about their likes and dislikes. Complete the table below using one tick for *likes* (**suki**), two ticks for *loves* (**totemo suki**) and × for *doesn't like* (**amari suki dewa/ja arimasen**). Leave the squares blank if no information is supplied.

	Anne	Takeshi	Emi	Mr Yamaguchi	Reiko
Tennis					
Japanese cookery					
TV news					
Soap drama					
Whisky					
Cartoons					

3 Read the three dialogues below and fill in the correct word: either **imasu** (for *people* and *animals*) or **arimasu** (for n*on-living/ moving objects* including *plants*).

(a) Q: Emi-san wa doki ni _____ ka.
   A: Ima tenisu kōto ni _____.
   Q: Doko no tenisu kōto desu ka.
   A: Takeshi-kun no gakkō no chikaku ni _____ .

(b) Q: Sumimasen, pōsuto wa kono chikaku ni _____ ka.
   A: Hai, _____ . Massugu itte kudasai. Pōsuto wa ano ginkō no mae ni _____ .

(c) Q: Sumimasen, Yamaguchi-san wa ima uchi ni _____ ka.
   A: Iie, _____ . Ima kaisha ni _____ .
   Q: Nan ji ni kaerimasu ka.
   A: Ano ... hachi ji kara uchi ni _____ .

4 In response to the questions, use the pictures below to describe where the people and items are:

(a) Sumimasen, ginkō wa doko desu ka.

(a)

(b)   An-san no tokei wa doko ni arimasu ka.

(c)   Takeshi-kun no inu wa ima doko ni imasu ka.

(d)   Reiko-san wa doko ni imasu ka.

(e)   Watashi no hon wa doko desu ka.

5   Below is a family photo of the Yamaguchi family and Anne, taken on a sightseeing tour around Tokyo. Can you make sentences about where they all are? The English sentences below will help you.

Mr Yamaguchi is behind Emi.
Reiko is next to Mr Yamaguchi.
Takeshi is next to Reiko.
The dog is in front of Takeshi.
Anne is next to the dog.
Emi is in front of Mr Yamaguchi.

6   Say these sentences in Japanese.

(a)   Takeshi is good at the 100 metres.
(b)   Mr Yamaguchi is very good at golf.
(c)   No, I'm no good at it yet.
(d)   I'm good at French.
(e)   Yesterday I didn't watch TV at all.
(f)   I don't often read the newspaper.

7   Mr Yamaguchi is being asked how often he does certain activities.
Use the prompts in the brackets to work out how he would
answer. Choose between **yoku** (*often*), **tokidoki** (*sometimes*),
amari (*not often*), **zenzen** (*never*).

Rei: Yoku tenisu o shimasu ka. (*No, not often*) Iie, amari shimasen.

(a)   Yoku eiga o mimasu ka. (*yes, sometimes*)
(b)   Yoku gorufu o shimasu ka. (*yes, often*)
(c)   Yoku hon o yomimasu ka. (*no, not often*)
(d)   Tokidoki basu de kaisha ni ikimasu ka. (*no, never*)
(e)   Tokidoki hōmu dorama o mimasu ka. (*no, not often*)
(f)   Yoku rokku ongaku o kikimasu ka. (*no, never*)

8 Word puzzle: Reiko-san wa _____ desu.

The highlighted column on the grid below will give you the information you need to complete this sentence about Reiko, but first you have to work out the missing words in the sentences below and fill them in on the grid. **Gambatte!**

(1) Takeshi-kun wa tenisu ga _____ _____ dewa arimasen. (*Takeshi doesn't like tennis very much.*)

(2) Yamaguchi-san wa _____ ga daisuki desu. (*Mr Yamaguchi loves the news.*)

(3) _____ ni ikitai desu. (*I want to go to Germany.*)

(4) An-san no hon wa terebi no ue _____ _____. (*Anne's book is on the TV.*)

(5) Zenzen manga o _____ . (*I never read comics.*)

(6) Nomimono wa _____ _____ _____ desu. (*The drink I like is cola.*)

(7) Supōtsu wa hokkē _____ _____ desu. (*The sport I am good at is hockey.*)

(8) Emi-san wa tenisu _____ _____ desu. (*Emi is good at tennis.*)

(9) Takeshi-kun wa _____ _____ demasen deshita. (*Takeshi didn't take part in the race.*)

(10) An-san wa _____ jazu ongaku o kikimasen. (*Anne never listens to jazz music.*)

▌ Fukushū tesuto *Revision test*

This is the last test in the units with **Setsumei** sections (Units 1–12), and so this revision test will be based on all these units! Each question will also indicate which unit it is based on so that you can look back at these units if you need to.

1   Units 1–4
Link the Japanese phrases on the left with the English meanings on the right.

(a) Musume wa futari desu. Jūroku sai to jūni sai desu.   (i) How do you do. My name is Takeshi Yamaguchi.

(b) Watashi wa yonjussai desu.   (ii) I am Japanese. I am from Osaka.

(c) Hajimemashite. Yamaguchi Takeshi desu.   (iii) I am a company employee at Nissan.

(d) Kanai wa sensei desu.   (iv) I am 40 years old.

(e) Watashi wa Nihonjin desu. Ōsaka kara desu.   (v) My birthday is on the 11th of September.

(f) Watashi wa Nissan no kaishain desu.   (vi) I have two daughters aged 12 and 16.

(g) Watashi no tanjōbi wa kugatsu jūichi-nichi desu.   (vii) My wife is a teacher.

Now write out your own self-introduction based on this pattern (*i – vii*) and try to learn it off by heart.

2   Units 5–6
How do you say these phrases in Japanese?

(a) May I have this one please?
(b) Please show me that book (over there).
(c) May I have an ice-cream and a coffee please?
(d) Excuse me, what time is it?
(e) The post office is open from 9 until 5.30.
(f) How much is this English newspaper?

    (g) How much is this letter to England?

    (h) Do you have any stamps?

    (i) May I have two bottles of beer please?

3 Unit 7

Scott is in Shinjuku looking for a bank.

    (a) How does he attract the attention of a passer-by and ask where the Japan bank is?

    (b) How does the passer-by direct him to go a little way and turn right at the traffic lights?

    (c) How does Scott ask him to repeat what he said?

    (d) How does the passer-by say that the bank is opposite 'Sogo' department store?

    (e) How does Scott say *thank you*?

4 Units 8–10

The pictures below show what Reiko did this morning. Describe her day using the pictures as prompts. (Remember to use **mashita** *did*.)

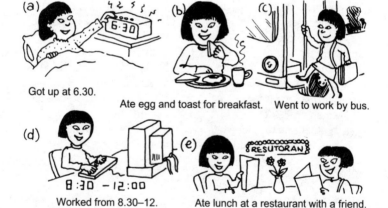

(a) Got up at 6.30.

(b) Ate egg and toast for breakfast.

(c) Went to work by bus.

(d) Worked from 8.30–12.

(e) Ate lunch at a restaurant with a friend.

Next, using the information below, can you describe what she is *going to do* for the rest of the day? (Use **masu**.)

(f) Return home by underground.

(g) Prepare the evening meal from 2 to 4. (**bangohan o tsukurimasu**)

(h) Have chicken and rice for dinner.

(i) Watch TV.

(j) Go to bed at about 11.30.

5 All units

Asking questions. How do you ask:

(a) Excuse me, where is the post office?
(b) How do you say *book* in Japanese?
(c) What do you do on Saturdays?
(d) What time do you get up?
(e) When are you going to France?
(f) What did you do last night?
(g) What do you have for breakfast?
(h) How long does it take by bullet train from Tōkyō to Ōsaka?

6 Units 9–10

Complete the correct endings to the **masu** words from a choice of **mashō** (*let's*), **mashō ka** (*shall we?*), **masen ka** (*would you like to?*), **tai desu** (*I want to*).

(a) Eiga o mi _____ . (*Shall we watch a film?*)
(b) Kaimono ni iki _____ . (*Let's go shopping.*)
(c) Nihon ni iki _____ . (*I want to go to Japan.*)
(d) Ano resutoran de kōhii o nomi _____ . (*Shall we drink coffee at that restaurant?*)
(e) **Issho ni** biiru o nomi _____ . (*Would you like to have a beer **with me?***)
(f) Omoshiroi hon o yomi _____ . (*I want to read an interesting book.*)
(g) Watashi no uchi de hirugohan o tabe _____ . (*Let's eat lunch at my house.*)

7 Units 11–12

The describing words are missing from the statements below. Choose one from the following list to make sense of the statement. Be careful! There is only one match for each sentence.

   Words to choose from: **shizuka, shizukana, atsui, samukatta, jōzu, tokui**

(a) Kyō wa _____ desu ne.
(b) Kinō wa _____ desu ne.
(c) Koko wa _____ tokoro desu ne.
(d) Kono resutoran wa _____ desu ne.
(e) An-san wa supōtsu wa amari _____ dewa arimasen.
(f) Watashi wa supōtsu ga _____ desu.

13

日本語を読みましょう！
— NIHONGO O YOMIMASHŌ —
Let's read Japanese!

In this unit you will learn

- about the Japanese writing system
- how to read the days of the week and numbers in Japanese characters
- how to read food and drink words and identify them on a menu

Hajime ni (はじめに)

It was explained in the *Introduction* that this unit is largely independent of the rest of the book, and so you can miss it out or come back to it later if you choose. However, for the learner who would like to know more about Japanese script, this unit will serve as an introduction, and you will also have an opportunity to use what you have learnt in an activity in Unit 15.

The Japanese language in this book is written in **rōmaji**. **Rōma** means *Roman* and **ji** means *letter* or *character*. In other words, **rōmaji** means the *Roman alphabet* (A, B, C ...). **Rōmaji** is used to write Japanese sounds in a written form that people who don't know Japanese script can read.

Although all Japanese people learn to read and write the Roman alphabet, Japanese is read and written in a different form. There are three writing forms which make up the whole Japanese writing system. Let's look at each of these in turn.

1 Kanji (漢字)

Kan is an old word for *Chinese* and **ji** means *letter* or *character*. This is because the Japanese writing system was introduced to Japan from China just under 2000 years ago and was adapted to the Japanese language.

Kanji were developed originally from pictures of natural objects such as the sun, the moon, water, etc. Each kanji represents a meaning or idea. For example, the word *Japan* (**Nihon**) is written like this in kanji: 日本.

日 means *sun* and developed from a picture of the sun:

本 means *root* and developed from a picture of the roots of a tree:

Therefore, the word *Japan* means *root/origin of the sun*, so Japan is the place where the sun rises. In other words: *land of the rising sun* (named by the Chinese because Japan lies to the east of China).

You will be introduced to more kanji later in this unit. There are several thousand kanji in the Japanese language, and you need to know about 2000 to read a Japanese newspaper properly! The Japanese spend their school years building up their knowledge of kanji, so don't be daunted by the amount. You will learn just a few in this unit.

2 Hiragana *and* Katakana

The other two scripts are known collectively as kana. In the *Pronunciation guide* (*Introduction*, page 8) you were introduced to the Japanese sounds which make up the Japanese language. Each of these sounds is represented by a symbol or **kana**. An important difference between this system and the Roman alphabet can be shown like this:

In English, the word *house* is made up of five letters: H-O-U-S-E.
In Japanese, the word for house is **uchi** and is made up of two sounds: U-CHI.
These sounds are represented by these two **kana** symbols: うち

There are two kana scripts: hiragana and katakana. They both represent the same set of sounds but the symbols are written differently. For example, this is how the sound **a** is written in the two scripts:

Hiragana **a** = あ

Katakana **a** = ア

In a similar way, but for different reasons, the Roman alphabet also has two symbols representing one letter, known as capitals and lower case: A, a; B, b; C, c; and so on.

Below is an explanation of the different ways in which hiragana and katakana are used:

(a) **Hiragana** (ひらがな)

Hiragana is used mainly to write Japanese words which don't have a kanji, and to write the grammatical parts of words and sentences. Here is an example:

I (she, they, etc.) look is written: 見   ま   す

                         mi   ma   su

見 is a kanji meaning *look*, and ます are two hiragana representing **ma** and **su** and show that it is a present or future action: *I look* or *I will look*.

I looked is written: 見 ま し た

                mi ma shi ta

The same kanji is used to convey the meaning of *look*. The hiragana ま **ma**, し **shi**, た **ta** are used to show that it is a past action (*I looked*). In other words, hiragana has a grammatical function. In this case it shows you whether the action word is **masu** or **mashita** (as you learnt in Units 8 and 10).

When Japanese children first go to school, they write all Japanese words in hiragana, and then gradually replace some of these words with kanji as they learn them.

(b) **Katakana** (カタカナ)

Katakana is used mainly for writing foreign (non-Japanese) words which have been introduced into the Japanese language. In Unit 2 you were introduced to the idea of foreign words being adopted into and adapted to the Japanese language. Here are some examples of these words, written in the katakana script:

Resutoran (*restaurant*) = レストラン

                        re su to ra n

Sutereo (*stereo*) = ステレオ

                        su te re o

Notice that these two words have two symbols in common: ス (**su**) and レ (**re**). See if you can find them and underline them.

As well as using katakana to write all foreign words, it has also become increasingly fashionable in recent times to write Japanese words in katakana, especially in advertising, and it has the effect of making words stand out.

Now you have been introduced to the three Japanese scripts, look at the extract from a Japanese magazine to see how Japanese looks in the written form. It shows examples of all three scripts.

The article is from a school newsletter and is introducing a new teacher from England to the school. Note that the writing is printed from top to bottom. This is how Japanese is traditionally written; you begin reading from the top right-hand corner. However, Japanese can also be written 'western-style' – from left to right – and Japanese people are familiar with both styles.

The four kanji in the first column (top right-hand side) mean *English instruction*, and the hiragana make up the word **yoroshiku** (you met this word in Units 1 and 20). In English we might say *the school looks forward to receiving English instruction.*

The katakana in the second column make up the teacher's name (non-Japanese names are always written in katakana), and the final two hiragana make the word **san** (*Mr*).

When you have completed this unit, look back at this article and see which other words and symbols you can pick out – numbers, dates, katakana words. You won't be able to understand the whole article (and it is in small print), but it's fun and good practice to be able to identify some Japanese characters!

漢字を読みましょう!
Kanji o yomimashō!
Let's read kanji!

 ——————— **Renshū** ———————

1   You learnt in the introduction to this unit that kanji were developed from pictures of natural objects. Can you work out the meanings of these seven kanji from the pictures of objects that they developed from?

Picture	Development	Kanji

Answers

日 means *sun* and also *day* (the rising and setting of the sun defines a day).

月 means *moon* and also *month* (the cycle of the moon takes one month).

火 means *fire*.

水 means *water* (the picture shows the splashing of water).

木 means *tree* or *wood/timber*

金 means *gold* or *money* (the picture shows a mountain with a gold mine in it).

土 means *earth* or *soil* (the picture shows plants growing from the earth).

These seven kanji are also used to represent days of the week. You learnt to say the days of the week in Unit 8 page 107. Now you are going to learn how to read them.

Kanji		English	Rōmaji
日	=	*Sunday*	Nichi (yōbi)
月	=	*Monday*	Getsu (yōbi)
火	=	*Tuesday*	Ka (yōbi)

水	=	*Wednesday*	Sui (yōbi)
木	=	*Thursday*	Moku (yōbi)
金	=	*Friday*	Kin (yōbi)
土	=	*Saturday*	Do (yōbi)

Yōbi is in brackets because it is written with two other kanji, but you can identify the days of the week from the first kanji.

❇ Hinto

To help you link the correct kanji with the correct day of the week:

日 (*Sunday*) and 月 (*Monday*) are easy because they have the same meanings in English (Monday is short for *Moon day*).

金 (*Friday*) means *money* – and Friday is often pay day!

土 (*Saturday*) means *earth day* – perhaps you do the gardening on Saturdays

水 (*Wednesday*) means *water* – and both begin with *w*!

木 (*Thursday*) means *tree* – both begin with *t*.

☑ 2   Without looking at the kanji chart above, see if you can match the correct day with its kanji representation by writing the letters (a)–(f) in the brackets next to the English meaning.

(a) 水   Monday ( )

(b) 木   Friday ( )

(c) 日   Saturday ( )

(d) 火   Wednesday ( )

(e) 土   Sunday ( )

(f) 月   Tuesday ( )

(g) 金

There is one remaining kanji. Which day of the week does it represent? _____day. And which letter is it?

☑ 3   The calendar below is for the month of June. Use the information from it to answer the questions below, as in the example. (You may want to look back at Units 4 and 9 first to remind yourself how to say the days of the month in Japanese.)

Rei: Jūku-nichi wa nanyōbi desu ka. (*What day of the week is the 19th?*) = Mokuyōbi desu.

日	月	火	水	木	金	土
1	2	3	4	5	6	7
8	9	10	11	12	13	14
15	16	17	18	19	20	21
22	23	24	25	26	27	28
29	30					

(a) Nijūsan-nichi wa nanyōbi desu ka.
(b) Nijūkū-nichi wa nanyōbi desu ka.
(c) Tōka wa nanyōbi desu ka.
(d) Nijūichi-nichi wa nanyōbi desu ka.
(e) Hatsuka wa nanyōbi desu ka.
(f) Yōka wa nanyōbi desu ka.
(g) Yokka wa nanyōbi desu ka.

Sūji *Numbers*

In Unit 2 you learnt to count from 1–12, and you have been using numbers throughout the units in different ways (months, dates, time, money, etc.). Now you are going to learn how to read them in kanji! There are some hints on the right to help you remember them.

Number	Kanji	Rōmaji	Hinto
1	一	ichi	One stroke
2	二	ni	Two strokes
3	三	san	Three strokes
4	四	shi/yon	Four sides
5	五	go	This looks like the numeral 5 – 5
6	六	roku	Looks like a rocket (**roku**) taking off –
7	七	nana/shichi	looks like a French 7 upside-down –
8	八	hachi	looks like a ha-t (**ha-chi**) –
9	九	kyū/ku	
10	十	jū	Like the roman numeral for 10 at an angle – x
11	十一	jūichi	10 + 1
12	十二	jūni	10 + 2 (and so on)

✳ Hinto

Pictures and sound association are very effective for helping you to remember new symbols (you learnt to remember some new words in the same way in earlier units). Can you think of something to help you remember 九 *(9)*?

4 When you feel confident that you can recognise the numbers, try the following activity.

Link the kanji number on the left with the correct rōmaji in the middle column and the correct numeral on the right, as in the example. Then check your answers with the chart above (there are no answers at the back of the book).

Kanji	Rōmaji	Numeral
一	shi	5
五	shichi	3
十二	ichi	4
七	san	1 2
三	go	1
四	jūni	7

✔ *Dates and months*

You have already learnt that the kanji 日 is used to represent the day *Sunday* and that the kanji 月 is used to represent the day *Monday*. These two kanji also have another meaning:

日 means *day/date* as in 4th, 12th, etc. So 四日 = 4th; and 十二日 = 12th.

月 means *month*. You learnt to say the months in Unit 2 by adding the word **gatsu** to the numbers 1–12. For example, **Ichigatsu** = *1st month* = *January*. This is written 一月 in kanji.

5 Match the months on the left with the kanji on the right. Write the correct letter in the brackets.

(a)	March	六月	( )
(b)	November	八月	( )
(c)	June	十二月	( )
(d)	September	十一月	( )
(e)	December	三月	( )
(f)	August	九月	( )

More about numbers

You have learnt to recognise the kanji for the numbers 1–12 in this unit. The numbers 11–99 are made of a combination of 1–10. Here are some examples:

十五	= 15	=	jūgo (10 + 5)
二十	= 20	=	nijū (2 × 10) – you learnt this rule in Unit 3
二十三	= 23	=	nijūsan (2 × 10 + 3)

6 You have already learnt the kanji 日 is added to a number to make a date. For example: 二十日 = **hatsuka** = *20th*. (Look back to Units 4 and 9 if you need to revise how to say the days of the month.)

Match the kanji date on the left with the rōmaji in the middle by writing the correct letter in the brackets. Then write the date in English in the right-hand column. The first one has been done for you.

	Kanji	**Rōmaji**		**English**
(a)	二十三日	sanjūichi-nichi	( )	
(b)	一日	yōka	( )	
(c)	十四日	nijūsan-nichi	(a)	23rd
(d)	二十日	tsuitachi	( )	
(e)	十二日	itsuka	( )	
(f)	五日	jūyokka	( )	
(g)	八日	hatsuka	( )	
(h)	三十一日	jūni-nichi	( )	

7 Below are the dates of some special events in Britain and in Japan. Can you link up the correct date with the correct event? Write the correct letter in the brackets next to the event.

	Date	**Event**	
(a)	十二月二十四日	Bonfire night	( )
(b)	五月五日	Girls' day (Japan: March 3rd)	( )
(c)	十一月十五日	Christmas Eve	( )
(d)	一月一日	Boys' day (Japan: May 5th)	( )
(e)	三月三日	Shichigosan (Japan: Nov. 15th)	( )
(f)	十一月五日	New Year's Day	( )

8 Below is part of an advertisement for a Japanese theatre production. Can you pick out the month, date and day of the performance?

平成七年十月二十一日土

薪能

カタカナを読みましょう
Katakana o yomimashō
Let's read katakana

You learnt in the introduction to this unit that the katakana script is used to write non-Japanese words that have been adopted into the Japanese language. You have learnt many of these words in the earlier units, and Unit 2 introduced you to the way that such words are adopted and adapted. Look back at this unit if you need to revise this before proceeding with the following section.

9 You haven't learnt to read any katakana yet, but try this recognition activity to get you used to what katakana symbols look like.

It is a simple matching activity. Look at the katakana words (a)–(g), find the same word in the right-hand column and write the correct letter (a)–(g) in the brackets.

(a)	コーヒー	ケーキ	( )
(b)	アイス	ミルク	( )
(c)	チーズ	サラダ	( )
(d)	ピザ	アイス	( )
(e)	ケーキ	チーズ	( )
(f)	サラダ	ピザ	( )
(g)	ミルク	コーヒー	( )

In the *Pronunciation guide* in the *Introduction* there is a chart of the Japanese sounds (page 9). Below is a chart of the same sounds, but written in katakana (Look back at the *Pronunciation guide* to remind yourself how to say the sounds.)

Katakana chart

ア (a)	イ (i)	ウ (u)	エ (e)	オ (o)
カ (ka)	キ (ki)	ク (ku)	ケ (ke)	コ (ko)
サ (sa)	シ (shi)	ス (su)	セ (se)	ソ (so)
タ (ta)	チ (chi)	ツ (tsu)	テ (te)	ト (to)
ナ (na)	ニ (ni)	ヌ (nu)	ネ (ne)	ノ (no)
ハ (ha)	ヒ (hi)	フ (fu)	ヘ (he)	ホ (ho)
マ (ma)	ミ (mi)	ム (mu)	メ (me)	モ (mo)
ヤ (ya)		ユ (yu)		ヨ (yo)
ラ (ra)	リ (ri)	ル (ru)	レ (re)	ロ (ro)
ワ (wa)				ン (n/m)

The katakana below, taken from the above chart, change their sound when they have the symbol ゛ added to them. Here are the rules:

Rule 1: **k** sounds become **g** sounds.

ガ (ga)   ギ (gi)   グ (gu)   ゲ (ge)   ゴ (go)

Rule 2: **s** sounds become **z** sounds.

ザ (za)   ジ (ji)   ズ (zu)   ゼ (ze)   ゾ (zo)

Rule 3: **t** sounds become **d** sounds.

ダ (da)   デ (de)   ド (do)

Rule 4: **h** sounds become **b** sounds.

バ (ba)   ビ (bi)   ブ (bu)   ベ (be)   ボ (bo)

These last five katakana change their sounds when the symbol ° is added:

パ (pa)   ピ (pi)   プ (pu)   ペ (pe)   ポ (po)

You are not expected to learn all these katakana in order to do the actitivies in this unit! The activities will keep referring you back to the chart. However, the chart is there if you want to start memorising the katakana. Try just a few (about five) at a time and try to link the shapes of each katakana with a picture or sound that will help you to remember it more easily. Here are a few ideas to get you started.

ア (**a**) looks like an antelope

イ (**i**) is a leaning **T** which rhymes with **i**

ウ (**u**) looks like a **uisukii** (*whisky*) flask

エ (**e**) looks like elevator doors

キ (**ki**) looks like a door key

✳ Hinto

Katakana symbols which look similar:

シ (**shi**) and ツ (**tsu**). The long stroke of **shi** slopes down more gently.

ン (**n**) and ソ (**so**). Again, the long stroke of **n** slopes down more gently.

Be aware of these similarities and if one sound doesn't seem to work in a word, try the other.

— : This dash is used to indicate long sounds. In **rōmaji** this has been indicated with a macron or a double **ii** as in this example:

kōhii (*coffee*) is written コーヒー in katakana.   — represents the macron and the extra **i**.

10 In Exercise 9 you matched pairs of katakana words. Here are those same words again, but this time you are going to find out how you say them and what they mean. Look back at the chart, match each symbol, write down the rōmaji, then work out what it

means in English and select the correct word from the list on the right. The first word has been done for you.

	Katakana	Rōmaji	English	
(a)	コーヒー	kōhii	salad	( )
(b)	アイス		cake	( )
(c)	チーズ		milk	( )
(d)	ピザ		coffee	(a)
(e)	ケーキ		ice	( )
(f)	サラダ		cheese	( )
(g)	ミルク		pizza	( )

Katakana food and drink words

Below are ten common food and drink words that are found on Japanese menus, for example, in coffee shops. Try to remember them by making sound and picture associations as explained above. Say the words out loud to yourself, then try covering the rōmaji and reading the katakana words. Finally, see how well you have remembered them by trying Exercise 11. (But don't worry if you need to look back at this list!)

Katakana word	Rōmaji	English meaning
コーヒー	kōhii	coffee
アイスコーヒー	aisukōhii	iced coffee
ミルク	miruku	milk
コーラ	kōra	cola
ケーキ	kēki	cake
カレー	karē	curry
ステーキ	sutēki	steak
ピザ	piza	pizza
サラダ	sarada	salad
ハンバーガー	hambāgā	hamburger

11 Below is a coffee shop menu written in katakana. Use the menu to answer the questions (a)–(d).

メニュー　MENU

コーヒー	￥500
アイスコーヒー	￥600
コーラ	￥400
ケーキ	￥500〜700
● ●	
ピザ	￥800
カレー	￥900
ハンバーガー	￥700

(a) How much is a cup of coffee?
(b) How much is a pizza?
(c) How much is a hamburger and a glass of cola?
(d) You and your friend each have up to 1300 yen to spend and you both want something to eat and a drink but you don't want to order the same items. What different combinations could you order?

 12 The ten food words you have learnt are hidden in this word-search. See how many you can find without looking back at the list above. Words are written left to right and top to bottom. Tick the words off as you find them, on the English list on the right:

ア	イ	ス	コ	ー	ヒ	ー
コ	サ	テ	｜	ミ	ル	ハ
ラ	ダ	｜	ヒ	ル	ピ	ン
ケ	ー	キ	｜	ク	シ	バ
サ	コ	ク	マ	ア	ウ	｜
キ	｜	ヒ	カ	レ	ー	ガ
サ	ラ	ダ	イ	ピ	ザ	｜

iced coffee
coffee
milk
cola
cake
curry
hamburger
salad
pizza
steak

◢ Tesuto テスト

1 Write the English equivalent next to the dates (month, date and day) below. The first one has been done for you.

(a) 八月一日（水）　　　　　　　Wednesday 1st August

(b) 六月十一日（土）

(c) 一月三日（火）

(d) 九月二十五日（日）

(e) 四月七日（月）

(f) 二月十八日（金）

(g) 五月五日　　　　（What special day is this in Japan?）

2 Select the correct katakana word from each of the choices (i)–(iii) below.

(a) Salad: (i) サンド (ii) サラダ

(iii) ピザ

(b) Steak: (i) ステーキ (ii) ケーキ

(iii) ステレオ

(c) Ice: (i) コーヒー (ii) ケーキ

(iii) アイス

(d) Milk: (i) ホテル (ii) ミルク

(iii) ミート

(e) Hamburger: (i) ハンバーガー (ii) チキンバーガー

(iii) チーズバーガー

14

KAIMONO
Shopping

As mentioned in the 'Introduction', Units 14–20 offer you the opportunity to *put into practice* the language you have learnt in the first 12 units, and to further your knowledge of Japanese in the context of situations you may find yourself in if you visit Japan or have contact with Japanese people.

Each unit is more or less independent so, for example, if you are going to eat out with Japanese friends or business colleagues, study unit 15; or if you are meeting a Japanese person in your or their home, look at unit 20.

Even if you do not have contact with Japanese people, these units will help you to develop your confidence in using Japanese and you will learn more about this fascinating language and culture.

In this unit you will learn

● how to find out more about shops in Japan
● how to practise buying clothes and other goods
● about typical Japanese souvenirs and presents

Fukushū

- Numbers (Units 2, 3)
- Saying it's a bit (small, expensive) (p. 140)
- Asking for something (p. 63)
- Asking the price (p. 76)
- Have you got/do you have? (p. 77)
- Counters for different objects (p. 77)
- Describing words (big, small, etc.) (Unit 11)

Nihon no depāto *Japanese department stores*

To find out about Japanese department stores, read the passage below. Answering the questions to **Renshū 1** will help you to understand it.

Nihon no depāto wa daitai kuji kara shichiji made desu. Nichiyōbi **demo aiteimasu**. **Iroirona** mono o **utteimasu**. **Tatoeba, nichiyōhin**, tabemono, **yōfuku** to **denki seihin** o utteimasu. Ten'in no seifuku wa totemo suteki desu. Ten'in no Nihongo mo totemo **teinei** desu. Kireina depāto wa Tōkyō no Ginza ni takusan arimasu ga totemo takai desu.

demo	even, also
aiteimasu	open
iroirona	various
utteimasu	sell
tatoeba	for example
nichiyōhin	everyday goods
yōfuku	clothes
denki seihin	electrical goods
seifuku	uniform
teinei	polite

Renshū

1 (a) What time do Japanese department stores open and close?
   (b) Do they open on Sundays?
   (c) What does the passage say about the shop assistants' uniforms? What else does it say about these assistants?
   (d) In which area of Tokyo would you find beautiful but very expensive department stores?

Tango-Hyō

Hinto

There are key vocabulary lists (**Tango-hyō**) at the beginning of each of the sections in this and future units. The best way to familiarise yourself with these words is to memorize a few words or a section at a time. Say them out aloud to practise your pronunciation, then cover up the Japanese side and test yourself using the English words as prompts. Try this the other way round as well; cover the English side and see how many Japanese words you recognise. These words and phrases will recur throughout the unit and so there will be plenty of opportunity for reinforcement.

Useful questions and phrases

_____ arimasu ka	do you have _____?
_____ uriba wa doko desu ka	where is the _____department?
Chotto takai (chiisai/ōkii/yasui) desu	it's a bit expensive (small/big/cheap)
motto yasui (ōkii/chiisai/takai)	do you have a cheaper (bigger/smaller/
no wa arimasu ka	more expensive) *one*?
saizu wa?	what size is it?
kore de yoroshii desu ka	is that all?
sore de kekkō desu	that's all, thank you
onegaishimasu	please
otsuri	change

Useful shop vocabulary

uriba	department, counter
kutsu uriba	shoe department
kamera uriba	camera department
tōki uriba	china/pottery department
fujinfuku uriba	women's clothes department
____ wa nankai ni arimasu ka	what floor is the _____ located on?
ikkai	ground floor
nikai	first floor
sankai	second floor
yonkai	third floor
chikai	basement
chika ikkai	first floor of basement (B1 – where there is more than one floor in the basement)
okujō	rooftop
erebētā	elevator/lift
esukarētā	escalator

---

kaidan	stairs
reji	cash desk
annaijo	information desk
sutoa gaido	store guide
pāsento	per cent
waribiki	discount

Phrases used by shop assistants

shōshō omachi kudasai	please wait a moment
maido arigatō gozaimasu	thank you for your custom

Nihon ni tsuite

You will have noticed in the **Tango-hyō** section above that the floors in Japanese don't follow the British system: for example, **nikai** is translated as *first floor* (and not second floor as you might expect). This is because in Japan you count from the first floor, not the ground floor. The diagram below illustrates this:

yonkai	(3rd floor)
sankai	(2nd floor)
nikai	(first floor)
ikkai	(ground floor)
chika ikkai	(B1)

Renshū

2   The two activities below are designed for you to start using the new words you have learnt in the **Tango-hyō** lists above straight-

away. Use them like a test to see how many words you can remember. Use the vocabulary lists above to check your answers (there are no answers in the back of the book). Speak out aloud.

(a) Can you say these phrases in Japanese? Use the example to guide you, but replace the underlined words with the alternative words given in (i)–(iii).

Rei: It's a little <u>expensive</u>. Do you have a <u>cheaper</u> one? Chotto <u>takai</u> desu. Motto <u>yasui</u> no wa arimasu ka.

(i) Small, bigger
(ii) Big, smaller
(iii) Cheap, more expensive

(b) Imagine you are in a Japanese department store and practise asking for the places below, as in the example.
Rei: (Camera department): Sumimasen, kamera uriba wa doko desu ka.

(i) China department
(ii) Women's clothes department
(iii) Shoe department
(iv) Elevator
(v) Lift
(vi) Stairs
(vii) Cash desk
(viii) Information desk

Depāto no kaimono *Department store shopping*

Items to buy

yōfuku	clothes
bōshi	hat
zubon	trousers
shatsu	shirt
wanpiisu	dress
burausu	blouse
sukāto	skirt
sētā	jumper
T. shatsu	T-shirt
kutsu	shoes

Colour and size

akai	red
aoi	blue
shiroi	white
kuroi	black
eru (L)	large size
emu (M)	medium size
esu (S)	small size

3 In this activity you are going to practise the new words for clothes and colours in the vocabulary list above, so make sure you are familiar with the words.

Practise asking for the items (a)–(g) below using the example as your guide but replacing the underlined part with the alternative items. Then check your answers by looking back at the vocabulary above (there are no answers at the back of the book.)

Rei: Do you have any <u>red jumpers</u>? <u>Akai sētā</u> ga arimasu ka.

(a) Red trousers
(b) Black shoes
(c) White T-shirts
(d) Blue trousers
(e) Blue skirts
(f) Red dresses
(g) White blouses

Some of these useful phrases from activities 2 and 3 are also on the cassette for you to practise.

Kaiwa 1

Emi is going to England during her university holidays and she has gone with Anne to a department store in Shinjuku to buy some new clothes.

Read out aloud the new vocabulary for this dialogue, then listen to the cassette (or read the dialogue if you don't have a cassette) and, without looking back at the text, try Exercise 4.

Annaijo de:
Emi   Sumimasen, fujinfuku uriba wa doko desu ka.
Ten'in   Hai. Nikai ni arimasu. Dōzo, sutoa gaido o **otori kudasai**.

Fujinfuku uriba de:

Ten'in Irasshaimase.

Anne Emi, **mite**! Kono akai sēta wa suteki desu ne.

Emi Ē, kirei desu ne.

Ten'in Sore wa hyaku pāsento **yōmō** desu.

Emi Sō desu ka. Ikura desu ka.

Ten'in Nisen gohyaku-en desu.

Emi Saizu wa?

Ten'in Saizu wa emu desu.

Emi Emu wa chotto ōkii desu. Motto chiisai no wa arimasu ka.

Ten'in Hai. Shōshō omachi kudasai. Sō desu ne. Kore wa esu desu ga aoi desu.

Anne Sore mo suteki desu yo.

Emi Ja, chotto **kitemimasu**.

A little later:

Anne Dō desu ka. Aa! Hontō ni **niaimasu** yo.

Emi Sō desu ka. Ja kore o kaimasu.

Ten'in Hai. Kore de yoroshii desu ka.

Emi Ē, sore de kekkō desu.

Ten'in Nisen gohyaku-en **de gozaimasu**.

Emi Ja, **gosen-en de onegaishimasu**.

Ten'in Shōshō omachi kudasai. Nisen gohyaku-en no otsuri desu.

Emi Domo arigatō.

Ten'in Maido arigatō gozaimasu.

otori kudasai	please take (one)
mite	look
yōmō	wool
kitemimasu	I'll try it on
niaimasu	it suits you
de gozaimasu	very polite form of **desu** (*is*)
gosen-en de onegaishimasu	please take it out of 5000 yen

Renshū

4 After you've listened to the cassette (you may want to listen more than once), see if you can say the Japanese for the phrases overleaf, then write them down.

(a) Excuse me, where is the women's clothes department?
(b) How much is it?
(c) Do you have a smaller one?
(d) Right, I'll just try it on.
(e) Right, I'll buy this one.
(f) That's all, thank you.
(g) Please take it out of 5000 yen.
(h) Thank you very much for your custom.

Now read through the dialogue (remember to read out aloud) and check you have understood it (check your answers in the back of the book as well) before progressing to Exercise 5.

5 Next imagine you are a customer in the department store and use the above dialogue and the **Tango-hyō** to help you create the following scenario.

You ask to see a pair of black trousers, you ask how much they are and are told they are 3000 yen.

You then ask the size. When you are told the size is S, you ask if they have a larger size.

You then decide to buy them and pay out of a 10,000 yen note.

Imagine the shop assistant's comments as well as your own and say the dialogue out aloud.

6 The larger department stores in Tokyo also stock store guides in English, as with this example of the Seibu department store below. Use this store guide to answer the questions in Japanese below. You should note that there are two buildings, A and B. Indicate this with **A no** or **B no**, as in the example. Also note that the sixth floor is pronounced **rokkai**.

Rei: Q: Nekutai wa nankai ni arimasu ka. A: **B no** sankai ni arimasu.

(a) Q: Sukāto wa nankai ni arimasu ka.
(b) Q: Resutoran wa nankai ni arimasu ka.
(c) Q: Tokei wa nankai ni arimasu ka.
(d) Q: Kimono wa nankai ni arimasu ka.
(e) Q: Shatsu wa nankai ni arimasu ka.
(f) Q: Sakana wa nankai ni arimasu ka.
(g) Q: **Otoko no** kutsu wa nankai ni arimasu ka.

	A			**B**	
R	GARDENINGS		**R**	PLAY GROUNDS & PET SHOP	
8	RESTAURANTS		**8**	SAISON SQUARE & SPECIAL EVENT SPACE	
7	SPECIALITIES Jewelry, Watches, Boutiques		**7**	FURNITURE & ART GALLERY	
6	KIMONO & LADIES' FASHION		**6**	FURNITURE & FABRICS	
5	PRÊT-A-PORTER & INNER WEAR		**5**	HOUSE WARE	

	A			**B**	
4	INTERNATIONAL BOUTIQUES		**4**	CHILDREN'S WEAR & TOYS	
3	LADIES' FASHION Shoes		**3**	MEN'S FASHION Shirts, Neckties, Belts, Bags, etc.	
2	LADIES' FASHION Skirts, Blouse, Pants, etc.		**2**	MEN'S FASHION	
	M2 BAG ZONE				
1	LADIES' FASHION Accessories, Cosmetics. etc.		**1**	MEN'S FASHION Shoes, Bags	
B1	FOODS Fish, Vegetables, Meat		**B1**	MEN'S FASHION	

otoko no	men's

Nihon ni tsuite

Discount electrical stores

These discount stores are some of the few places in Japan where you can barter. Akihabara in Tokyo is a particularly famous area, specialising in electrical and electronic goods. It's an amazing place simply to browse around, stocking all the most up-to-date equipment. You are able to buy goods tax-free if you intend to take them back to your own country and if you have a tourist visa on your passport.

Tango-hyō

denki seihin	electrical goods
rajio	radio
shii dii pureyā	CD player
sutereo	stereo
rajikase	radio cassette
tēpu rekōda	tape recorder
pasokon	PC

Kaiwa 2

Familiarise yourself with the **Tango-hyō** and the new vocabulary below this dialogue, then read the dialogue.

Scott is in an electrical store in Akihabara, looking for a CD player to take back to the States.

Ten'in Irasshaimase!

Scott **Miteiru dake desu.** (*after a while*) Ano, kono shii dii pureyā wa Nihon-**sei** desu ka.

Ten'in Ē, sore wa '*Nashonaru*' desu. Sore wa totemo ii shii dii pureyā desu yo.

Scott A, sō desu ka. Ikura desu ka.

Ten'in Sore wa niman-en desu.

Scott Chotto takai desu ne. (*points to shelf*) Ano shii dii pureyā wa ikura desu ka.

Ten'in Are wa ichiman gosen-en desu. Are wa 'Sanyō' desu.

Scott Ja, are o misete kudasai.

Ten'in Hai, shōshō omachi kudasai.

A little while later:

Scott Waribiki ga **dekimasu** ka.

Ten'in Sō desu ne. Go-pāsento no waribiki ga dekimasu.

Scott Mmm. Jū-pāsento wa?

Ten'in E! Sore wa totemo **muri** desu. Ja, nana-pāsento **ni shimashō**!

Scott Hai, sore wa ii desu.

Ten'in Sore wa hontō ni waribiki desu yo!

miteiru dake desu	I'm just looking
sei	made in (Nihon-sei = made in Japan)
Nashonaru	National (Japanese electrical company)
dekimasu	(I) can
waribiki ga dekimasu ka	can you do a discount?
muri	impossible
... ni shimashō	let's decide on ...
... ni shimasu	decide on ...

Renshū

7 Try to answer these questions without referring to the dialogue. You may need to read it through several times before attempting this exercise.

(a) 'Nashonaru' no shii dii pureyā wa ikura desu ka.

(b) 'Nashonaru' no shii dii pureyā wa doko-sei desu ka.

(c) Chotto _____ desu ne. (fill in the missing Japanese word)

(d) 'Sanyō' no shii dii pureyā wa ikura desu ka.

(e) Waribiki wa nan pāsento ni shimashita ka.

Now read through the dialogue (remember to read out aloud) and check you have understood it (check your answers in the back of the book as well) before progressing to Exercise 8.

8 Imagine that you are in a store in Akihabara. You want to buy a radio-cassette (**rajikase**). Fill in the gaps in the dialogue below using the dialogue above and its related vocabulary list to help you. Say your part out aloud (you could then write it down for reinforcement).

Ten'in Irasshaimase!

You *Say that you are just having a look around.*

Ten'in Hai, dōzo.

You *Ask to see that radio-cassette over there.*

Ten'in Hai!

You *Ask if it is made in Japan.*

Ten'in Iie, sore wa Amerika-sei desu.

You *Ask how much it is.*

Ten'in Niman-en desu.

You *Say that's a bit expensive and ask if they do a discount.*

Ten'in Sō desu ne. Go pāsento dekimasu.
You   *Say that you will have it (use 'kore').*

Omiyage-ya de *At the souvenir shop*

Tango-hyō

omiyage	souvenirs
kimono	Japanese kimono
ningyō	Japanese doll
sensu	fan
washi	Japanese paper
yukata	Japanese cotton dressing gown
chōchin	paper lantern
hashi	chopsticks

────── Renshū ──────

 9 To do this exercise you first need to think back to Unit 6 where you were introduced to some of the different words used for counting types of items. You learnt these in the form of two systems, A and B. You may find it useful to look back to Unit 6 (setsumei 5) and review these ways of counting before trying the activity below.

Using the vocabulary above, ask for each of the souvenirs below, using the correct counter/number and **o kudasai** (*may I have?*). Remember that the counter is said between **o** and **kudasai**.

Rei:
Kimono o hitotsu kudasai.
(*or:* Kimono o ichimai
                  kudasai)

(yukata)

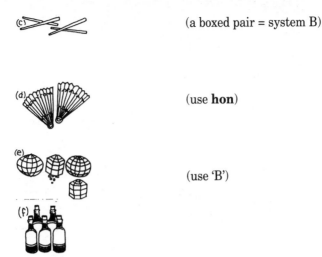

(a boxed pair = system B)

(use **hon**)

(use 'B')

10 Emi is at a souvenir shop looking for typical Japanese gifts to take to England. Listen to the conversation on the cassette and then put the dialogue below into the right order, starting with **Irasshaimase!** (You may need to listen to the cassette several times.)

(a) Sō desu ka. Ikura desu ka.
(b) Hai. Kore de yoroshii desu ka.
(c) Hai, dōzo. Hyaku pāsento **men** desu.
(d) Irasshaimase!
(e) Ano ... kono o-hashi mo kudasai.
(f) Sore wa kirei desu ne. Ja sore o futatsu kudasai.
(g) Rokusen-en desu.
(h) Hai, kore wa yonsen-en desu. Gojū pāsento men desu.
(i) Ano aoi yukata o misete kudasai.
(j) Chotto takai desu ne. Motto yasui no wa arimasu ka.

men	cotton

🗹 Tesuto

How do you say in Japanese:

- (a) It's a bit big?
- (b) What size is it?
- (c) Do you have a cheaper one?
- (d) What floor is the camera department on?
- (e) Where is the electrical goods department?
- (f) Please take it out of 10,000 yen?
- (g) Please show me the black T-shirt over there?
- (h) May I have three pairs of chopsticks?

15

BIIRU O IPPON KUDASAI
A bottle of beer, please

In this unit you will learn

- how to find out about eating in Japan
- how to practise ordering drinks and snacks
- how to practise ordering a meal
- how to read a coffee shop menu

Fukushū

- Ways of counting people (p. 42) and items (p. 77)
- Saying *may I have* ... (p. 63)
- Asking to see something (p. 63)
- Asking and saying prices (p. 75)
- Asking *do you have any* ...? (p. 77)
- Food and drink items (Unit 8)
- Making suggestions and accepting (Unit 9)
- Saying what you want to do (p. 127)
- Expressing likes and dislikes (p. 148)

Famirii resutoran de *At a family restaurant*

Below is Reiko's account of eating out at a family restaurant. Before you read this account you need to understand the following phrase:

... ga taberaremasu   *you (I, they, etc.) can eat ...*

It works like the other **masu** words you have learnt except that instead of using **o** before the **masu** word, you use **ga**. For example:

Gohan ga taberaremasu.   *I can eat rice.*
Niku ga taberaremasen.   *I can't eat meat.*

Now read the passage, then check your understanding by answering the questions (in English) in Exercise 1.

Kinō kazoku to **famirii resutoran** ni ikimashita. **Kono yōna** resutoran de **washoku** kara **yōshoku** made **iroirona** tabemono ga taberaremasu. Watashi wa **katsudon** o tabemashita. Shujin wa **biifu sutēki** o tabemashita. Sorekara biiru o nihon nomimashita. Takeshi, Emi to An-san wa **mina**, **hambāgā** o tabemashita. **Genzai** no **wakamono** wa yōshoku ga totemo suki desu. Washoku wa amari tabemasen.

Sore ni mina kōhii o nomimashita. Kono famarii resutoran wa '**wan kappa sābisu**' ga arimashita. Shujin wa takusan kōhii o nomimashita.

famirii resutoran	family restaurant
	(American diner-style restaurants)
kono yō (na)	this type (of)
washoku	Japanese cuisine
yōshoku	western (European and American) cuisine
iroirona	various sorts
katsudon	pork cutlets and egg on rice
biifu sutēki	beef steak
mina	all of them, everybody
hambāgā	hamburger
genzai	these days
wakamono	young people
wan kappu sābisu	one cup service (your cup is re-filled as many times as you want at no extra charge)

Renshū

1   (a)   Fill in the gap, in English: Yesterday I went with _____ to a family restaurant.
    (b)   What range of food can you eat at this type of restaurant?
    (c)   What did each person have to eat?
    (d)   How many bottles of beer did Mr Yamaguchi drink?
    (e)   What does Reiko say about young people these days?

Gaishoku ni tsuite (1)   *About eating out (1)*

The wide range of dishes, cookery styles and eating places can be quite overwhelming for the visitor to Japan. This unit will only cover a few of the dishes and types of restaurant which exist in Japan. You can divide the types of eating places into categories:

- Speciality restaurants – these offer one particular kind of cuisine, for example, a **sushi-ya** specialises in Sushi, and a **soba-ya** specialises in Japanese noodles.

- **Nihon-ryōri** (*Japanese cuisine*) – these restaurants serve a variety of dishes and range from very expensive, high-class places to relatively inexpensive ones.

- Pubs and **izakaya** (*drinking places*) – these serve inexpensive food with drinks.

- 'Family' and western-style restaurants – these can be less expensive, particularly at lunchtime (this is the case with many restaurants) when they serve special **setto** (*set meals*).

- Coffee shops – these serve light snacks and coffee. You pay a higher price for coffee, so you can sit and relax for as long as you like, even if you buy only one cup.

Japanese restaurants are becoming more popular in Britain, especially in London, and so you can have the opportunity to experience Japanese food without going to Japan. However, they can be expensive.

Tango-hyō

Useful expressions

chūmon shimasu	make an order
... ni shimasu	I've decided on ... I'll have ... (when ordering)
kampai!	cheers!
oishisō!	it looks delicious
oishikatta	it was delicious
mō kekko desu	I'm fine, I've had enough, thank you

Vocabulary used in restaurants

nannin-sama desu ka	how many people?
kochira e, dōzo	over here, please
o-kimari desu ka	have you decided?

Yōshoku *Western food*

tabemono	*food*
chiizu sandoitchi	cheese sandwich
supagetti naporitan	spaghetti neapolitan
sarada	salad
piza	pizza
karē raisu	curry on rice
dezāto	desert
chiizukēki	cheesecake
nomimono	*drink*
aisu kōhii	iced coffee
orenji jūsu	orange juice
miruku	milk
remon tii	lemon tea

 ——————————— **Renshū** ———————————

2 Practise ordering the items below, using **... o kudasai** (*may I have ...?*) and the correct counter or number (use **hitotsu**, **futatsu**, etc. except for *bottle of beer*).

Rei: Piza o hitotsu kudasai.

Gaishoku ni tsuite (2)   *About eating out (2)*

Many of the restaurants and coffee shops in Japan display the types
of food they serve in the form of plastic models (**shokuhin sampuru**
– *food samples*). These are displayed in glass cases outside the
entrance to the shop. This helps potential customers decide what food
they want to eat and at which restaurant. It also can be helpful if you
can't read the menu. Instead you can point to the dish you want and
say **kore o kudasai**. If you are unsure what a dish is, you can point
to it and say **kore wa nan desu ka**. Often the menus have pictures
of all the dishes. The menus of some family restaurants and fast-food
places also name the dishes in English.

Renshū

3   Listen to the cassette, then switch it off and read the dialogue
below. Put the dialogue into the right order, beginning with
Irasshaimase. Listen to the cassette as many times as you need
to before trying this.

If you don't have a cassette, read through the sentences (a)–(p)
and see if you can put them into the right order.

**An-san to Haidi-san wa *issho* ni kissaten de hiru gohan o
tabemasu**.
(*Heidi and Anne are going to eat lunch **together** at a coffee shop.*)

(a) Futari desu.
(b) Hai! Sandoitchi hitotsu, supagetti hitotsu, to kōhii o futatsu desu ne.
(c) E! **Dōshite?** Haidi-san wa dezāto ga totemo suki desu ne!
(d) (A little later) O-kimari desu ka.
(e) Hai, dōzo.
(f) Irasshaimase! Nannin-sama desu ka.
(g) Hai, onegaishimasu.
(h) Hai, chiizu sandoitchi o hitotsu kudasai.
(i) Sō desu ne. **Demo**, **saikin** chotto **futorimashita**.
(j) Watashi wa supagetti naporitan ni shimasu.
(k) Watashi wa mō kekko desu.
(l) Kōhii o futatsu kudasai.
(m) Menyū o misete kudasai.
(n) (After lunch) Watashi wa dezāto o tabetai desu. Haidi-san wa?
(o) O-nomimono wa?
(p) Hai, kochira e, dōzo.

dōshite	why?
saikin	recently
demo	but
futorimashita	I've put on weight

Renshū

4   How do you say the following phrases in Japanese? Use the dialogue and new vocabulary above, and speak out aloud!

(a) How many people? Three people.
(b) May I see the menu please?
(c) Have you decided?
(d) I'm going to decide on a cheese sandwich and salad.
(e) I love spaghetti.
(f) I want to eat cheesecake.
(g) I've had enough, thank you.

5   Use the example of a coffee shop menu below to say your side of the dialogue below. It is written in katakana (the writing used for non-Japanese words).

If you have studied Unit 13, see if you can remember how to read this menu. Alternatively, use the katakana chart in Unit 13 (page 171) to help you work out the items on the menu. There is also a rōmaji version of the menu after this exercise, but try not to look at it until you've finished the exercise!

~ ルーナ コーヒー ショップ ~

コーヒー	¥400	ハンバーガー	¥650
アイスコーヒー	¥500	ピザ	¥700
ミルク	¥500	サラダ	¥600
ケーキ	¥500-700	カレー	¥900

Waiter Irasshaimase! Nannin-sama desu ka.
You *Say that you are on your own.*
Waiter Hai, kochira e, dōzo.
You *Ask to see the menu.*
Waiter Hai, dōzo.
You *Order two savoury dishes from the menu.*
Waiter Wakarimashita. O-nomimono wa?
You *Order something appropriate.*
A little later:
You *Say that it was delicious.*
Waiter Dezāto wa?
You *Say that you're full, thank you.*

Rōmaji version:

Rūna kōhii shoppu

Kōhii	400	Hambāgā	650
Aisu kōhii	500	Piza	700
Miruku	500	Sarada	600
Kēki	500–700	Karē	900

Fāsuto fūdo *Fast food*

Tango-hyō

Phrases used by shop assistants (ten'in) and waitresses (uētoresu)

o-meshiagari desu ka	to eat in?
o-mochikaeri desu ka	to take away?
esu, emu, eru	small, medium, large
dochira desu ka	which one?
kashikomarimashita	certainly, sir/madam
de gozaimasu	polite alternative to **desu**

Phrases used by the customer

koko de tabemasu	I'm going to eat here
mottekaerimasu	I'm going to take away
... o onegaishimasu	please (an alternative to 'o kudasai')
... no esu (emu/eru)	a small (medium/large)...
kōra no esu o onegaishimasu	a small cola please

✴ Hinto: *Pronunciation tip*

Practise saying these words. Each syllable should run smoothly into the next.

O-meshiagari = o-me-shi-a-ga-ri
O-mochikaeri = o-mo-chi-ka-e-ri
Onegaishimasu = o-ne-ga-i-shi-ma-su
Mottekaerimasu – pause slightly between **mo** and **tte**

Tabemono *Food*

furaido poteto	chips
chiizubāgā	cheeseburger
teriyakibāgā	teriyakiburger
chikinbāgā	chickenburger
apuru pai	apple pie

Nomimono *Drink*

miruku shēku	milk shake
– **chokoretto**	– chocolate
– **banana**	– banana
– **sutoroberii**	– strawberry

———— Kaiwa ————

Takeshi-kun to tomodachi no Hiroshi-kun wa 'Happiibāgā' no resutoran de tabemono o kaimasu. (*Takeshi and his friend Hiroshi are going to buy some food at 'Happyburger' restaurant.*)

As you listen to the cassette (or read the dialogue below) see if you can complete the table in Exercise 6.

Uētoresu Irasshaimase! O-meshiagari desu ka. O-mochikaeri desu ka.
Takeshi Mottekaerimasu.
Uētoresu Wakarimashita. Menyū o dōzo.
Takeshi Zembu oishisō! Hiroshi-kun, nan ni shimasu ka.
Hiroshi Boku wa chikinbāgā to furaido poteto ni shimasu.
Uētoresu Esu to emu to eru to, dochira desu ka.
Hiroshi Emu o onegaishimasu.
Uētoresu O-nomimono wa?

Hiroshi   Sutoroberii miruku shēku no emu o onegaishimasu.

Takeshi   Boku wa chiizubāgā to furaido poteto no eru o onegaishimasu. Soshite, banana miruku shēku ni shimasu. Saizu esu o kudasai.

Uētoresu Kashikomarimashita. Zembu de sen yonhyaku-en de gozaimasu.

 ———————— **Renshū** ————————

6   Fill in the table below to indicate what each boy ordered and what size (where appropriate). Use 'T' for Takeshi and 'H' for Hiroshi. Then circle the correct total price that they paid.

	Item ordered?	Small?	Medium?	Large?
Hamburger				
Cheeseburger				
Chickenburger				
Potato fries				
Banana milkshake				
Strawberry milkshake				
Chocolate milkshake				

Total: (a)   1700 yen
           (b)   400 yen
           (c)   1400 yen

7   The takeaway pizza menu below is written in English as well as Japanese. Use this menu and the pronunciation guide next to it (or try and work out how to say the words yourself by using the katakana chart in Unit 13) to say out aloud your part of the dialogue below. Use the dialogue above to help you (there are no answers at the back of the book).

DOMINO'S PIZZA COMBINATION

アメリカン・スペシャル
American Special
TOPPINGS
ペパロニ、オニオン、ダブルチーズ

🅼 ¥1600 🅻 ¥2400

フレッシュ・ベジー
Fresh Vegi
TOPPINGS
トマト、ピーマン、コーン、オニオン、
マッシュルーム、ダブルチーズ

🅼 ¥2000 🅻 ¥3000

デラックス
Deluxe
TOPPINGS
イタリアンソーセージ、ペパロニ、
マッシュルーム、オニオン、ピーマン

🅼 ¥2000 🅻 ¥3000

グレート・アメリカン
Great American
TOPPINGS
ダブルクリスピーベーコン、
ビーフビッツ、ダブルチーズ

🅼 ¥2000 🅻 ¥3000

メキシカンDX
Mexican DX
TOPPINGS
タコスミート、ハラピニオ、トマト、
オニオン、コーン、エキストラチーズ

🅼 ¥2000 🅻 ¥3000

Pronunciation guide:	English	Rōmaji
	American special	Amerikan supesharu
	Fresh vegi	Furesshu bejii
	Deluxe	Derakkusu
	Great American	Gurēto Amerikan
	Mexican DX	Mekishikan DX

Uētoresu Irasshaimase! O-meshiagari desu ka. O-mochikaeri desu ka.
You   *Say you want a takeaway; ask to see the menu.*
Uētoresu Hai, dōzo.
You   *Choose a pizza from the menu.*
Uētoresu Ēmu to eru to dochira desu ka.
You   *Say the size of pizza that you want.*
Uētoresu O-nomimono wa?
You   *Order a large coffee.*
Uētoresu Kashikomarimashita

Nihon-ryōri no resutoran *Japanese-cuisine restaurants*

Tango-hyō

washoku	Japanese food
sushi	vinegared rice with raw fish and other toppings
sashimi	raw fish
tempura	prawns and vegetables fried in light batter
yakitori	pieces of chicken and vegetables grilled on bamboo skewers
soba	buckwheat noodles
udon	thick noodles
miso shiru	miso (beanpaste) soup
tsukemono	pickled vegetables
teishoku	set meal (the main dish plus rice, miso soup and pickles)

Renshū

8 To help you practise these new words, imagine that the pictures below are the plastic models outside a restaurant. Explain to a friend what each one is in answer to the question **Kore wa nan desu ka**, as in the example.
Rei: Sore wa sushi desu.

SOBA

UDON
NOODLES

MISO SOUP

9 Mr Yamaguchi is entertaining an American client at a Japanese restaurant. Listen to the dialogue on the cassette as many times as necessary, then fill in the gaps in the dialogue below.

Uētoresu Irasshaimase! (a) _____ de gozaimasu ka.

Yamaguchi (b) _____ desu.

Uētoresu Hai, Kochira e. (c) _____ o dōzo.

Yamaguchi Ēto, biiru o (d) _____ kudasai.

Uētoresu Hai, (e) _____ _____ kudasai. (*she returns with the beer*)

Yamaguchi (f) _____ _____ _____ . (*he pours a drink for the client*)

Client (g) _____ _____ . Yamaguchi-san mo biiru o dōzo. (*he pours a drink for Mr Yamaguchi*)

Both men (*raising their glasses*) (h) _____.

Yamaguchi Menyū ga (i) _____ _____ .

Client Sō desu ne. (j) '_____ _____' wa nan desu ka.

Yamaguchi 'Sashimi teishoku' wa sashimi to (k) _____ __ _____ , _____ _____ _____ desu.

Client Ja, sashimi teishoku ni shimasu.

Yamaguchi Watashi wa (l) _____ teishoku _____ _____ .

Uētoresu (m) _____ desu ka.

Yamaguchi Ē, sashimi teishoku o (n) _____ to sushi teishoku o hitotsu _____. Sore ni biiru mo _____kudasai.

Uētoresu Kashikomarimashita.

Gaishoku ni tsuite (3)   *About eating out (3)*

You will have noticed in the dialogue above that Mr Yamaguchi and the American client pour each other's beer. This custom is strictly adhered to in Japan. You don't pour your own drink and you don't let another person's glass become empty.

When it comes to paying the bill (o-kanjō), this will normally be left at your table. You take it to the cash till (reji) on your way out. There is no need to tip in restaurants in Japan. The service is usually included in some way.

 —————————————— **Renshū** ——————————————

10 Put yourself in Mr Yamaguchi's place and answer the client's questions about the following dishes. Use the dialogue above as your model and speak out aloud.

(a) Client: 'Sushi teishoku' wa nan desu ka.
(b) Client: 'Yakitori teishoku' wa nan desu ka.
(c) Client: 'Tempura teishoku' wa nan desu ka.

 Tesuto

How do you say in Japanese:

(a) I've decided on a cheeseburger and potato fries?
(b) Have you decided?
(c) I can't eat meat?
(d) That was delicious?
(e) I've had enough, thank you?
(f) Three bottles of beer please?
(g) Cheers?

16

O-KANE
Money

In this unit you will learn

- more about Japanese money and prices
- how to change traveller's cheques at a bank
- how to send a parcel home at the post office
- how to use an international telephone

Fukushū

- Numbers (Units 2–4, Unit 6)
- Time: **kara – made** (p. 65)
- Japanese money (Unit 6)
- Saying and understanding prices (Unit 6)
- Counters and buying stamps (p. 77, 80)
- Giving and understanding directions (Unit 7)
- Saying you want to do something (p. 127)

Renshū

1   This exercise is a revision one to help you practise large numbers
    and prices. Look back to Exercise 1 in Unit 6 (page 82). This was

a listening activity. This time, just practise saying each amount out aloud in Japanese (answers are in the back of the book under Unit 16). If you still feel that you need more practice, try some of the other activities in Unit 6 again (for example Exercises 3, 5, 7).

2   The word for *note* in Japanese is **satsu** (for example *a five pound note* = **go-pondo satsu**) and the word for *coin* is **kōka** (for example, *a one pence coin* = **ichi-pensu kōka**).

Look back to Unit 6, setsumei 2 (page 75) at the various coins and notes in the Japanese currency. Cover the captions under each note or coin and say out aloud in Japanese the amount plus **kōka** or **satsu** as appropriate. For example a 1-yen coin is **ichi-en kōka** (there are no answers in the back of the book).

Nihon no ginkō, yūbinkyoku ni tsuite   *About Japanese banks and post offices*

To understand the passage below you first need to understand the key word **aiteimasu** (*is open*) and its negative form **aiteimasen** (*is not open*). For example:

Sūpa wa kuji kara rokuji   *The supermarket is open*
   made aiteimasu.   *from nine to six.*

Now read the passage below, then check your understanding by trying Exercise 3.

Nihon no ginkō wa getsuyōbi kara kinyōbi made daitai kuji kara sanji made aiteimasu. **Shūmatsu** wa aiteimasen. Nihon no yūbinkyoku wa getsuyōbi kara kinyōbi made kuji kara goji made desu. Doyōbi wa kuji kara jūniji goro made desu. Nichiyōbi wa aiteimasen.

| aiteimasu | is open |
| shūmatsu | weekend |

Renshū

3 Fill in the opening and closing times in the chart below using the information from the passage above.

	Bank	**Post office**
Monday – Friday	–	–
Saturdays	–	–
Sundays	–	–

Tango-hyō

Ginkō de *At the bank*

ryōgae-guchi	exchange window
kawase rēto	exchange rate
genkin	cash
kurejitto kādo	credit card
toraberāzu chekku	traveller's cheques
pasupōto	passport
bank kādo	bank card
sain	signature
kasshu mashiin	cashpoint
komisshon	commission

Useful phrases

... o kaetai desu	I want to change ...
... o ... ni kaetai desu	I want to change ... into ...
go-pondo o en ni kaetai desu	I want to change five pounds into yen
... en satsu de kudasai	may I have it in ... yen notes, please
... en satsu de yoroshiii desu ka	is it all right in ... yen notes?
koko ni sain shite kudasai	please sign here

Gaika *Foreign currency*

pondo	pounds
doru	dollars
furan	franc
maruku	marks

Hinto: *Pronunciation tips*

Here are some pronunciation tips to help you master the new vocabulary. Be especially careful when saying words which derive from

English. You need to make a special effort to pronounce them 'Japanese-style'. For example:

maruku	ma-ru-k(u)	}	The last **u** is soft, almost not pronounced
doru	do-r(u)		The **r** is always soft – somewhere between **r** and **l**.
pondo	po-n-d(o)		The **o** is soft, almost not pronounced.
kurejitto	ku-re-ji (*pause*) to		The pause is like that in *headdress*.
ryōgae	ryo-u-ga-e		Run the **r** and **y** together in **ryō**; **e** is pronounced as in *pen*.
kaetai	ka-e-ta-i		**E** as in *pen*; i as in *cheese*.

Renshū

4 Before you begin this exercise, familiarise yourself with the new words. Keep saying them out aloud, then use this exercise as a way of testing how well you have remembered them. (There are also some useful phrases on the cassette.) Say out aloud in Japanese:

(a) I want to change some traveller's cheques.
(b) I want to change traveller's cheques into cash (or: I want to cash traveller's cheques).
(c) May I have it in 5000 yen notes, please?
(d) Please sign here.
(e) Excuse me, where is the exchange window?

5 **Kaiwa**

Anne has gone to the bank to change some money. Listen to the cassette (or read the dialogue) and work out the answers to these questions.

(a) Where is Anne told the exchange window is?
(b) What amount of traveller's cheques does Anne want to change?
(c) What is the exchange rate on that day, and how much will Anne's cheques be in yen?
(d) What is the rate of commission?
(e) How does Anne want the money?

Ginkō de:
Anne   Sumimasen, ryōgae-guchi wa doko desu ka.
Ginkō-in   Asoko desu. Ano kasshu mashiin no chikaku ni arima-
               su.
Anne   Dōmo arigato.
Ryōgae-guchi de:
Anne   Sumimasen, kono toraberāzu chekku o en ni kaetai
               desu.
Ginkō-in   Hai. Zembu de hyaku pondo desu ne.
Anne   Ē, sō desu.
Ginkō-in   Kawase rēto wa ichi pondo wa hyaku yonjū-en desu.
               Hyaku pondo wa ichiman yonsen-en **ni narimasu**.
Anne   Komisshon wa ikura desu ka.
Ginkō-in   Komisshon wa san pāsento desu.
Anne   Hai. Ēto, gosen-en to sen-en satsu de kudasai.
Ginkō-in   Hai, wakarimashita. Koko ni sain shite kudasai.
               Soshite pasupōto o misete kudasai.
Anne   Hai, dōzo.

... ni narimasu	will be

6   Listen to the cassette again, but this time stop the cassette each
time the bank clerk has spoken and say out aloud Anne's part
using the English prompts below (**Ginkō-in** in brackets indicates
when the bank clerk is speaking). You can then check your
answer by continuing the tape.

Alternatively you can read the dialogue, covering Anne's part
each time. (There are no answers in the back of the book.)

You   *Ask which is the exchange window.*
Ginkō-in ...
You   *Say thank you. Say you want to change these traveller's
            cheques into yen.*
Ginkō-in ...
You   *Agree about the amount.*
Ginkō-in ...
You   *Ask how much the commission is.*
Ginkō-in ...
You   *Ask for 5000 and 1000 yen notes.*

Ginkō-in ...
You   *Hand over your passport.*

Tango-hyō

<table>
<tr><td colspan="2">Yūbinkyoku de   At the post office</td></tr>
<tr><td>hagaki</td><td>postcard</td></tr>
<tr><td>tegami</td><td>letter</td></tr>
<tr><td>earoguramu</td><td>aerogram</td></tr>
<tr><td>kozutsumi</td><td>parcel</td></tr>
<tr><td>funabin de</td><td>by seamail</td></tr>
<tr><td>kōkūbin de</td><td>by airmail</td></tr>
<tr><td>kiro</td><td>kilo</td></tr>
<tr><td>guramu</td><td>gramme</td></tr>
<tr><td>... o okuritai desu</td><td>I want to send ...</td></tr>
<tr><td>okurimasu</td><td>send</td></tr>
<tr><td>tegami o kōkūbin de okuritai desu</td><td>I want to send a letter by airmail</td></tr>
<tr><td>naka wa nan desu ka</td><td>what's inside?</td></tr>
</table>

✳ Hinto: *Pronunciation tips*

kōkūbin	ko-u-ku-u-bi-n	Make sure you say the long sounds.
kozutsumi	ko-zu-tsu-mi	**Tsu** is one syllable – it may help you if you attach the **t** to **zu**.)

 ——————— **Renshū** ———————

7   Using the vocabulary above work out how to say these sentences in Japanese.

(a) I want to send a postcard.
(b) I want to send this postcard.
(c) I want to send a letter.
(d) I want to send this parcel.
(e) I want to send this parcel by seamail.
(f) I want to send this parcel by airmail.

 8   **Haidi-san wa kozutsumi o Doitsu ni okurimasu** (*Heidi is sending a parcel to Germany*)

Listen to the cassette a few times while considering these questions:

- How heavy is the parcel?
- How does she want to send it?
- What is in it?
- What else does she buy?
- How much is the total amount?

Now, without the aid of the cassette, see if you can put the dialogue below into the correct order. Use the cassette (or the answers at the back of the book if you don't have one) to check that you are right.

✳ Hinto

- Start by matching questions with answers
- (*i*) follows (*b*)

(a) Sanzen sambyaku gojū-en desu.
(b) Nihon no kimono to iroirona hon desu.
(c) Funabin de onegaishimasu.
(d) Kono kozutsumi o Doitsu ni okuritai desu.
(e) Wakarimashita. Kono kozutsumi no naka wa nan desu ka.
(f) Hai. Zembu de ikura desu ka.
(g) Hai. Ichi-kiro nanahyaku-guramu desu ne. Sore wa sanzen-en ni narimasu.
(h) Soshite hagaki wa Doitsu made ikura desu ka.
(i) Sorekara, koko ni sain shite kudasai.
(j) Funabin desu ka. Kōkūbin desu ka.
(k) Ja, nanajū-en no kitte o gomai kudasai.
(l) Nanajū-en desu.
(m) Gosen-en de onegaishimasu.

9 Now it's your turn. You want to send an aerogram and a parcel to England and purchase some stamps.

You   *Say you want to send this parcel to England.*
Kyoku-in Funabin desu ka. Kōkūbin desu ka.
You   *Say by airmail.*
Kyoku-in Gohyaku-guramu desu. Sore wa sen nihyaku-en ni narimasu. Kono naka wa nan desu ka.
You   *Say there are some Japanese souvenirs and a letter.*
Kyoku-in Wakarimashita. Koko ni sain shite kudasai.
You   *Next find out how much an aerogram to England is.*
Kyoku-in Hachijū-en desu.
You   *Now ask for ten postcard stamps.*

Kyoku-in Hai, dōzo. Zembu de sen kyūhyaku hachijū-en ni narimasu.

You *Hand over a 5000 yen note.*

Nihon ni tsuite

Kōshū denwa *Public telephones*

As well as public phone boxes, you can also find phones in coffee shops, bars, outside newspaper kiosks and so on. These phones (usually yellow or green) are for domestic calls only and take 10 yen or 100 yen coins. The green phones also accept **terehon kādo** (*telephone cards* – see the example below).

To make an international phone call you have to use special international phones; new-style grey phones even have a monitor screen in English to help you.

Phone cards come in a variety of designs – this card depicts the Japanese badger (**tanuki**) at a summer festival. '50' indicates there are 50 units on this card (you can buy up to 105 units).

Renshū

10 Anne is trying to buy a phone card. Read the dialogue below, then fill in the route Anne must take to find the kiosk, including any landmarks, on the following map (X is where Anne starts from).

Anne   Sumimasen, terehon kādo o kaitai desu. Doko de **utteimasu** ka.

Passer-by   Sō desu ne. **Baiten** wa terehon kādo o utteimasu. Ichiban chikai baiten wa ... so desu ne. Koko kara massugu itte, tsugi no kōsaten o hidari ni magatte kudasai. Soshite, chotto itte kudasai. Baiten wa migi-gawa ni arimasu. Eki no mae desu.

Anne   Hai, wakarimashita. Dōmo arigatō gozaimasu.

utteimasu	sells
baiten	kiosk

11 Now imagine that Anne has stopped you in the street and give her these directions: tell her to go a little way, then turn right at the next traffic lights. Then tell her to go straight on and turn left at the crossroads. The kiosk is next to the bank.

—————————— **Fukushū tesuto** ——————————

The following test is based on Units 14, 15 and 16.

1 Match the Japanese items on the left with the correct English description on the right.

(a) Sashimi	(i)	Seamail
(b) Baiten	(ii)	Set meal
(c) Hashi	(iii)	Paper lantern
(d) Teishoku	(iv)	Raw fish
(e) Washoku	(v)	Western food
(f) Chōchin	(vi)	Chopsticks
(g) Funabin	(vii)	Kiosk
(h) _____ ?	(viii)	Japanese food

There is one extra item on the right. When you've identified it, write it in the gap (h), in Japanese.

2 Match the correct phrase with its English meaning.

(a) The exchange rate is one dollar to 70 yen:
  (i) Kawase rēto wa ichi maruku wa nanajū-en desu.
  (ii) Kawase rēto wa ichi doru wa nanajū-en desu.
  (iii) Toraberāzu chekku o genkin ni kaetai desu.

(b) How much is the commission?
  (i) Komisshon wa ikura desu ka.
  (ii) Bank kādo wa ikura desu ka.
  (iii) Pasupōto wa ikura desu ka.

(c) What is in this parcel?
  (i) Kono tegami no naka wa nan desu ka.
  (ii) Sono kozutsumi no naka wa nan desu ka.
  (iii) Kono kozutsumi no naka wa nan desu ka.

(d) Kiosks sell phone cards.
  (i) Baiten wa aiteimasu.
  (ii) Baiten wa terehon kādo o utteimasu.
  (iii) Baiten wa terehon kādo o kaimasu.

3 How do you say in Japanese:

(a) It's a bit small. Do you have a larger one?
(b) Please take it out of 1000 yen?
(c) A small (portion of) chips please?

(d)   I'll decide on a tempura set meal?
(e)   I want to change some traveller's cheques?
(f)   I want to change 10 dollars into yen?
(g)   I want to send this letter by airmail?

17

YOYAKU SHITAI DESU
I want to make a reservation

In this unit you will learn

- about accommodation in Japan
- how to ask for information at the tourist office
- useful phrases (how many nights, type of room, etc.)
- how to make a reservation over the phone
- how to check in and out of a hotel

───────────── **Fukushū** ─────────────

- Giving your phone number (p. 32)
- Saying dates (Units 2, 4, 9)
- Counting people (p. 42)
- Asking *do you have ... ?* (Unit 6)
- Asking *how much?* Prices (Unit 6)
- Saying you want to do something (p. 127)

In the next three units you will follow Scott, Anne, Heidi and Han as they plan and carry out a trip to Hokkaido, the north island of Japan.

Familiarise yourself with the new words, then read the dialogue and try Exercise 1.

Tango-hyō

Shukuhaku *Accommodation*

ryokan	Japanese inn
hoteru	western-style hotel
minshuku	family-run inn
bijinesu hoteru	business hotel
penshon	pension (family-run lodgings)
yūsuhosuteru	youth hostel
washitsu	Japanese-style room
yōshitsu	western-style room
washoku	Japanese food
yōshoku	western food
tsuin	twin
daburu	double
ippaku	one night
nihaku	two nights
sanpaku	three nights
nanpaku desu ka	how many nights?
heya	room
hitori (ni tsuki)	per person
annai	information
annaisho	information guide book

Hinto: *Remembering new words*

The words for Japanese/western-style room, and Japanese/western food may seem similar and hence confusing. The first thing to remember is that **wa** refers to something Japanese, and **yō** refers to something western. (Another example is **yōfuku** – *clothes* – which you learnt in Unit 14 and actually means western-style clothes; **wafuku** is the word used for Japanese-style clothes such as **kimono**.)

The other thing to remember is that **shoku** means *food* (there are two further examples of this in the next **Tango-hyō** in this unit) and **shitsu** means *room*.

———— Kaiwa 1 ————

Read the following dialogue, then try Exercise 1.

An-san to Haidi-san wa tsūrisuto infomēshon sentā (TIC) ni imasu (*Anne and Heidi are at the TIC (tourist information centre).*)

Kakari-in	Irasshaimase!
Anne	Sumimasen. Raishū Hokkaidō ni ryokō shimasu. Hokkaidō no shukuhaku annai ga arimasu ka.
Kakari-in	Hai, wakarimashita. Washitsu to yōshitsu to **dochira ga yoroshii desu ka**.
Anne	Mada **kimeteimasen**.
Kakari-in	Ja, kono Hokkaidō no annaisho o dōzo. Ni-**pēji** wa ryokan no annai desu. Ryokan no heya wa daitai washitsu desu ne. Tabemono mo washoku desu. Ippaku wa hitori ni tsuki rokusen-en kara desu.
Heidi	Chotto takai desu ga ii **keiken** desu ne.
Kakari-in	Sō desu ne. Soshite san-pēji wa hoteru no annai desu. Hoteru no heya wa yōshitsu desu. Tabemono mo yōshoku desu.
Anne	Tsuin no heya wa ikura desu ka.
Kakari-in	Tsuin wa gosen-en kara desu. Soshite yūsuhosuteru wa yon-pēji desu. Ippaku wa hitori ni tsuki nisen-en kara desu. Heya wa yōshitsu de tabemono wa yōshoku desu.
Heidi	Sore wa yasui desu ne.
Anne	Sō desu ne. Watashi no uchi de kono annaisho o yomi-mashō.
Kakari-in	Hokkaidō no **chizu** mo dōzo.
Anne	Dōmo arigatō.

kakari-in	attendant, person in charge
dochira ga yoroshii desu ka	which would you prefer?
kimeteimasen	(we) haven't decided
pēji	page
keiken	experience
chizu	map

 ———————— **Renshū** ————————

1   Fill in the table below using the information in the dialogue. Write Y for *yes* and N for *no*.

	Japanese inn	Hotel	Youth hostel
Price/night Per person? Per room? Japanese room? Western room? Japanese food? Western food? Page number (in guide book)			

2 Using the above dialogue and vocabulary, how would you say the following phrases in Japanese?

(a) Do you have any accommodation information for Hokkaido?

(b) Do you have a map of Tokyo?

(c) Which do you prefer – Japanese or western-style rooms?

(d) How much is a twin room?

(e) How much is a single room (**shinguru**)?

(f) Let's read this guide book at my house.

Anne, Heidi, Scott and Han are planning their trip at the Yamaguchi house. First familiarise yourself with the new words and phrases below.

Tango-hyō

moshi moshi	hello (used on the phone)
yoyaku (shimasu)	reservation (make a reservation)
shokuji	meals
haitteimasu	it is included
chōshoku	breakfast
yūshoku	evening meal
... o onegaishimasu	please (like **... o kudasai**)

Polite language (used by receptionists, shop assistants, etc.)

de gozaimasu	(polite form of **desu** – is)
gozaimasu	(polite form of **arimasu** – have)
deshō	(polite form of **desu**)
kashikomarimashita	certainly
wakarimashita	certainly (I've understood)
nannin-sama	how many people? (polite form of **nannin**)

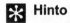 **Hinto**

You've already learnt that **asagohan** means *breakfast* and **bangohan** means *evening meal* (Unit 8, setsumei 5). The words **chōshoku** and **yūshoku** tend to be used in hotels and restaurants.

And remember that **shoku** means *food* (see **Hinto** on page 217 of this unit).

 ———————————— **Renshū** ————————————

 3 **Han-san wa Sapporo yūsuhosuteru ni denwa o shimasu.**
Han is phoning Sapporo youth hostel. Listen to the conversation on the tape (or read the dialogue) and find out the following information.

(a) What date is Han making the reservation for?
(b) How many nights is it for?
(c) How much is it per person per night?
(d) How much is breakfast? And how much is the evening meal?
(e) What information is requested of Han at the end?

Kakari-in Moshi moshi. Sapporo yūsuhosuteru de gozaimasu.
Han Sumimasen, nigatsu mikka ni yoyaku o shitai desu. Heya ga arimasu ka.
Kakari-in Hai, shōshō omachi kudasai. Nannin-sama de gozaimasu ka.
Han Yonin desu. **Onna no hito** ga futari to **otoko no hito** ga futari desu.
Kakari-in Hai, gozaimasu. Nanpaku de gozaimasu ka.
Han Sanpaku desu. Mikka, yokka to itsuka o onegaishimasu. Ippaku wa ikura desu ka.
Kakari-in Hitori ni sen gohyaku-en de gozaimasu.
Han Shokuji wa haitteimasu ka.
Kakari-in Iie, chōshoku wa roppyaku-en de yūshoku wa sen-en de gozaimasu.
Han Ja, chōshoku mo onegaishimasu.
Kakari-in Hai, wakarimashita. O-namae to o-denwa bangō o onegaishimasu.

| onna no hito | woman |
| otoko no hito | man |

Now listen to the conversation again while reading the dialogue to check your understanding before moving on Exercise 4.

4   Anne, Scott, Han and Heidi are also planning to go skiing in Hokkaidō; they plan to stay in another youth hostel in a place called Ōnuma, near a ski resort. You are going to make the reservation for them using the information provided in the dialogue below.

Listen to the receptionist on the cassette, then pause the cassette and say your part. Then switch on the cassette again and check that you said it correctly (if you don't have a cassette, the answers are also at the back of the book). Try not to refer back to the dialogue in Exercise 3. **Gambatte!**

Kakari-in   Moshi moshi, Ōnuma yūsuhosuteru de gozaimasu.
You   *Say you want to make a reservation for February 6th.*
Kakari-in   Hai, nannin-sama de gozaimasu ka.
You   *Say it's for four people.*
Kakari-in   Hai, gozaimasu. Nanpaku de gozaimasu ka.
You   *Say it's for two nights.*
Kakari-in   Hai, wakarimashita.
You   *Ask how much it is per night.*
Kakari-in   Hitori sanzen-en de gozaimasu.
You   *Ask if meals are included.*
Kakari-in   Iie, chōshoku wa gohyaku-en de yūshoku wa sen nihyaku-en de gozaimasu.
You   *Say you'll have breakfast and dinner then.*
Kakari-in   Kashikomarimashita. O-namae to o-denwa-bangō onegaishimasu.
You   *Give your name and phone number.*

Ryokan ni tsuite *About Japanese inns*

Heidi said that although it was expensive, it would be a good experience to stay in a **ryokan**. Staying in a Japanese inn is certainly a unique experience. Guests have the opportunity to sleep on futon, bathe in communal baths (and in spa water at hot-spring resorts), and generally to receive a very high standard of service. Meals are usually served in your room and provide you with the opportunity to try a wide range of traditional Japanese dishes.

Staying in a **ryokan** can be very expensive, but there are other Japanese inns and pensions at lower prices which will give you a similar experience.

Renshū

5 Here is an example of a cheaper style of Japanese inn.

Japanese inn group Ryokan Toki

Listen to the phone conversation on the cassette between a customer and a receptionist and fill in the gaps in the dialogue below.

If you don't have a cassette, see how much you can work out from the advert and other dialogues, then fill in the gaps using the answers at the back of the book and use the dialogue as a reading activity to check your understanding.

Tango-hyō

yokushitsu	bathroom
yokushitsu ga aru heya	a room with a bathroom
yokushitsu ga nai heya	a room without a bathroom

Receptionist   (a)   _____ _____, Ryokan Toki _____ _____ .

Customer   (b)   _____ _____ ni yoyaku shitai desu.

Receptionist   (c)   _____ _____ de gozaimasu ka.

Customer   (d)   _____ desu. Ippaku wa _____ _____ _____.

Receptionist   (e)   _____ deshō ka. _____ deshō ka.

Customer   (f)   Washitsu o _____.

Receptionist   (g)   _____ ga aru heya wa hassen _____ de, yokushitsu ga nai heya wa _____ de gozaimasu.

Customer   (h)   _____ wa haitteimasu ka.

Receptionist   (i)   Iie, _____ wa happyaku-en de, _____ wa sen gohyaku-en de gozaimasu.

Customer   (j)   Ja, _____ no heya to shokuji o _____.

Receptionist   (k)   Kashikomarimashita. _____ to _____ o onegaishimasu.

——————— Renshū ———————

6   Anne, Scott, Han and Heidi have decided, as part of their trip to Hokkaidō, to treat themselves to one night's stay at a reasonably priced **ryokan** in the famous hot spring resort of Noboribetsu. The information about the **ryokan** is printed below.

You are the receptionist, and when Scott phones the **ryokan** you use this information to answer his questions.

Use the dialogues from Exercises 4 and 5 to help you if necessary, but see how much you can understand without referring to them. (You can use the polite alternatives of **desu** – **de gozaimasu** – and **arimasu** – **gozaimasu** – if you are feeling brave, answers are given in both styles.)

Noboribetsu ryokan advert

You	*Say 'hello' and the name of the inn.*
Scott	Nigatsu nanoka ni yoyaku shitai desu.
You	*Ask how many people it is for.*
Scott	Yonin desu. Ippaku wa ikura desu ka.
You	*Ask him if he wants Japanese or western-style rooms.*
Scott	Washitsu o onegaishimasu.
You	*Give the information for four people (use 2 × 2 people) with and without a bathroom.*
Scott	Shokuji wa haitteimasu ka.
You	*Say 'no' and give the prices of meals.*
Scott	Ja, niman-en no heya to shokuji o onegaishimasu.
You	*Now ask for his name and telephone number.*

Nihon no hoteru ni tsuite *About Japanese hotels*

There is a wide variety of western-style hotels, ranging from the expensive and high-class type such as the New Otani Hotel in Tokyo, to the inexpensive business-style hotel aimed at business travellers in need of basic and reasonably priced rooms. A well-known type of business hotel is the capsule hotel – so-called because the rooms are usually the size of the single bed within them, plus a television and light. They are usually located near to stations and are popular with city workers who have missed the last train home and need somewhere cheap to stay the night.

Kaiwa 2

Read the dialogue below then try Exercise 7.

Mr Yamaguchi has been working late, entertaining some clients, and has missed the last train home. He tries to book in at a **kapuseru hoteru** (capsule hotel).

Yamaguchi	Konban heya ga arimasu ka.
Kakari-in	Sumimasen, konban heya wa arimasen ga asoko no hoteru wa heya ga arimasu.
Yamaguchi	Dōmo arigatō.

At the next hotel:

Yamaguchi	Sumimasen, heya ga arimasu ka.
Kakari-in	Hai, gozaimasu.
Yamaguchi	Ippaku o onegaishimasu.
Kakari-in	O-hitori de gozaimasu ka.
Yamaguchi	Hai, hitori desu.
Kakari-in	Koko ni o-namae to **go-jūsho** o onegaishimasu.
Yamaguchi	Hai, dōzo.
Kakari-in	Dewa, kochira e dōzo.

The next morning:

Yamaguchi	**O-kanjō** o onegaishimasu.
Kakari-in	Hai, kashikomarimashita. Zembu de kyūsen-en de gozaimasu.
Yamaguchi	Ja, ichiman-en de onegaishimasu.
Kakari-in	Arigatō gozaimasu. Sen-en no **otsuri** o dōzo.

go-jūsho	address (**go** is used when asking for someone else's address)
o-kanjō	bill
otsuri	change

Renshū

7   Read the Japanese statements below and circle **hai** if it is true, and **iie** if it is false.

saisho	first

(a) Saisho no kapuseru hoteru ni wa heya ga arimashita. (hai/iie).

(b) Tsugi no hoteru ni wa heya ga arimashita. (hai/iie)

(c) Yamaguchi-san wa nihaku shimashita. (hai/iie)

(d) Yamaguchi-san wa namae to denwa-bangō o kakimashita. (hai/iie)

(e) Heya wa zembu de 9000-en deshita. (hai/iie)

8 Without looking at the dialogue above, how do you say the following phrases in Japanese?

(a) Excuse me, do you have a room for tonight?

(b) One night, please.

(c) May I have your name and address?

(d) May I have the bill, please?

(e) Please take it out of 10,000 yen.

(f) Here's 1000 yen change.

Now check your answers with the dialogue. (There are no answers at the back of the book.)

☑ Tesuto

1 Select the correct Japanese phrase for each of these English phrases.

(a) Hello, I'd like to make a reservation.
  (i) Moshi moshi, heya ga arimasu ka.
  (ii) Moshi moshi, washitsu o onegaishimasu.
  (iii) Moshi moshi, yoyaku o shitai desu.

(b) Are meals included?
  (i) Chōshoku wa haiteimasu ka.
  (ii) Shokuji wa haitteimasu ka.
  (iii) Shokuji wa haitteimasen.

(c) How much is it for three nights?
  (i) Ippaku wa ikura desu ka.
  (ii) Sanpaku onegaishimasu.
  (iii) Sanpaku wa ikura desu ka.

(d) May I have your name and phone number?
  (i) O-denwa bangō o onegaishimasu.

     (ii) O-namae to go-jūsho o onegaishimasu.

     (iii) O-namae to o-denwa bangō o onegaishimasu.

(e) A room with a bathroom costs 5000 yen.

     (i)   Yokushitsu ga nai heya wa gosen-en desu.

     (ii) Yokushitsu ga aru heya wa yonsen-en desu.

     (iii) Yokushitsu ga aru heya wa gosen-en desu.

2 Match the Japanese words with their English meanings.

(a)	Minshuku	(i)	A double room
(b)	Yōshitsu	(ii)	A Japanese inn
(c)	Ryokan	(iii)	A Japanese-style room
(d)	Washoku	(iv)	A business hotel
(e)	Daburu	(v)	Family-run, Japanese-style inn
(f)	Washitsu	(vi)	A western-style room
(g)	Bijinesu hoteru	(vii)	Japanese cuisine
(h)	_____	(viii)	Per person

There is one English phrase extra. How do you say this in Japanese? (Complete (h).)

18

KONO DENSHA WA
— **SAPPORO-YUKI DESU KA** —
Is this the train for Sapporo?

In this unit you will learn

- how to buy train and underground tickets
- how to ask where the platform is
- about food on trains
- how to catch a taxi and give directions to the driver

─────────── **Fukushū** ───────────

Familiarise yourself with these new words (test yourself by covering first the English words and then the Japanese words), then read out aloud the conversation below.

Tango-hyō

jidōkippu uriba	automatic ticket machine
... made ikura desu ka	how much is it to ...?
hōmu	platform
kippu	ticket
seisanjo	fare adjustment office
haraimasu	pay

———————— Kaiwa 1 ————————

It's the first day of the trip to Hokkaidō and Anne and Heidi are at Shimbashi underground station

Jidō kippu uriba de *(at the ticket machines)*:

Anne   Ueno eki made ikura desu ka.

Heidi   Ano **chizu** o mimashō!

Anne   'Ueno' no **kanji** ga wakarimasu ka.

Heidi   Wakarimasen. *(sees a passer-by)* Sumimasen, Ueno made ikura desu ka.

Passer-by Ueno desu ka. Hyaku nijū-en desu.

Heidi   Arigatō gozaimasu.

Hōmu de *(on the platform)*:

Anne   A! Sukotto-san wa asoko desu. Sukotto-san!

Scott   Ohayō.

Heidi   Ohayō. **Anata no** kippu wa ikura deshita ka.

Scott   Gojū-en deshita.

Anne   Are! Ueno made hyaku nijū-en desu yo.

Scott   **Shimpai shinai de**! Ueno eki no seisanjo de **nokori** o haraimasu.

chizu	map
kanji	Japanese writing
anato no ...	your ...
shimpai shinai de!	don't worry
nokori	the rest

———————————— **Renshū** ————————————

1 Answer these questions in English.
   (a) Where do Anne and Heidi want to travel to?
   (b) What can't they understand?
   (c) How much does a ticket cost?
   (d) How much did Scott pay and why isn't he worried about this?

Nihon no chikatetsu ni tsuite *About the Japanese underground*

There is an underground (or 'subway') system in ten of the major cities in Japan, including Tokyo, Kyoto, Osaka and Sapporo. The Tokyo system is the most complex, and often there is no English written on the ticket machines. If you don't know how much to pay, you can buy the cheapest ticket, as Scott did, and pay the difference at the **seisanjo** (*fare adjustment office*) at your destination. There are no penalties for doing this. Alternatively, you can do as Anne and Heidi did – ask someone!

Unlike the ticket machines, all the station names are written in **rōmaji** (Japanese written in English) as well as Japanese (see the example below). Not only are the station names supplied, but the previous and the next station are also shown so that you can check when your station is coming up.

Renshū

2 Without looking back at the dialogue, can you work out how Anne, Heidi and Scott said these phrases in Japanese?

(a) Excuse me, how much is it to Ueno station?
(b) Let's look at that map over there!
(c) Do you understand the Japanese writing (kanji) for 'Ueno'?
(d) It's 120 yen to Ueno.
(e) I will pay the rest at the fare adjustment office.

3 Now it's your turn! You are at Shinjuku station and you want to go to Ginza (exclusive and expensive shopping area). Stop a passer-by and say:

You	*Excuse me, how much is it to Ginza?*
Passer-by	150-en desu.
You	*Excuse me, could you repeat that please?*
Passer-by	150-en desu.
You	*Repeat the price and say 'thank-you'.*

Tango-hyō

sen	line
(example) **Hibiya-sen**	the Hibiya line
nani sen	which line?
eki-in	rail employee
norikaemasu	change, transfer
norikaete kudasai	please change
... sen ni norikaete kudasai	please change to the ... line
doko de norikaemasu ka	where do I change at?

Hinto: *Pronunciation tips*

Norikaemasu No-ri-ka-e-ma-su (**e** is spoken as the *e* in *met*; the final **su** is soft – the **u** is hardly spoken)

Kaiwa 2

Han has a more complicated journey to make to Ueno from Kiba. He is asking how to get there at the information office. Look at the map below as you listen to the cassette (or read the dialogue).

Han   Sumimasen, Ueno ni ikitai desu. Doko de norikaemasu ka.
Eki-in Hai, koko kara Kayabachō ni itte kudasai. Soshite, Hibiya-sen ni norikaete kudasai.
Han   Kayabachō de norikaemasu ne?
Eki-in Hai, sō desu. Hibiya-sen ni norikaemasu.
Han   Wakarimashita. Arigatō gozaimasu.

Renshū

4   Can you match the Japanese questions with the correct answers without looking at the dialogue above? (You may need to listen to the cassette several times first.)

(a) Han-san wa doko ni ikimasu ka.

(b) Doko de norikaemasu ka.

(c) Nani sen ni norikaemasu ka.

(i) Kayabachō de norikaemasu.

(ii) Hibiya-sen ni norikaemasu.

(iii) Ueno ni ikimasu.

Hinto: Notice **doko de** (*at which station?*)

nani sen ni (*to which line?*)

5 Look again at the map and this time imagine that Han is making the journey to Ueno from Kuramae. Say out aloud the conversation between Han and the station employee using the English prompts below (? indicates information you must find from the map).

Han (a) *Says excuse me and that he wants to go to Ueno.*

Eki-in (b) *Tells him to go from here (Kuramae) to ? station. Then to change to the ? line.*

Han (c) *Checks that he changes at ? station.*

Eki-in (d) *Says 'that's right' and repeats which line he should change to.*

Han (e) *Says he's understood and thank you.*

Ueno eki de *At Ueno station*

Tango-hyō

midori no mado-guchi	green window
kaimasu	buy
kaisatsu-guchi	ticket gate
kippu uriba	ticket office
katamichi	single
ōfuku	return
shitei seki	reserved seat
jiyū seki	unreserved seat
... yuki	destined for ...
Sapporo-yuki	destined for Sapporo
waribiki kippu	discount ticket

Familiarise yourself with the new words above, then read the dialogue. Try Exercise 6 when you have read it at least once.

Kaiwa 3

Ueno eki de Han-san wa An to Haidi to Sukotto ni aimasu *(At Ueno station Han meets up with Anne, Heidi and Scott):*

Anne	Han-san, ohayō!
Han	A! Yokatta. Ja, shinkansen no kippu o kaimashō.
Heidi	Doko de kippu o kaimasu ka.
Anne	Asoko desu. Ano midori no mado-guchi de.
Scott	Boku ga kippu o kaitai desu.
Anne	Dōzo!
Scott	Sumimasen, Sapporo-yuki no kippu o yonmai kudasai.
Eki-in	Katamichi desu ka, ōfuku desu ka.
Scott	Chotto …
Anne *(whispers)*	Ōfuku desu.
Scott	E? Hai, ōfuku o onegaishimasu.
Eki-in	Shitei seki desu ka, jiyū seki desu ka.
Scott	Ēto …
Heidi	Jiyū seki wa **motto yasui** desu ne.
Scott	Ja, jiyū seki o onegaishimasu.
Eki-in	Hai, zembu de …
Han *(whispers)*	Sukotto-san, waribiki kippu desu yo!
Scott	A! Sumimasen, **watashitachi** wa gakusei desu. Waribiki kippu ga arimasu ka.
Eki-in	Arimasu yo. **Pasupōto** o misete kudasai … Arigatō gozaimasu. Ja, zembu de rokuman nisen-en desu.
Scott	Hai, nanaman-en de onegaishimasu.
Anne, Han, Heidi	Sukotto-san, **omedetō**!

motto yasui	cheaper
watashitachi	we
pasupōto	passport
omedetō	congratulations

Renshū

6 Try this activity without referring back to the dialogue. Some of the Japanese sentences below are true and some are false. Write a circle (**maru**) in the brackets next to the ones you think are true, and a cross (**batsu**) next to the ones you think are false.

(a) Sukotto-san wa Sapporo-yuki no kippu o kaimashita.   ( )
(b) Kaisatsuguchi de kippu o kaimashita.   ( )
(c) Kippu o go-mai kaimashita.   ( )
(d) Katamichi no kippu o kaimashita.   ( )
(e) Gakusei no waribiki kippu ga arimasen deshita.   ( )
(f) Jiyū seki no kippu o kaimashita.   ( )
(g) Kippu wa zembu de 6200-en deshita.   ( )

7   Use the dialogue and new words as necessary to work out how to say the following.

(a) Where do we buy the tickets for the Shinkansen?
(b) I'd like four tickets for Kyōto, please.
(c) Return or single?
(d) I'd like a reserved seat, please.
(e) Do you have any discount tickets?
(f) Please show me your passports.

8   Now it's your turn. You're going to Hiroshima by bullet train: you want two single tickets for unreserved seats; you want a discounted ticket for the person travelling with you who is a child (**kodomo**). Use this information to complete the conversation below. Speak out aloud.

You   *Say 'excuse me', then state your destination and how many tickets you want.*
Eki-in   Katamichi desu ka, ōfuku desu ka.
You   *Give the information required.*
Eki-in   Shitei seki desu ka, jiyū seki desu ka.
You   *Give the information required, then ask about the child discount ticket.*
Eki-in   Hai arimasu yo.

Waribiki kippu ni tsuite *About discount tickets*

Visitors to Japan can purchase a Japan rail pass which can be used during a trip to Japan on JR (Japan Railways) trains, buses and ferries. As Japan rail travel is very expensive, the rail pass can mean huge savings. You must purchase the voucher for the pass outside

Japan (travel agents will have details) and exchange it for a pass
when you arrive in Japan. You have to enter Japan under the status
of 'temporary visitor' to be eligible to use the pass. Anne, Scott, Heidi
and Han do not have passes because they have a study visa; however,
other discounts are available, for example for group travel or for long-
distance round-trips.

Tango-hyō

nanban-sen	what platform number?
	(Lit. what track number?)
tsugi no ...	the next ...
chotto matte kudasai	Please wait a while

Renshū

9 Han is asking for some information at the travel centre (**ryokō
sentā**) on the station. Look at the new words, then put the
dialogue below into the correct order. Begin with **Sumimasen ...**

(a) Rokuban-sen desu.
(b) Jūichiji desu.
(c) Sumimasen, Sapporo-yuki no densha wa nanban-sen desu ka.
(d) Tsugi no densha wa nanji desu ka.
(e) Arigatō gozaimasu.

10 Now it's your turn to find out about the Hiroshima train. Try to
say your part out aloud from memory.

You   *Say 'excuse me' and ask what platform your train goes from.*
Eki-in   Yonban-sen desu.
You   *Ask what time the next train is.*
Eki-in   4-ji desu.
You   *Repeat the time and say thank you.*

11 Read the following conversation.

Anne   Sumimasen, kono densha wa Sapporo-yuki desu ka.
Passer-by Iie, sono densha wa Yamagata-yuki desu. Tsugi no
              densha wa Sapporo-yuki desu. Chotto matte kudasai.

Now try to re-write the dialogue so that Anne asks if this is the
train for Hiroshima; the answer is 'no, it's the Ōsaka train'; it's
the next train that is for Hiroshima'.

Shinkansen no naka de *Inside the bullet train*

O-bentō or *packed lunches*, usually comprising rice with meat or fish and various pickles, and beautifully presented in a box with a small pair of wooden chopsticks, can be bought at railway stations or on board the bullet train and express train from as little as 600 yen. These **o-bentō** are known as **ekiben** (**eki** means *station* and **ben** is a shortened form of **o-bentō**). Many railway stations have their own speciality **ekiben** – the two mentioned in the dialogue below could actually be bought at stations along the train line between Hakodate and Sapporo, in South Hokkaidō.

Railway food vendors (**uriko**) walk up and down the length of the bullet train selling a wide assortment of **o-bentō** and **omiyage** (*souvenirs*). They use very polite Japanese language, bowing and apologising for the interruption as they enter and leave each carriage.

Tango-hyō

tōi	far
ikura	salmon roe
(o)-bentō	packed lunches
ekiben	packed train lunches
kani-meshi	crab and rice
tōchaku shimasu	arrive

Polite language (used by railway food vendors)

shitsurei itashimasu	excuse me (said when entering the train carriage)
... ikaga desu ka	how about ...? (polite version of **... dō desu ka** – Unit 9)
gozaimasu	have (polite version of **arimasu**)
de gozaimasu } **deshō**	is (polite version of **desu**)

Renshū

12 Listen to the conversation on the cassette and fill in the gaps in the dialogue below. Listen several times before you try to fill in the gaps.

Scott　(a) An-san! Sapporo made ＿＿＿＿＿ ＿＿＿＿＿ kakari-masu ka.

Anne　(b) ＿＿＿＿＿ ＿＿＿＿＿ gurai desu yo.

Scott　(c) ＿＿＿＿＿ desu ne! Nani o shimashō ka.

Uriko　(*enters carriage pushing food trolley*)
　　　Shitsurei itashimasu.

Scott　(d) A! O-bentō o ＿＿＿＿＿ .

Uriko　(*walking down carriage*)
　　　(e) ＿＿＿＿＿, o-bentō wa ＿＿＿＿＿ deshō ka.

Scott　Sumimasen.

Uriko　Hai!

Scott　(f) Ekiben wa ＿＿＿＿＿ ＿＿＿＿＿ ＿＿＿＿＿ ＿＿＿＿＿ .

Uriko　(g) Ikura-bentō to kani-meshi ga ＿＿＿＿＿ .

Scott　(h) E? An-san, 'kani' wa ＿＿＿＿＿ ＿＿＿＿＿ nan desu ka.

Anne　(i) 'Crab' desu. ＿＿＿＿＿ desu yo.

Scott　(j) Sō desu ka. Ja, kani-meshi o ＿＿＿＿＿ to ocha ＿＿＿＿＿ .

Uriko　(k) Kashikomarimashita. Zembu de ＿＿＿＿＿ de gozaimasu.

Scott　Sen-en de onegaishimasu.

Uriko　(l) Arigatō gozaimasu. Hyaku-en no ＿＿＿＿＿ de gozaimasu.

A little later:

Scott　(m) Aa! Oishikatta desu. An-san, nanji ni ＿＿＿＿＿ ＿＿＿＿＿ ka.

Anne　(n) ＿＿＿＿＿ ＿＿＿＿＿ desu.

Scott　Ima nanji desu ka.

Anne　(o) Ima ＿＿＿＿＿ desu.

Scott　(p) E! Mada desu ne. Hontō ni tōi desu. ＿＿＿＿＿ ＿＿＿＿＿ ＿＿＿＿＿ ＿＿＿＿＿ .

Anne,
Heidi
and Han　Sukotto-san, **Shizuka ni**!

shizuka ni	be quiet

Sapporo eki de *At Sapporo station*

Tango-hyō

takushii noriba	taxi rank
untenshu	driver
yoku dekimashita	well done
nan demo nai desu	it's nothing

Renshū

13 Listen to the dialogue on the cassette and, as Scott gives the directions to the taxi driver from Sapporo station, follow them on the map and decide whether the youth hostel is at the place marked a, b or c. (The arrows and points (i), (ii), (iii) refer to exercise 15; you don't need these for exercise 13.)

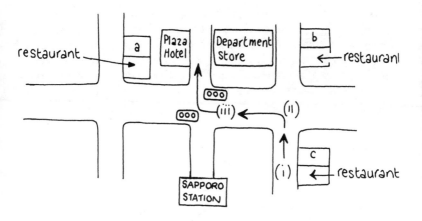

14 Kiku-renshū

Listen to the taxi dialogue on the cassette again, then see if you can say these phrases in Japanese.

(a) Let's go by taxi.
(b) Where is the taxi rank?

(c) I want to go to Sapporo youth hostel.

(d) Do you have a youth hostel map?

(e) The youth hostel is over there. It's next to that restaurant.

15 Now it's your turn. Use the map in exercise 13 to give the following directions. You are setting out from the restaurant next to (c) on the map and are taking a taxi to the *Plaza* Hotel.

You	*Say where you want to go.*
Untenshu	Sore wa doko deshō ka.
You	*Give the first direction (i). And then the next direction (ii)*
Untenshu	Koko desu ka.
You	*Say 'that's right'. Now give the third direction (iii).*
Untenshu	Hai, wakarimashita.
You	*Say that the hotel is over there, then give it's exact location.*
Untenshu	Koko desu ne. Roppyaku-en desu.
You	*Say 'thanks' and hand over a 1000 yen note.*
Untenshu	Yonhyaku-en no otsuri desu. Arigatō gozaimashita.

Takushi ni tsuite *About taxis*

Taxi ranks are found in main public places such as stations and large hotels. If a taxi is vacant there will be a red light in the windscreen; a green light shows that it is occupied. The doors of taxis are opened and closed automatically by the driver. In large cities it is a good idea to have a map or address of where you want to go, to show the driver. There is no custom of tipping – the exact fare will be shown on the meter.

Tesuto

1 Say the following sentences in Japanese.

(a) Ask a passer-by how much it is to Shinjuku station.

(b) Say that you want to go to Shibuya station.

(c) Ask where you change at.

(d) Ask where you buy tickets for the bullet train.

(e) Ask for one ticket to Kyōto.

(f) Tell a taxi driver to turn left at the next traffic lights.

(g) Ask which platform the train for Maebashi goes from.

2 Choose the correct English equivalent for each of the following Japanese phrases.

(a) Tōzai-sen ni norikaete kudasai.
- (i) Change to the Tozai line.
- (ii) Change at Tozai.
- (iii) Take the Tozai train.

(b) Katamichi desu ka. Ōfuku desu ka.
- (i) Do you want a single ticket?
- (ii) Do you want a single or a return?
- (iii) Do you want a packed lunch?

(c) Jiyūseki desu ka. Shitei seki desu ka.
- (i) I'll have a reserved seat, please.
- (ii) I'll have an unreserved seat, please.
- (iii) Do you want a reserved or unreserved seat?

(d) Hachi-ji ni tōchaku shimasu.
- (i) We arrive at 7 o'clock.
- (ii) We arrive at 8 o'clock.
- (iii) We leave at 8 o'clock.

(e) O-cha, o-bentō wa ikaga deshō ka.
- (i) Does anyone want green tea or packed lunches?
- (ii) May I have green tea and a packed lunch?
- (iii) We have green tea and packed lunches.

19

SUKII NI IKIMASHŌ
Let's go skiing!

In this unit you will learn

- how to ask for information about sightseeing
- how to find out about places and leisure activities
- how to practise hiring sports equipment
- how to book a theatre ticket by phone
- how to find out about traditional Japanese theatre

———————————— Fukushū ——————————

- Dates (Units 2, 4, 9)
- Time (Unit 5)
- Prices (Unit 6)
- Counters (Unit 6)
- Understanding and saying directions (Unit 7)
- Making suggestions and invitations (Unit 9)
- Time expressions (Units 9, 10)
- Saying what you want to do (Unit 10)
- Saying likes and dislikes (Unit 12)
- Saying what you are good at (Unit 12)
- Floors (Unit 14)

Kankō *Sightseeing*

Tango-hyō

ryokō annai-jo	tourist information office
gaido bukku	guide book
chizu	map
hakubutsukan	museum
kinenkan	memorial museum
kōen	park
Yuki-Matsuri	Snow Festival
matsuri	festival
basu noriba	bus stop
biiru-en	beer garden
... wa, doko desu ka/doko	
ni arimasu ka	where is the ...?
kankō	sightseeing
kankō basu	sightseeing bus

Kaiwa

On their first morning in Sapporo, Heidi, Anne, Scott and Han have gone to the tourist information office. Once you have learnt the new words above, listen to the cassette (or read the dialogue below) as you look at the map of Sapporo in Exercise 1. See if you can fill in the information required.

Ryokō annai-jo de *(at the tourist information office)*:

Heidi   Sumimasen, Sapporo no chizu ga arimasu ka.

Kakari-in Hai, dōzo.

Anne   Yuki-matsuri wa doko desu ka.

Kakari-in Koko desu. Ōdōri-kōen no naka desu.

Han   Kono machi ni omoshiroi hakubutsukan ga arimasu ka.

Kakari-in Ē. Hokkaidō daigaku no chikaku ni Ainu kinenkan ga arimasu.

Heidi   Sore ni, Sapporo no kankō o shitai desu. Kankō basu ga arimasu ka.

Kakari-in Arimasu yo. Kankō basu noriba wa koko ni arimasu. Eki no mae desu. Tsugi no basu wa jūichiji desu.

Scott   Ano ... **yūmeina** biiru-en wa doko ni arimasu ka.

Kakari-in Sapporo biiru-en desu ne. Koko desu. Sōgō depāto no chikaku ni arimasu. Gozen jūichi-ji kara gogo kuji made aiteimasu.

Han   Soshite, konban disuko ni ikitai desu.

Kakari-in Ja, **Susukino** no hen ni disuko ya bā ga takusan arimasu.
Koko kara chikatetsu de Susukino eki made itte kudasai.
Han Arigatō gozaimashita.

yūmei (na)	famous
Susukino no hen	the Susukino area

 ———————— **Renshū** ————————

1 Below is a street map of Sapporo. Use the information in the
dialogue to match the points 1–5 on the map with the places
(a)–(e) below. Write 1–5 in the brackets after the places.

(a) Sapporo beer garden (　)
(b) Sightseeing bus stop (　)

(c)   Disco area   ( )
(d)   Ainu memorial museum   ( )
(e)   Snow Festival   ( )
Now fill in these times:
(f)   Beer garden (opening time):
                  (closing time):
(g)   Next sightseeing bus:

Sapporo ni tsuite *About Sapporo*

Hokkaidō, the north island of Japan, has only been inhabited in a major way by the Japanese within the last 100 years or so. Before that it was almost exclusively inhabited by the Ainu, a group of people believed to be the original inhabitants of the Japanese islands. The climate is generally cooler than the rest of Japan, and winters are long and severe. Sapporo, the capital of Hokkaidō, is a modern city, laid out in a checker-board pattern. The Odori park slices east to west through the middle of the city, and it is here that the famous **Yuki-matsuri** or *Snow Festival* is held in February. Vast numbers of tourists descend on the city at this time to see the amazing snow and ice sculptures.

Renshū

2   Try to work out, without referring back to the dialogue, how the speakers said:

(a)   Do you have a map of Sapporo?
(b)   Where is the Snow Festival?
(c)   Are there any interesting museums in Sapporo?
(d)   I want to do a sightseeing tour of Sapporo.
(e)   Where is the famous beer garden?
(f)   We want to go to a disco this evening.

3   Now it's your turn to find out some information at the tourist office. This time you are in Tokyo, planning your day. Say out aloud your part of the conversation, then fill in the table below with the information you are given. Here is the vocabulary that you will need:

bijutsukan	art gallery
kokuritsu	national
toku ni	in particular
meiji jingū	meiji shrine
omiyage	souvenirs
utteimasu	sell
Sunshine 60 biru	Sunshine 60 building (Japan's highest building – 60 floors)
kabuki-za	kabuki theatre

Areas of Tokyo mentioned in the dialogue: Ueno, Yoyogi park, Asakusa, Ikebukuro, Ginza.

Ryokō annai-jo de:

You *Ask if they have a map of Tokyo.*

Kakari-in Hai, dōzo.

You *Ask if there are any interesting museums in Tokyo.*

Kakari-in Ē. Ueno no hen ni takusan arimasu. Toku ni, Tōkyō bijutsukan to kokuritsu hakubutsukan wa omoshiroi desu. Kuji kara yoji han made aiteimasu.

You *Ask where the Meiji shrine is.*

Kakari-in Koko desu. Yoyogi kōen no naka ni arimasu. Kuji kara yoji han made aiteimasu.

You *Say you want to buy some Japanese souvenirs.*

Kakari-in Sō desu ka. Ja, Asakusa de ii omiyage o utteimasu.

You *Ask where Asakusa is.*

Kakari-in Koko desu. Ueno kōen no chikaku desu.

You *Ask where the famous Sunshine 60 building is.*

Kakari-in Ikebukuro no hen ni arimasu.

You *Say you want to see kabuki this evening. Ask where the kabuki theatre is.*

Kakari-in Koko desu. Higashi-Ginza no chikaku ni arimasu. Kabuki wa shichiji han kara desu.

You *Say 'thank you'.*

Place	Location	Opening times (where relevant)
National Museum		
Tokyo Art Gallery		
Meiji shrine		
Japanese souvenirs		
Sunshine 60 building		
Kabuki theatre		

Sukii ni ikimashō *Let's go skiing*

Tango-hyō

sukii-jō	ski ground
nyūjōken	admission ticket
sukii yōgu	ski equipment
... o karitai	I want to rent ...
hitori ni tsuki	per person
rifuto	lift
muzukashisō	it looks difficult
sukii surōpu	ski slopes

Kaiwa

Anne, Heidi, Scott and Han have moved on from Sapporo to a youth hostel near a ski resort. Listen to the cassette (or read the dialogue below), then answer the questions in Exercise 4.

Scott Kyō wa nani o shimashō ka.
Han Sukii ni ikimashō!
Heidi Sō shimashō. Watashi wa sukii ga totemo suki desu.
Scott Boku wa amari ...
Anne Watashi mo chotto ...
Han An-san, Sukotto-san, hayaku! Sukii-jō ni ikimashō.
Sukii-jō de:
Han Sumimasen, nyūjōken wa ikura desu ka.
Kakari-in Ichi-jikan wa sen-en desu. Ichinichi wa gosen-en desu.
Han Ja, ichinichi no nyūjōken o yonmai kudasai. Sore ni, sukii

yōgu o karitai desu. Ikura desu ka.
Kakari-in Hitori ni tsuki sen-en desu.
Han Hai, sukii yōgu mo onegaishimasu.
Kakari-in Zembu de niman yonsen-en desu.
A little later:
Heidi Ja, rifuto de sukii surōpu ni ikimashō ne.
Scott Chotto ... muzukashisō desu ne.
Han E! Sukotto-san, Amerika de yoku sukii ni ikimashita ka.
Scott Iie, amari shimasen deshita. Amari jōzu dewa arimasen.
Anne Watashi mo amari jōzu dewa arimasen.
Han Hontō desu ka. Dō shimashō ka.
Anne Ja, Sukotto-san, issho ni sukii no renshū o shimashō.
Scott Ii desu ne. Sō shimashō.

Renshū

4 Answer the questions below in Japanese.

(a) Haidi-san wa sukii ga suki desu ka.
(b) Yūsuhosuteru kara doko ni ikimashita ka.
(c) Ichinichi no nyūjōken wa ikura desu ka.
(d) Han-san wa nani o karitai desu ka.
(e) Nan de sukii surōpu ni ikimashita ka.
(f) Sukotto-san wa Amerika de yoku sukii o shimashita ka.
(g) An-san wa sukii ga jōzu desu ka.
(h) Dare ga sukii no renshū o shimashita ka.

5 Using the dialogue above, say these phrases out aloud in Japanese:

(a) What shall we do today?
(b) Excuse me, how much is an admission ticket?
(c) May I have four one-day admission tickets, please.
(d) Also, I want to hire ski equipment.
(e) I'm not very good at skiing.

6 Anne and Scott have finished their ski lesson and have decided to try ice-skating at a nearby outdoor ice rink. Imagine that you are the ice rink attendant; answer their questions using the following information.

Admission ticket cost:	One hour = 500 yen	One day = 2000 yen
Skate hire:	300 yen per person	
Skating lessons:	1000 yen per hour	

sukēto gutsu	ice skates
sukēto no ressun	skating lessons
soku	a pair (shoes, socks, etc.)
ni-soku	two pairs

Sukēto-jō de:

Scott Sumimasen, nyūjōken wa ikura desu ka.
You *Give both costs.*
Scott Sore ni sukēto gutsu o karitai desu. Ikura desu ka.
You *Give the information required.*
Scott Sukēto no ressun wa ikura desu ka.
You *Give the information required.*
Scott Chotto takai desu ne. Ja, ichijikan no nyūjōken o nimai to sukēto gutsu o ni-soku karitai desu.
You *Say how much it is altogether.*
Scott Nisen-en de onegaishimasu.
You *Say how much change you are giving.*
Scott Dōmo arigatō.

Renshū

7   Reiko is booking tickets by phone for the kabuki theatre as a surprise for Anne when she comes back from Hokkaidō. Read through the new words, then listen to the conversation on the cassette a few times. Then switch off the cassette and see if you can fill in the gaps in the dialogue below. Check your answers by replaying the cassette (or look at the answers at the back of the book.)

If you don't have the cassette, fill in the gaps from the answers at the back, then use the dialogue as a reading activity to test your understanding before going on to Exercise 8.

kabuki-za	the kabuki theatre in Tokyo
kūseki	vacant seats
man-in	full house (sold out)
seki	seats
kodomo	children
hangaku	half the price
otona	adults
makuai	interval
sankai	three times
Eigo no gaido	English guide
iyahōn	earphones

Kakari-in (a) _____ _____. Kabuki-za de gozaimasu.

Reiko   (b) Sumimasen, _____ _____ _____ ni kūseki ga arimasu ka.

Kakari-in (c) Sō desu ne. Doyōbi no ban wa _____ desu ga doyōbi no _____ wa dō desu ka. Mada _____ ga arimasu.

Reiko   (d) Seki wa _____ desu ka.

Kakari-in (e) _____ _____ seki wa gosen-en to _____ de, ni-kai no seki wa _____ en to _____-en de gozaimasu. _____ _____ _____ wa hangaku de gozaimasu.

Reiko   (f) Ja, _____ en no seki o _____ mai kudasai. Sore ni kodomo no seki o _____ mai kudasai.

Kakari-in (g) Kashikomarimashita, Zembu de _____ _____ _____ en de gozaimasu.

Reiko   (h) Kabuki wa _____ _____ desu ka.

Kakari-in (i) _____ ji kara _____ ji made desu. Makuai wa _____ arimasu.

Reiko   (j) Eigo no _____ ga arimasu ka.

Kakari-in (k) Ē, eigo no _____ to _____ o utteimasu.

Reiko   A! yokatta desu ne.

Kakari-in (l) Sore de wa _____ to _____ o onegaishimasu.

Reiko   (m) Yamaguchi Reiko desu. Denwa-bangō wa Tōkyō _____ desu.

Kakari-in Arigatō gozaimashita.

Renshū

8 Match the Japanese phrases on the left with the correct English phrases on the right.

(a) Kūseki ga arimasu ka.
(b) Doyōbi no ban wa man-in desu.
(c) Seki wa ikura desu ka.
(d) Rokusen-en no seki o yonmai kudasai.
(e) Kabuki wa nanji kara desu ka.
(f) Eigo no gaido ga arimasu ka.
(g) O-namae to o-denwa-bangō o onegaishimasu.

(i) What time does the kabuki performance start?
(ii) Your name and phone number, please.
(iii) Do you have any guides in English?
(iv) Do you have any seats?
(v) How much is a seat?
(vi) May I have 4 × 6000-yen seats, please.
(vii) Saturday night is sold out.

Gekijō ni tsuite *About the theatre*

The three main traditional forms of Japanese theatre are **kabuki**, **bunraku** and **noh**. Kabuki theatre offers its audience exciting and intriguing drama accompanied by a colourful and varied display of music, costume, stage sets and dance. All parts, including those of women, are played by men, and the actors usually have a long family tradition of involvement in the kabuki theatre.

Bunraku is similar in style to kabuki theatre, however, its actors are puppets. The puppets are about 4 feet tall and are very life-like, with many moving parts including eyes, eyebrows and fingers. They are each operated by three puppeteers who are visible on stage. It takes many years to train as a puppeteer. A group of narrators tell the story and provide the voices of the puppets, and music accompaniment is provided by a shamisen player.

Noh theatre is a more controlled style of drama. It uses a minimum of props, actors and sets, and its stories are performed through the medium of controlled dance, movement, poetry and song. A Greek-style chorus tells the story, and musicians accompany the action with flutes and drums. Some of the actors wear intricate masks, and the costumes are very sumptuous.

Although these forms of theatre go back several centuries, some of the forms have been transferred to modern or western theatre such as the kabuki-style Macbeth which toured Europe and the States to high acclaim.

 ——————— **Renshū** ———————

9   The Bunraku theatre occasionally tours Britain. Imagine that you are working at your local theatre and a Japanese person phones to inquire about tickets. Use the schedule below to answer these questions.

> **Performances:** Saturday 12 and Sunday 13 September at 7.30 p.m.
> **Tickets:**   Stalls (ground floor) £8/£10;
>   balcony (1st floor) £6/£9
> **Children:**   Half the above prices.

Customer Moshi, moshi. Konshū no doyōbi ni kūseki ga arimasu ka.
You   *Saturday is sold out; there are still seats for Sunday.*
Customer Seki wa ikura desu ka.
You   *Give the information asked for.*
Customer Ja, hachi-pondo no seki o nimai to kodomo no seki o nimai kudasai.
You   *Say how much that will be altogether.*
Customer Bunraku wa nanji kara desu ka.
You   *Give the information required.*
Customer Dōmo arigatō.
You   Ask for his/her name and phone number.

 ——————— **Fukushū tesuto** ———————

1   **Units 17–19**
    Find 12 words which you have learnt in Units 17–19. There are some English clues to help you. Words can be found left to right, right to left, top to bottom, and bottom to top.

    Clues: Japanese cuisine, Japanese-style room, reservation, two nights, reserved seat, return (ticket), train lunch, discount, museum, entrance ticket, art gallery, tour bus.

H	A	K	U	B	U	T	S	U	K	A	N
A	I	E	R	I	J	O	H	R	I	N	U
U	N	Y	U	J	O	K	E	N	R	E	S
K	I	S	Y	U	K	O	H	S	A	W	A
A	S	H	I	T	E	I	S	E	K	I	B
Y	O	W	A	S	H	I	T	S	U	K	O
O	F	U	K	U	N	Y	U	H	R	A	K
Y	U	S	H	K	A	U	H	A	H	I	N
A	R	U	W	A	R	I	B	I	K	I	A
J	O	H	N	N	E	B	I	K	E	S	K

2 Units 17–19

Select one word from the box below to complete the Japanese phrases. You can only use each word once.

(a) Kyōto no chizu ga _____ ka.

(b) Nigatsu futsuka ni yoyaku o _____ desu.

(c) Shokuji wa _____ ka.

(d) Ōsaka-yuki no kippu o _____ kudasai.

(e) Hiroshima-yuki no densha wa _____ desu ka.

(f) Sapporo made dono gurai _____ ka.

(g) Nichiyōbi no ban _____ ga arimasu ka.

(h) Nyūjōken wa _____ desu ka.

(i) O-namae to o-denwa-bangō o _____.

---

gomai   onegaishimasu   ikura   arimasu   kakarimasu
haitteimasu   kūseki   shitai   nanban-sen

---

3 Units 17–19

Can you ask:

(a) For a Tokyo accommodation guide?

(b) The price of a double room?

(c) If there are any rooms for tonight?

   (d) For a single ticket?

   (e) Whether there are discount tickets for students?

   (f) If there are any art galleries in *this area* (**kono hen**)?

   (g) Where to change trains?

4 Units 17–19

Complete the following sentences by choosing the endings (i), (ii) or (iii).

   (a) Tsugi no shingō o migi ni
      (i)   itte kudasai.
      (ii) norikaete kudasai.
      (iii) magatte kudasai.

   (b) Hakubutsukan wa kuji kara yoji han made
      (i)   aiteimasu.
      (ii) haitteimasu.
      (iii) utteimasu.

   (c) Sukēto gutsu o
      (i)   shitai desu.
      (ii) karitai desu.
      (iii) ikitai desu.

   (d) Watashi wa sukii ga amari
      (i)   suki desu.
      (ii) jōzu desu.
      (iii) jōzu dewa arimasen.

20

ASOBI NI KITE KUDASAI
Please come and visit

This unit will look at a few formal Japanese phrases you may come across in the Japanese home and in working life. It is particularly useful if you are planning to go to Japan or if you have Japanese friends in this country.

In this unit you will learn

- about visiting a Japanese home
- about Japanese houses
- how to invite a Japanese person to your home
- how to introduce yourself in a business or formal situation
- about the exchange of business cards
- how to make a phone call to a Japanese home and office

Fukushū

- Greetings (Unit 1)
- Days of the week (p. 107)
- Inviting someone (p. 116)
- Asking if someone is well (p. 136)
- Describing words (Unit 11)
- Useful expressions (p. 194)

Satō-sensei no ie de *At Mrs Sato the teacher's house*

The new phrases below are recorded on the cassette for you to practise your pronunciation. Switch on the cassette, listen to one word or phrase, pause the cassette and repeat it. When you have listened and repeated all the words once, wind back and this time say the word first, then play the cassette to check your pronunciation. Try recording yourself and compare this with the cassette. This will help you to correct and improve your pronunciation – and it will help you to remember the words too!

Tango-hyō

gomen kudasai	may I come in? (Lit. excuse me – said when entering the entrance of a home)
genkan	the entrance porch
Ima	living room
yoku irasshaimashita	welcome (to my home)
o-genki desu ka	are you well? (used if someone has been ill or if you haven't see them for some time)
o-kagesama de	I'm fine, thank you (in reply to **o-genki desu ka**)
o-hairi kudasai	please come in
hairimasu	enter
shitsurei shimasu	pardon me for interrupting (said when entering a home or room)
surippa	slippers
o-kake kudasai	please sit down
tsumaranai mono	it's nothing much (said when handing over a gift) (Lit a boring thing)
ikaga desu ka	how about…? would you like? (formal version of **dō desu ka**)
dochira ga ii desu ka	which would you prefer?
itadakimasu	(said before a meal – like 'Bon appétit')
gochisōsama deshita	(said after a meal – *Lit.* 'That was a feast!')
oishisō desu	it looks delicious
… no okawari	another helping of …
mō kekkō desu	I'm full, thank you
o-ki o tsukete!	take care

Kaiwa

Read the conversation below and/or listen to it on the cassette; focus particularly on Anne's part.

An-san wa Satō-sensei no ie e asobi ni ikimashita. (*Anne has gone to visit Satō-sensei's home.*)

Anne (*sliding open the front door*) Gomen kudasai!

Satō-sensei	Aa, An-san! Yoku irasshaimashita. O-genki desu ka.
Anne	Ē, o-kagesama de.
Satō-sensei	Dōzo, o-hairi kudasai.
Anne	Shitsurei shimasu. (*Anne enters the genkan*)
Satō-sensei	Surippa o dōzo. (*Anne takes off her shoes and steps into the slippers*)
Satō-sensei	Kochira e dōzo.

Ima ni hairimasu (*they enter the living room*):

Satō-sensei	O-kake kudasai.
Anne	Shitsurei shimasu.
Satō-sensei	Hokkaidō wa dō deshita ka.
Anne	Totemo tanoshikatta desu. Kireina tokoro desu ne.
Satō-sensei	Sō desu ne. Samukatta desu ka.
Anne	Ē, chotto samukatta desu. Ano, tsumaranai mono desu ga, dōzo.
Satō-sensei	**Ara! Nan deshō?**
Anne	Hokkaidō no omiyage desu.
Satō-sensei	Dōmo arigatō gozaimasu. An-san, o-cha to kōhii to dochira ga ii desu ka.
Anne	Ocha o onegaishimasu.
Satō-sensei	Kēki wa ikaga desu ka.
Anne	Oishisō desu ne. Itadakimasu.

Later:

Satō-sensei	An-san, itsu Igirisu ni kaerimasu ka.
Anne	Mō sugu desu ne. Raigetsu desu.
Satō-sensei	Nihongo ga jōzu **ni narimashita** ne.
Anne	Iie, mada dame desu.
Satō-sensei	Jōzu desu yo. Ocha no okawari wa ikaga desu ka.

Anne	Mō kekkō desu.
As Anne is leaving:	
Anne	Gochisōsama deshita. Kēki wa oishikatta desu.
Satō-sensei	Mata asobi ni kite kudasai.
Anne	Arigatō gozaimashita.
Satō-sensei	O-ki o tsukete!
Anne	Oyasumi nasai.

| **ara! nan deshō?** | hey, what's this? |
| **... ni narimashita** | you have become ... |

Renshū

1 Can you link the Japanese phrases on the left with their English meanings on the right? See if you can do this exercise without referring back to the dialogue.

(a) Ocha o onegaishimasu.   (i) May I come in?

(b) Shitsurei shimasu.   (ii) I'm fine, thank you.

(c) Tsumaranai mono desu ga, dōzo.   (iii) Pardon me for interrupting.

   (iv) It's nothing, but please accept this.

(d) Gochisōsama deshita.

(e) Hokkaidō no omiyage desu.   (v) It's a souvenir from Hokkaido.

(f) Gomen kudasai.   (vi) May I have green tea, please.

(g) Kēki wa oishikatta desu.   (vii) They look delicious.

(h) O-kagesama de.   (viii) That was delicious (a feast), thank you.

(i) _____

   (ix) The cakes were delicious.

There is one English phrase remaining. Can you supply the Japanese for it (i)?

2 Now that you have familiarised yourself with the new words and the dialogue above, try taking Anne's part in the conversation. If you have a cassette, pause it after each of Satō-sensei's lines and say Anne's part out aloud. Try to do this from memory, but don't worry if you need to look back at the dialogue to prompt you. When you've said the line, play it on the cassette to check how you did. Continue like this through the dialogue.

If you don't have a cassette, use a piece of paper to cover each part of Anne's dialogue until you have said it, then uncover it and check.

3 What do you say in Japanese:

(a) As you slide open the front door of a Japanese home?
(b) As you enter the house?
(c) After your host/ess asks you to sit down?
(d) When you hand over a gift?
(e) Before you start to eat or drink?
(f) If you are offered a choice of drinks and you want coffee?
(g) If you are offered more and you are full?
(h) When you want to say something was delicious?
(i) At the end of a meal?

Nihon no ie ni tsuite   *About Japanese homes*

The Japanese live in a variety of accommodation ranging from apartment blocks and 'mansions' (blocks of flats) in the cities through single-storey wooden or pre-fabricated houses in the suburbs and smaller cities, to larger houses for those who can afford them, and farmhouses in the country areas.

Standard to all Japanese homes is the **genkan** or *porch* which separates the outside from the interior of the home. There is often a step up from the genkan to the main body of the house, and it is in the genkan that you must remove your shoes and step up into the slippers that are set out for you beyond the genkan. This reinforces the idea of a separation between the outside and the interior, and of course, in practical terms, it keeps the home freer from dirt.

Many, but not all, Japanese homes have rooms with **tatami** floors. Tatami mats are made from rice straw and rushes woven around a frame. When you enter a tatami room you always take off the slippers and leave them in the hallway. Many homes (and restaurants too) also have a pair of plastic slippers or wooden clogs for use only in the toilet.

Due to the lack of land space Japanese houses tend to be smaller than their western counterparts. They also tend to be much less cluttered with furniture, and rooms, particularly the main living room, are often multi-functional. It is not unusual, for example, for the living room to be turned into the parents' bedroom at night simply by laying out the futon bedding. The next day it is aired outside and then put away again in the cupboard.

 ——————————— **Renshū** ———————————

4 Look at the dialogue again and this time take the role of Satō-sensei. Listen to the cassette (or read the dialogue) and repeat Satō-sensei's lines after her. Then, as you did in Exercise 2, try pausing the tape after Anne's lines and saying Satō-sensei's lines out aloud.

5 Link the English phrases on the left with their Japanese equivalents on the right.

(a)	Welcome (to my home).	(i)	Biiru to wain to dochira ga ii desu ka.
(b)	Are you well?		
(c)	Please come in.	(ii)	Dōmo arigatō gozaimasu.
(d)	Come this way.	(iii)	Mata asobi ni kite kudasai.
(e)	Please sit down.	(iv)	O-ki o tsukete.
(f)	Thank you very much.	(v)	Yoku irasshaimashita.
(g)	Would you prefer beer or wine?	(vi)	Kōhii wa ikaga desu ka.
		(vii)	O-genki desu ka.
(h)	Would you like some coffee?	(viii)	Dōzo o-hairi kudasai.
		(ix)	Kochira e, dōzo.
(i)	Would you like some more coffee?	(x)	O-kake kudasai.
		(xi)	_____
(j)	Please visit again.		
(k)	Take care.		

There is one extra English phrase. Can you say the Japanese equivalent (xi)?

6 Emi is in England and is planning to visit Anne's mother. Anne's mother has been studying Japanese by herself so that she can welcome Emi in Japanese. Take the part of Anne's mother and say out aloud your part in the dialogue below.

Emi   Gomen kudasai!
Mrs Jenkins *Welcome Emi to your house and invite her in.*

Emi	Shitsurei shimasu.
Mrs Jenkins	*Guide her to the living room, then ask her to sit down.*
Emi	Shitsurei shimasu.
Mrs Jenkins	*Ask her how London was.*
Emi	Omoshirokatta desu.
Mrs Jenkins	*Ask her where she went.*
Emi	'Madame Tussauds' to **'Daiei hakubutsukan'** ni ikimashita. Ano, tsumaranai mono desu ga, dōzo.
Mrs Jenkins	*Thank her very much for the gift.*
Emi	Nihon no **ningyō** desu.
Mrs Jenkins	*Ask her if she'd prefer tea or coffee.*
Emi	Kōcha o onegaishimasu.
Mrs Jenkins	*Then offer her some sandwiches.*
Emi	Hai, itadakimasu.
Mrs Jenkins	*Ask her if Anne is well.*
Emi	Hai, totemo genki desu. Nihongo ga jōzu ni narimashita.
Mrs Jenkins	*Ask her if she'd like some more tea.*
Emi	Iie, mō kekkō desu. Gochisōsama deshita. **Sorosoro shitsurei shimasu**.
Mrs Jenkins	*Ask her to visit again.*
Emi	Arigatō gozaimasu. Totemo tanoshikatta desu.
Mrs Jenkins	*Tell her to take care and say goodbye.*
Emi	Sayōnara.

daiei hakubutsukan	British Museum
ningyō	doll
sorosoro	soon
sorosoro shitsurei shimasu	I shall be leaving (excusing myself) soon

Nihon ni tsuite

Gift-giving

When you visit a Japanese home for the first time, take a small gift to show your appreciation. If you are planning a trip to Japan, 'typical' British gifts such as small items of china, tea-towels or drink coasters would be adequate. For a more important person such as a company head or someone who has or is going to do you a great favour, a good quality bottle of whisky would be greatly appreciated. The Japanese usually have gifts specially wrapped when they buy them. We don't generally have this custom in England, and so you can either wrap the gift yourself or simply present it in the shop bag.

You may find that when you offer your gift, your host/ess will put it to one side and not open it in front of you. This is a Japanese custom and certainly doesn't mean that the person is not pleased to receive it. On the other hand, if a Japanese person visits you, it's quite good to follow the British tradition and open the present in front of him or her so that you can show your appreciation and maybe ask some questions about it.

Watashi wa Yamaguchi to mōshimasu *I am called Mr Yamaguchi*

In this section you will learn some useful phrases for more formal and business situations. First of all, familiarise yourself with the new words below and then look at Unit 1 again – how to introduce yourself.

Tango-hyō

... to mōshimasu	I am called ...
meishi	business card
Eikoku	England (also Igirisu)
yoroshiku onegaishimasu	pleased to meet you
	(also **dōzo yoroshiku**)
watashi no desu	This is/it's mine

 ─────────── **Kaiwa** ───────────

Listen to the conversation on the cassette (or if you don't have a cassette read the dialogue), then fill in the table in exercise 7 with the information required.

Mr Yamaguchi is meeting a British business client at a reception in Tokyo.

Business client Hajimemashite, **Eikoku** Ginkō no Maiku Robinson **to mōshimasu**. Dōzo yoroshiku. (*they both bow*)

Yamaguchi Hajimemashite, Nihon Ginkō no Yamaguchi to mōshimasu. Yoroshiku onegaishimasu.

Business client Watashi no meishi o dōzo.

Yamaguchi **Watashi no desu**. Dōzo. (*they both exchange business cards*)

Renshū

7

	Business client	Mr Yamaguchi
Name		—
Place of work		

Meishi ni tsuite   About business cards

The information on a **meishi** or *business card* helps the Japanese business person to quickly establish the rank of the other person, and thus how formally they should greet someone or how deeply they should bow (a deeper bow to a more senior person). In meetings with non-Japanese people, however, this information is less necessary, as non-Japanese people do not have a place within this ranking. Nevertheless, a business card, especially if it is in Japanese as well as English, helps a Japanese person in pronouncing your name and understanding your position.

There is a certain etiquette involved in the exchanging of **meishi**. You offer the card to the other person with the writing facing them, and usually with both hands. When you receive a business card, you should read it carefully and treat it with respect, putting it away carefully once you have studied it. If things become a little confused, you can use **sumimasen** or **shitsurei shimasu** (*excuse me*) to show that the situation is unfamiliar to you.

───────────────── **Renshū** ─────────────────

8 When a Japanese person introduces him or herself within a work situation, he or she invariably says the name of the company they belong to before their own name. This demonstrates the importance which is attached in Japan to identifying yourself with your place of work. Mr Yamaguchi introduced himself like this: **Nihon Ginkō no Yamaguchi to mōshimasu**. The English equivalent of this is: *I am Mr Yamaguchi of the Bank of Japan.*

Below is a list of work places. Imagine you work at these places and practise introducing yourself (use your own name). Speak out aloud and practise bowing too. (But remember that the Japanese are well aware of the western custom of shaking hands and may do this with a foreign client.)

(a) Eikoku Ginkō (*The Bank of England*)
(b) Eikoku Taishikan (*The British Embassy*)
(c) Higashi Denki (*East Electric*)
(d) Eikoku Gasu (*British Gas*)
(e) Mainichi Shinbun (*The 'Mainichi' newspaper*)
(f) Rondon Daigaku (*London University*)
(g) Nihon Shōji (*Japan Trading*)
(h) Daiei Hakubutsukan (*The British Museum*)

Denwa o suru koto   *Making phone calls*

 Say these new words out loud. There are also some phrases on the cassette for you to practise. Play one at a time, pause the tape and repeat it. Listen carefully to the pronunciation.

Tango-hyō

moshi moshi	hello (when telephoning)
irasshaimasu ka	is he in? (polite version of **imasu**)
rusu desu	he's not in (the house)
kaigi-chū	in a meeting
denwa-chū	on the phone
shutchō-chū	on a business trip
gaishutsu-chū	out (of the office)
dengon	a message

dengon o onegai dekimasu ka	may I leave a message?
watashi ni denwa o onegaishimasu	please phone me
yoroshiku onegaishimasu	I'm indebted to you (used when meeting someone for the first time and when someone is going to do you a favour)
mata denwa o shimasu	I'll phone again
o-taku	home (someone else's)
shitsurei shimasu	sorry for interrupting (said by the caller at the end of a call)

Renshū

9 **Yamaguchi-san wa Robinson-san ni denwa o shimasu**. (Mr Yamaguchi telephones Mr Robinson.)

Read the dialogue below, then indicate whether the following statements are correct or not by placing a circle (**maru**) by the correct ones and a cross (**batsu**) by the incorrect ones.

Yamaguchi Moshi moshi, Tōkyō Ginkō no Yamaguchi desu ga Robinson-san wa irasshaimasu ka.

Hisho Sumimasen, ima kaigi-chū desu. Go-dengon ga arimasu ka.

Yamaguchi Hai, watashi ni denwa o onegaishimasu. Kaisha no denwa-bangō wa zero san no hachi san kyū no go ichi ichi go desu. Shichiji made koko ni imasu. Soshite uchi e kaerimasu. Uchi no denwa-bangō wa zero san ichi no hachi san roku no nana kyū ichi nana desu.

Hisho Hai, wakarimashita.

Yamaguchi Yoroshiku onegaishimasu.

(a) Robinson-san wa Yamaguchi-san ni denwa o shimashita. ( )
(b) Robinson-san wa denwa-chū deshita. ( )
(c) Yamaguchi-san wa dengon ga arimashita. ( )
(d) Yamaguchi-san no kaisha no denwa-bangō wa 03-836-7917 desu. ( )
(e) 7-ji made kaisha ni imasu. ( )
(f) Soshite resutoran e ikimasu. ( )

10 Can you say the conversation below between the receptionist and Ms Gates, in Japanese? Speak out aloud.

Ms Gates (a) *Hello, this is Ms Gates of **London Insurance**. Is Mr Suzuki in?*

Hisho (b) *I'm sorry, he's out at the moment. Do you have a message?*

Ms Gates (c) *Yes, please could he phone me? My work (company) number is 0171-663-2198. I will be here until 5.30.*

Hisho (d) *Yes, certainly.*

Ms Gates (e) *Thanks for your help (I'm indebted to you).*

Rondon Hoken	London insurance

Kiku-renshū

11 Robinson-san wa Yamaguchi-san no uchi ni denwa o shimasu. (Mr Robinson telephones Mr Yamaguchi's house.)

Listen to the cassette, then fill in Mr Robinson's weekly diary below.

hima	free, not busy
tanoshimi ni shiteimasu	look forward to something

Tesuto

1   Fill in the gaps in the dialogue below:

Visitor (a) (*Slides open door*) _____ _____!
Host   (b) Aa! Tanaka-san, _____ _____.
Visitor (c) (**Says** '*Hello*') _____.
Host   (d) (*Asks her to come in*) _____ _____ _____.
Visitor (e) (*As enters house*) S_____ s_____.
Host   (f) (*Offers slippers*) _____ _____ _____.

2   Making phone calls. What do you say in Japanese:

(a) When you ask if it's the Yamaguchi residence?
(b) If you want to leave a message?
(c) If you're going to phone again?
(d) If you want the person to phone you?
(e) When you ask someone if they want to leave a message?
(f) If someone calls and the person they want to speak to is on the phone?
(g) At the end of a call (two choices)?

Omedetō gozaimasu! (*Congratulations!*) You have completed *Teach Yourself Beginner's Japanese* and are now a competent speaker of basic Japanese. You should now be able to carry out conversations in Japanese in a variety of different situations, whether in Japan or with a Japanese person in this country. Japanese is an exciting language and is becoming more and more popular to learn. So why not try to increase your knowledge and ability by taking your study further with the full *Teach Yourself Japanese* course or *Teach Yourself Business Japanese*?

Gambatte! *Good luck!*

Sayōnara

ANSWERS TO THE ——— EXERCISES ——— AND TESTS

Unit 1

Renshū

1 (a) Konnichiwa (b) Sayōnara (Ja, mata ne) (c) Konbanwa (d) Oyasumi (nasai) (e) Ohayō (gozaimasu) (f) Hajimemashite (Dōzo yoroshiku) **2** (a) Kochira wa Tanaka Machiko-san desu. Kochira wa Suzuki Fumi-san desu. (b) Kochira wa Yamamoto Masaki-san desu. Kochira wa Sue Teesdale-san desu. (c) Kochira wa Yamaguchi Reiko-san desu. Kochira wa An Jenkinsu-san desu. (d) Kochira wa Kimura Ichirō-san desu. Kochira wa Hayashi-san desu. **5** (a) 0 (b) 2 (c) 2 (d) 1 (e) 1 (f) 1 (g) 0 (h) 2 (i) 1   **6** (a) X (b) san (c) san (d) san

Tesuto

1 (a) Ohayō (gozaimasu) (b) Hajimemashite (Dōzo yoroshiku) (c) Oyasumi (nasai) (d) Sumimasen   **2** Hajimemashite, (*your name*) desu. Dōzo yoroshiku. **3** Kochira wa An Jenkinsu-san desu.

Unit 2

Hanashimashō

(a) Whisky (b) Cake (c) Ice-cream (d) Tape recorder (e) Stereo (f) Computer (g) Bus (or bath) (h) Taxi (i) Pants (meaning *trousers*) (j) Coat (k) Bed (l) Restaurant (m) Pen

Renshū

1 All start with 'zero (rei) san no' (a) san ni nana roku no go yon go san (b) hachi hachi kyū san no san ni ni ichi (c) nana nana roku ni no ichi ni san yon (d) hachi ni hachi san no yon yon go go   **2** (a) T (b) F (c) T (d) T (e) F   **3** (a)

March (b) January (c) August (d) November   **5** (a) Japan (b) Germany (c) Ireland (d) America (e) France (f) Italy

Tesuto

1 (a) 'Hat' wa nihongo de nan desu ka. (b) Shitsurei shimasu. (c) Watashi wa Igirisujin desu. (d) Nihongo no hon desu. **2** Crossword **3** (a) yon (shi) = 4 (b) nana (shichi) = 7 (c) san = 3 (d) nana (shichi) = 7

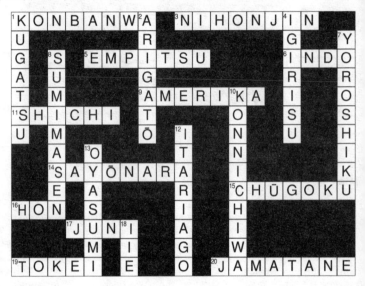

Unit 3

Hanashimashō

Sukotto-san wa Amerikajin desu; Han-san wa Chūgokujin desu; Takeshi-kun wa Nihonjin desu; Tani-san wa Furansujin desu; Haidi-san wa Doitsujin desu.

Renshū

1 (a) (Mr) Suzuki, 5, company employee, golf (b) Yuki, 3, student, swimming (c) Hanako Yamada, 4, shop assistant, gardening (d) Reiko Yamaguchi, 4, housewife, flower arranging   **2** All begin with 'Kochira wa *name* desu' (a) Susan-san wa shufu desu. Shumi wa dansu desu. (b) Andrew-san wa ten'in desu. Shumi wa sakkā desu. (c) Peter-san wa isha desu. Shumi wa gorufu desu. (d) John-san wa kaishain desu.   **3** (a) isha (b) shufu (c) ten'in (d) gakusei   **4** (a) 15 (b) 40 (c) 17 (d) 03-1353-0154 (e) 03-663-1289 (f) 3 (g) March   **5** An-san mo Haidi-san mo gakusei desu. (b) Tani-san mo Henri-san mo Furansujin desu. (c) Haha mo chichi mo haisha desu.

Tesuto

1 nana (shichi), jūnana (jūshichi), jūni, nijū, jūyon (jūshi), ni, ku (kyū), jūsan, jūroku, yonjū, gojū, rokujū **2** (a) Mōichido itte kudasai. (b) Yukkuri itte kudasai. **3** (c) **4** Watashi wa sensei dewa (ja) arimasen. Gakusei desu. **5** gonin, yonin, sannin, futari, hitori

Unit 4

Hanashimashō

1 Kazoku wa rokunin desu. **3** (a) okaasan (b) haha; ani (c) otōto (d) go-kazoku

Renshū

1 (a) 9 (b) 11 (c) 61 (d) 89 (e) 20 (f) 9 **2** (a) 18th, 11th (b) 20th, 23rd (c) 14th (d) 21st, 31st, 27th **3** Each begins with '(*Name*) no tanjōbi wa ...' (a) gogatsu jūichi-nichi (b) hachigatsu nijūichi-nichi (c) jūichigatsu hatsuka (d) kugatsu nijūgo-nichi (e) ichigatsu jūyokka (f) shigatsu sanjū-nichi **4** (a) Kazoku wa yonin desu. Haha, chichi, otōto to watashi desu. (b) Kazoku wa sannin desu. Haha, ani to watashi desu. (c) Kazoku wa yonin desu. Kanai, musume, musuko to watashi desu. (d) Kazoku wa yonin desu. Shūjin, futari no musuko to watashi desu. **5** Rei: Imōto wa jūnana-sai desu. Watashi wa nijūni-sai desu. (a) Chichi wa gojū-sai desu. Otōto wa jūroku-sai desu. Watashi wa hatachi desu. (b) Haha wa yonjūsan-sai desu. Ani wa sanjūissai desu. (c) Musume wa jūkyū-sai desu. Musuko wa jūgo-sai desu. **6** Rei: Oneesan wa nijūgo-sai desu. Imōtosan wa jūnana-sai desu. An-san wa nijūni-sai desu. (a) Otōsan wa gojū-sai desu. Otōtosan wa jūroku-sai desu. Sukotto-san wa hatachi desu. (b) Okaasan wa yonjūsan-sai desu. Oniisan wa sanjūissai desu. (c) Musume-san wa jūkyū-sai desu. Musuko-san wa jūgo-sai desu. **7** (a) 4 (c) 1 (d) 2 (e) 3

Tesuto

1 (a) sangatsu nijūku-nichi (b) hachigatsu jūichi-nichi (c) jūnigatsu nijūgo-nichi (d) ichigatsu jūsan-nichi (e) Gogatsu sanjūichi-nichi **2** haha = own mother, ane = own older sister, okaasan = someone else's mother, kazoku = own family, futari no imōto = two younger sisters, sannin no musuko = three sons, otōsan = someone else's father **3** kyūjukyū, kyūjūhachi, kyūjūshichi, etc.

Unit 5

Hanashimashō

1 (a) san-ji (b) hachi-ji (c) jūichi-ji (d) ichi-ji (e) jūni-ji **2** tabako o kudasai; hon o kudasai; sandoitchi o kudasai; kōhii o kudasai.

Renshū

1 (a) 8 o'clock (b) 11 a.m. (c) 12 p.m. (d) 12 p.m. (e) 6 a.m. (f) 3 a.m. **2** (a) (iii), (b) (vi), (c) (iv), (d) (ii), (e) (v), (f) (i) **3** (a) Getsuyō kurasu wa gozen jūji kara jūniji made desu. (b) Kinyō kurasu wa gogo shichiji kara kuji made desu. (c) Doyōkurasu wa gogo niji kara yoji made desu. **4** (a) Are wa Nihon no tokei desu. (b) Kore wa empitsu desu. (c) Sore wa kaban desu. (d) Kore wa shimbun desu. **5** Drinks: coffee, milk, beer, iced coffee, juice. Food: sandwich(es), spaghetti, pizza, ice-cream, cake(s).

Menyū o misete kudsasai./*Your choice* o kudasai.

6 (a) sore (b) kore (c) ano (d) sore (e) dono   **7** (a) Sono hon o misete kuda-sai./Dore desu ka./ Sore desu. (b) Irasshaimase./Ano tokei o misete kudasai./Dono tokei desu ka./Are desu./Hai, dōzo./Dōmo arigatō.

Tesuto

1 (a) Gogo rokuji (b) Gozen hachiji (c) Gozen jūji (d) jūichiji (e) shichiji han (f) yoji han   **2** Nihongo wa jūji kara jūichiji made desu. Furansugo wa jūichiji han kara jūniji han made desu. Eigo wa ichiji han kara niji han made desu. Tenisu kurabu wa sanji kara yoji made desu.   **3** (a) Menyū o misete kudasai. (b) Kore o kudasai. (c) Sono tokei o misete kudasai. (d) Ano tokei o misete kuda-sai. (e) Dore desu ka.

Unit 6

Hanashimashō

2 (a) yonhyaku gojū (b) kyūhyaku gojū (c) gohyaku gojū (d) nisen nihyaku (e) nisen gohyaku (f) nisen nihyaku gojū

Setsumei

9 – fishmonger's; electrical shop; bakery; butcher's; chemist's; Hinto: hanaya, sakanaya, denkiya, ginko, kusuriya, panya, yūbinkyoku

Renshū

1 (a) 200 yen (b) 600 yen (c) 950 yen (d) 1000 yen (e) 1050 yen (f) 40,000 yen (g) 25,000 yen   **2** (a) 2 (b) 12 (c) 1 (d) 6 (e) 3 (f) 20 (g) 6 (h) 8   **3** (a) (Rei) and (i) hyaku nijū-en (ii) nihyaku jū-en (iii) hyaku gojū-en (iv) hyaku nijū-en (b) Name of place + 'made ikura desu ka'.   **4** (a) *price* + 'no kitte o kudasai.' (i) kyūjū-en (ii) hachijū-en (iii) nihyaku-en (iv) gohyaku-en (v) hyaku-en (vi) jū-en. (b) (i) sanmai (ii) jūmai (iii) gomai (iv) ichimai (v) yonmai (vi) nijūmai   **5** All begin with 'Tōkyō kara ...'. (b) ... Narita made nisen happyaku kyūjū-en desu. (c) ... Kyōto made ichiman nisen kyūhyaku nanajū-en desu. (d) ... Shin-Ōsaka made ichiman sanzen yonhyaku hachijū-en desu. (e) ... Hiroshima made ichiman nanasen nanahyaku-en desu. (f) ... Nagasaki made niman sanzen gohyaku jū-en desu. (g) ... Sapporo made niman issen sambyaku hachijū-en desu.   **6** (a) Hagaki o sanmai kudasai. (b) Biiru o ippon kudasai. (c) Miruku o futatsu kudasai. (d) Pen o roppon kudasai. (e) Nihyaku-en no kēki o mittsu kudasai. (f) Sen-en no kippu o nimai kudasai.   **7** (a) sen kyūhyaku kyūjū roku-nen (b) sen rokujū roku-nen (c) sen kyūhyaku roku-jūsan-nen (d) sen kyūhyaku hachijū-nen (e) sen kyūhyaku yonjūgo-nen   **8** (a) Yūbinkyoku (b) Yaoya (c) Sakaya (d) Sakaya (e) Sakanaya (f) Panya

Unit 7

Hanashimashō

(a) Sumimasen (b) ginkō wa doko desu ka (c) Mōichido itte kudasai (d) (Dōmo) arigatō (gozaimasu)

Renshū

1 (a) Sumimasen, yūbinkyoku wa doko desu ka. (b) Sumimasen, hanaya wa doko desu ka. (c) Sumimasen, ginkō wa doko desu ka. (d) Sumimasen, eki wa doko desu ka. (e) Sumimasen, sūpā wa doku desu ka. (To say *the nearest* add 'Ichiban chikai' before the place as in: (a) Sumimasen, ichiban chikai no yūbinkyoku wa doko desu ka, etc.) **2** (1) (e), (2) (b), (3) (d), (4) (c), (5) (a) **3** (a) (i) Massugu itte kudasai. (ii) Migi ni magatte kudasai. (iii) Hidari ni magatte kudasai. (iv) (Tsugi no) shingō o massugu itte kudasai. (v) (Tsugi no) shingō o migi ni magatte kudasai. (vi) Kōsaten o massugu itte kudasai. (vii) Kōsaten o hidari ni magatte kudasai. (viii) Nibanme no shingō o migi ni magatte kudasai. (ix) Nibanme no kōsaten o hidari ni magatte kudasai. (x) Kado o migi ni magatte kudasai. (b) Massugu itte, migi ni magatte kudasai, etc. **4** (a) T (b) F (c) F (d) T (e) T (f) F **5** (a) chikaku (b) tonari (c) tonari (d) sakanaya (e) mukaigawa (f) panya/sūpā/depāto **7** (a)

(b) Ohayō gozaimasu (*good morning*)

Tesuto

1 Check Unit 6, **Tango-hyō**. **2** (b) **3** (a) Ohayō gozaimasu. (b) Massugu itte, kōsaten o migi ni magatte kudasai. (c) Yaoya wa ginkō no mukaigawa desu. (d) Kōhii to kēki o kudasai. (e) Ichiban chikai panya wa doko desu ka.

Unit 8

Hanashimashō

1 (a) rokuji (b) yoji han (c) gogo kuji (d) gozen shichiji han (e) jūniji (f) gozen jūichiji han. **2** (a) Ginkō wa kuji kara sanji made desu. (b) Sūpā wa hachiji kara hachiji made desu (c) Yūbinkyoku wa kuji kara rokuji made desu (d) Panya wa hachiji kara rokuji made desu.

ANSWERS TO THE EXERCISES

Renshū

1 (a) (ii), (b) (i), (c) (ii)   **2** (a) studies French; afternoon (b) Friday, from 8 p.m.
(c) morning; evening (d) all day; eats dinner (e) Monday–Friday; eats lunch   **3**
(a) (vii), (b) (iv), (c) (i), (d) (viii), (e) (ii)/ (vi), (f) (iii), (g) (v), (h) Sunday   **4** All
begin with '(Name)-san wa asagohan ni ... (a) ... pan o tabemasu. Sore ni kōhii
o nomimasu. (b) ... tamago o tabemasu. Sore ni kōcha o nomimasu. (c) ...
gohan o tabemasu. Sore ni ocha o nomimasu. (d) ... tōsuto o tabemasu. Sore ni
miruku o nomimasu. (e) ... kudamono o tabemasu. Sore ni jūsu o nomimasu.
5 Shichiji han goro okimasu. Daitai asagohan ni tamago o tabemasu. Soshite
kōcha o nomimasu. Sorekara kuji kara yoji made nihongo o benkyō shimasu.
Daitai jūniji han ni hirugohan o tabemasu. Doyōbi ni tenisu o shimasu. Yoru
tokidoki terebi o mimasu. Sore ni jūichiji goro nemasu.   **6** (a) Nanji ni okimasu ka. (b) Asagohan ni nani o tabemasu ka. (c) Nanyōbi ni kaimono o shimasu
ka. (d) Yoru nani o shimasu ka. (e) Itsu benkyō shimasu ka.

Tesuto

1 (a) Kinyōbi (b) Kayōbi (c) Getsuyōbi (d) Mokuyōbi   **2** Okimasu; asagohan;
tabemasu; o nomimasu; kara; ji made; Hirugohan; Bangohan o; mimasu; ji;
nemasu; ni; yomimasu

Unit 9

Hanashimashō

(1) shimashō (2) shimashō (3) tabemashō (4) nomimashō (5) mimashō (6)
benkyō shimashō

Renshū

1 3rd November (f); 7th July (c); 15th November (d); 3rd March (a); 4th
February (e) 10th October (h); 5th May (b); 1st October (g)   **2** (a) (i) Ashita
Rondon ni ikimasu. (ii) Konban konsāto ni ikimasu. (iii) Kyō Furansu ni ikimasu. (iv) Mainichi uchi ni kaerimasu. (b) As in (a) but add 'Tani-san wa ...'
at the start of each sentence. (c) (i) Ashita doko ni ikimasu ka. (ii) Konban
doko ni ikimasu ka. (iii) Kyō doko ni ikimasu ka. (iv) Mainichi doko ni kaerimasu ka.   **3** (a) ni (b) X (c) X (d) ni (e) X (f) ni   **4** (a) Ashita eiga o mimashō
ka. (b) Raishū doraibu ni ikimashō! (c) Kono zasshi o yomimasen ka. (d) Kyō
hirugohan o tabemashō ka. (e) Konban watashi no uchi ni kimasen ka. (f)
Raishū no doyōbi ni kaimono ni ikimashō! (g) Kōhii o nomimasen ka. (h)
Ashita no ban resutoran ni ikimashō ka   **5** Konnichi wa./Raishū watashi no
uchi ni kimasen ka. (Raishū no) suiyōbi wa dō desu ka./Mokuyōbi wa? (dō
desu ka)./Doyōbi wa ii desu. Yoji wa dō desu ka./Ja mata ne, sayōnara!

Tesuto

1 (c)   **2** (a) ikimashō ka (b) kimasen ka (c) mimashō (d) tabemashō ka (e) ikimashō ka (f) mimasen ka   **3** (a) Ashita tomodachi to Rondon ni ikimasu. (b)
Zannen desu ga nichiyōbi wa chotto ... (c) Biiru o nomimasen ka. (d)
Mokuyōbi wa dō desu ka. (e) Doyōbi wa ii desu. Yorokonde. (f) Watashi no
tanjōbi wa hachigatsu yōka desu. (g) Doko ni ikimashō ka.

Unit 10

Hanashimashō

(1) nomimashita (2) shimashita (3) mimashita (4) yomimashita (5) ikimashita
(6) kaerimashita

Renshū

1 (i) (a), (ii) (d), (iii) (b), (iv) (f), (v) (e), (vi) (c), (vii) (h)   **2** (a) (iii), (b) (ii), (c)
(iv), (d) (i), (e) (v)   **3** (b) gojikan (c) yonjuppun (d) ichijikan (e) gofun. (b)
Tōkyō kara Kyōto made shinkansen de gojikan gurai kakarimasu. (c) Dābii
kara Shefirudo made densha de yonjuppun gurai kakarimasu. (d) An-san no
uchi kara Sukotto-san no uchi made chikatetsu de ichijikan gurai kakarimasu. (e) An-san no uchi kara sūpā made aruite gofun gurai kakarimasu.   **4** (a)
(iv), (b) (vii), (c) (iii), (d) (vi), (e) (ii), (f) (i), (g) (v)   **5** (a) Senshū no doyōbi ni
Ginza de kaimono o shimashita. (b) Senshū no suiyōbi ni uchi de eigo o
benkyō shimashita. (c) Ashita tomodachi to resutoran de bangohan o tabemasu. (d) Kyonen Kyōto de ryokō o shimashita. (e) Kinō no ban eigakan de eiga o
mimashita. (f) Sengetsu no tōka ni Tōkyō no gekijō de nihon no odori o
mimashita.   **6** (a) Eki made jitensha de gofun kakarimasu. (b) Ashita kaimono o shitai desu. (c) Chichi wa kuruma de kaisha ni ikimasu. (d) Kesa no
asagohan ni tōsuto o tabemashita. (e) Kotoshi Furansu ni ikitai desu. (f)
Rainen no kugatsu ni Nihon ni ikimasu. (g) Kayōbi no ban gekijō ni ikimashō
ka.

Tesuto

1 (a) Ohayō gozaimasu (b) Hajimemashite (c) Oyasumi nasai (d) Sumimasen
(e) (Dōmo) arigatō gozaimasu. (f) Ja mata ne!   **3** (a) (iii), (b) (ii), (c) (iii)   **4** (a)
shimashita (b) no; ni; shi (c) de; o; shimasu (d) o tabemasu/mashita (e) wa/to;
ikimashita (f) o mimashita (g) no; ni; mashita; (h) kara; made; de; iki

Unit 11

Hanashimashō

(a) wakai desu ne (b) Kawaii desu ne (c) Sono tokei wa suteki desu ne (d)
Nihongo ga jōzu ne (e) Hayai desu ne (f) ii desu ne

Renshū

1 (a) Yasui kuruma desu ne. (b) Omoshiroi eiga desu ne. (c) Shizukana resutoran desu ne. (d) Shinsetsuna hito desu ne. (e) Oishii aisukuriimu desu ne.
(f) Ōkii terebi desu ne. (g) Chiisai terebi desu ne. (h) Genkina hito desu ne.   **2**
(a) Yasukatta desu. (b) Omoshirokatta desu ne. (c) Shizuka deshita ne. (d)
Shinsetsu deshita ne. (e) Oishikatta desu ne. (f) Ōkikatta desu ne. (g)
Chiisakatta desu ne. (h) Genki deshita ne.   **3** (a) Atsui desu. (b) Shizukana
gakkō desu. (c) Tanoshii desu. (d) ... ii desu. (e) ... oishii desu. (f) ... shinsetsu
desu. (g) Sutekina sētā desu. (h) ... kawaii desu.   **4** (a) Shizukana hito deshita ga omoshirokatta desu. (b) Kono aisukuriimu wa oishii desu ga chotto
takai desu. (c) Nihon ni ikitai desu ga takai desu. (d) Kyonen no haru wa
chotto samukatta desu ga kotoshi no haru wa chotto atsui desu. (e) Kono sētā

wa chotto ōkii desu ga sono (ano) sētā wa chotto chiisai desu. **5** (a) small (b) hot (c) convenient (d) smart (e) kind (f) expensive (g) nice **6** Sapporo: 15°C, a bit cold; Tōkyō 25°C, rain; Ōsaka: 27°C, rain later fine; Hiroshima: 26°C, nice weather; Nagasaki: 33°C, very hot

Tesuto

1 (a) wakai (b) tanoshikatta (c) shizukana (d) benri (e) desu **2** (a) (iv), (b) (v), (c) (ii), (d) (i), (e) (iii) **3** Senshū Nihongo no eiga o mimashita./ Omoshirokatta desu./Ashita no ban eigakan ni ikimashō (ka)/Yorokonde (ii desu ne). 'Rūna' kissaten ni ikimashō ka./Chotto takai desu ga aisukuriimu wa totemo oishii desu.

Unit 12

Hanashimashō

1 Nomimasen – *I don't drink*; gorufu o shimasen – *I don't play golf*; okimasen – *I don't wake up*; nemasen – *I don't sleep*, yomimasen – *I don't read*; ikimasen – *I don't go* **2** (a) Ginkō wa yūbinkyoku no tonari desu. (b) Eki wa eigakan no chikaku desu. (c) Depāto wa ginkō no mukaigawa desu. (d) Hanaya wa depāto no mae desu.

Renshū

1 Dialogue (a) Tokei wa tēburu no ue ni arimasu. (b) Inu wa kuruma no shita ni imasu. (c) Tamago wa kaban no naka ni arimasu. (d) Takeshi-kun wa uchi ni imasu. (e) Yūbinkyoku wa ginkō no mukaigawa desu. (f) An-san wa Emi-san no tonari ni imasu.

Answers: (a) maru (b) batsu (c) maru (d) maru (e) batsu (f) batsu

2 Dialogue:

Reiko	An-san, Nihon no ryōri wa dō desu ka.
Anne	Totemo suki desu.
Reiko	Yokatta desu ne. Nihon no terebi wa?
Anne	Sō desu ne. Nyūsu wa hotondo wakarimasen no de amari suki dewa arimasen. Demo hōmu dorama wa suki desu. Reiko-san wa?
Reiko	Ē, watashi mo hōmu dorama ga suki desu. Demo Takeshi wa hōmu dorama ga amari suki dewa arimasen.
Takeshi	Kirai desu. Boku wa manga ga suki desu. Soshite supōtsu bangumi mo suki desu ga tenisu wa amari suki dewa arimasen. Mochiron, Emi wa tenisu bangumi ga totemo suki desu.
Anne	Yamaguchi-san, nan no bangumi ga suki desu ka.
Mr Yamaguchi	Sō desu ne. Nyūsu ga suki desu. Nyūso o mitari uisukii o nondari suru to rirakkusu dekimasu. Boku wa uisukii ga totemo suki desu.

	Anne	Takeshi	Emi	Mr Yamaguchi	Reiko
Tennis		×	✓✓		
Japanese cookery	✓✓				
TV news	×			✓	
Soap drama	✓	×			✓
Whisky				✓✓	
Cartoons	✓				

Answers

3 (a) imasu; imasu; arimasu (b) arimasu; arimasu; arimasu (c) imasu; imasen; imasu; imasu **4** (a) Yūbinkyoku no tonari desu. (b) Terebi no ue ni arimasu. (c) Kuruma no shita ni imasu. (d) Daidokoro ni imasu. (e) Isu no ushiro desu. **5** Yamaguchi-san wa Emi-san no ushiro ni imasu. Reiko-san wa Yamaguchi-san no tonari ni imasu. Takeshi-kun wa Reiko-san no tonari ni imasu. Inu wa Takeshi-kun no mae ni imasu. An-san wa inu no tonari ni imasu. Emi-san wa Yamaguchi-san no mae ni imasu. **6** (a) Takeshi-kun wa hyaku mētoru ga jōzu desu. (b) Yamaguchi-san wa gorufu ga totemo jōzu desu. (c) iie, mada dame desu. (d) Watashi wa Furansugo ga tokui desu. (e) Kinō zenzen terebi o mimasen deshita. (f) Amari shimbun o yomimasen. **7** (a) Hai, tokidoki mimasu. (b) Hai, yoku shimasu. (c) Iie, amari yomimasen. (d) Iie, zenzen basu de ikimasen. (e) Iie, amari mimasen. (f) Iie, zenzen kikimasen.

8 Word puzzle

Fukushū tesuto

1 (a) (vi), (b) (iv), (c) (i), (d) (vii), (e) (ii), (f) (iii), (g) (v) **2** (a) Kore o kudasai. (b) Ano hon o misete kudasai. (c) Aisukuriimu to kōhii o kudasai. (d) Sumimasen, ima nanji desu ka. (e) Yūbinkyoku wa kuji kara goji han made desu. (f) Kono Eigo no shimbun wa ikura desu ka. (g) Kono tegami wa Igirisu made ikura desu ka. (h) Kitte ga arimasu ka. (i) Biiru o nihon kudasai. **3** (a) Sumimasen, Nihon ginkō wa doko desu ka/doko ni arimasu ka. (b) Chotto itte, shingō o migi ni magatte kudasai. (c) Sumimasen, mōichido itte kudasai. (d) Ginkō wa 'Sōgō' depāto no mukaigawa desu/ni arimasu. (e) (Dōmo) arigatō gozaimasu.   **4** (a) Rokuji han ni okimashita. (b) Asagohan ni tamago to tōsuto o tabemashita. (c) Basu de kaisha (shigoto) ni ikimashita. (d) Hachiji han kara jūniji made shigoto o shimashita. (e) Tomodachi to resutoran de hirugohan o tabemashita (or: Resutoran de tomodachi to hirugohan o tabemashita). (f) Chikatetsu de (uchi ni) kaerimasu. (g) Niji kara yoji made bangohan o tsukurimasu. (h) Bangohan ni toriniku to gohan o tabemasu. (i) Terebi o mimasu. (j) Jūichiji han goro nemasu.   **5** (a) Sumimasen, yūbinkyoku wa doko desu ka/ni arimasu ka. (b) 'Book' wa Nihongo de nan desu ka. (c) Doyōbi ni nani o shimasu ka. (d) Nanji ni okimasu ka. (e) Itsu Furansu ni ikimasu ka. (f) Kinō no ban nani o shimashita ka. (g) Asagohan ni nani o tabemasu ka. (h) Tōkyō kara Ōsaka made shinkansen de dono gurai kakarimasu ka.   **6** (a) mashō ka (b) mashō (c) tai desu (d) mashō ka (e) masen ka (f) tai desu (g) mashō   **7** (a) atsui (b) samukatta (c) shizukana (d) shizuka (e) jōzu (f) tokui

Unit 13

Renshū

2 In order from top to bottom (f), (g), (e), (a), (c), (d); Extra kanji = (b) = Thursday   **3** (a) Getsuyōbi desu. (b) Nichiyōbi (c) Kayōbi (d) Doyōbi (e) Kinyōbi (f) Nichiyōbi (g) Suiyōbi   **5** From top to bottom (c), (f), (e), (b), (a), (d)   **6** From top to bottom: (h) 31st (g) 8th (a) 23rd (b) 1st (f) 5th (c) 14th (d) 20th (e) 12th   **7** From top to bottom: (f), (e), (a), (b), (c), (d)   **8** Saturday 21st October   **9** From top to bottom: (e), (g), (f), (b), (c), (d), (a)   **10** From top to bottom: salad = (f) = sarada; cake = (e) = kēki; milk = (g) = miruku; ice = (b) = aisu; cheese = (c) = chiizu; pizza = (d) = piza   **11** (a) 500 (b) 800 (c) 1100 (d) Coffee plus pizza/hamburger/ cake; iced coffee plus hamburger/cake; cola plus any food on the menu.

12

Tesuto

1 (b) Saturday June 11th (c) Tuesday 3rd January (d) Sunday 25th September (e) Monday 7th April (f) Friday 18th February (g) 5th May (Boys' Day)   **2** (a) (ii), (b) (i), (c) (iii), (d) (ii), (e) (i)

Unit 14

Renshū

1 (a) 9–7 (b) Yes (c) They wear very smart uniforms and their Japanese is very polite. (d) Ginza 4 (a) Sumimasen, fujinfuku uriba wa doko desu ka. (b) Ikura desu ka. (c) Motto chiisai no wa arimasu ka. (d) Ja, chotto kitemimasu. (e) Ja, kore o kudasai. (f) Sore de kekkō desu. (g) Gosen-en de onegaishimasu. (h) Maido arigatō gozaimasu. 5 Possible answers (shop assistant in brackets): (Irasshaimase.)/Ano kuroi zubon o misete kudasai./(Hai, dōzo.)/Ikura desu ka./(Sanzen-en desu.)/Saizu wa?/(Esu desu.)/Motto ōkii no wa arimasu ka./(Hai, shōshō omachi kudasai.)/Ja, kore o kudasai. Ichiman-en de onegaishimasu. 6 All answers end with '... ni arimasu'. (a) A no nikai. (b) A no hachikai. (c) A no nanakai. (d) A no rokkai. (e) B no sankai. (f) A no chika ikkai (or A no chikai). (g) B no ikkai. 7 (a) Niman-en desu. (b) Nihon-sei desu. (c) Takai. (d) Ichiman gosen-en desu. (e) Nana pāsento ni shimashita. 8 Miteiru dake desu./Ano rajikase o misete kudasai./Nihon-sei desu ka./Ikura desu ka./Chotto takai desu ne. Waribiki ga dekimasu ka./Ja, kore o kudasai. 9 All answers end in 'kudasai'. (a) Yukata o mittsu (sanmai). (b) Washi o jūmai. (c) Hashi o futatsu. (d) Sensu o nihon. (e) Chōchin o yottsu. (f) O-sake o gohon. 10 (d) (i) (c) (a) (g) (j) (h) (f) (b) (e)

Tesuto

(a) Chotto ōkii desu. (b) Saizu wa? (c) Motto yasui no wa arimasu ka. (d) Kamera uriba wa nankai ni arimasu ka (nankai desu ka). (e) Denki seihin uriba wa doko desu ka. (f) Ichiman-en de onegaishimasu. (g) Ano kuroi T. shatsu o misete kudasai. (h) O-hashi o mittsu kudasai.

Unit 15

Renshū

1 (a) the family (b) A variety from Japanese to western-style cuisine. (c) Reiko: pork cutlets and egg on rice; Mr Yamaguchi: beef steak; Emi, Anne and Takeshi: hamburgers. (d) Two bottles. (e) They really like western food and don't eat Japanese cuisine very much. 2 All end in '... kudasai'. (a) Kōhii o futatsu (b) Sarada o mittsu (c) Hambāgā o yottsu (d) Aisukuriimu o hitotsu to chiizukēkii o futatsu (e) Remon tii o futatsu to biiru o ippon 3 (f), (a), (p), (m), (e), (d), (h), (j), (o), (l), (b), (g), (n), (k), (c), (i) 4 (a) Nannin-sama desu ka. Sannin desu. (b) Menyū o misete kudasai. (c) O-kimari desu ka. (d) Chiizu sandoitchi to sarada ni shimasu. (e) Supagetti ga totemo suki desu. (f) Chiizukēki o tabetai desu. (g) (Watashi wa) mō kekko desu. 5 Hitori desu./Menyū o misete kudasai./(*Your choice*) o kudasai./(*drink*) o kudasai./Oishikatta desu./Mō kekko desu. 6 H = chickenburger, medium chips, medium strawberry shake; T = cheeseburger, large chips, small banana shake; Price = (c) 1400 yen 8 All start with 'Sore wa ...'. (a) sashimi desu. (b) tempura desu. (c) soba desu. (d) yakitori desu. (e) miso shiru desu. (f) udon desu. 9 (a) Nannin-sama (b) Futari (c) (O-)menyū (d) Nihon (e) shōshō o-machi (f) Biiru o dōzo (g) Arigatō gozaimasu (h) Kampai (i) wakarimasu ka (j) sashimi teishoku (k) miso shiru, gohan to tsukemono (l) sushi, ni shimasu (m)

O-kimari (n) hitotsu; onegaishimasu; Nihon   **10** (a) Sushi teishoku wa sushi to miso shiru, gohan to tsukemono desu. (b) Yakitori teishoku wa yakitori to miso shiru, gohan to tsukemono desu. (c) Tempura teishoku wa tempura to miso shiru, gohan to tsukemono desu.

Tesuto

(a) Chiizubāgā to furaido poteto ni shimasu. (b) O-kimari desu ka. (c) Niku ga taberaremasen. (d) Oishikatta desu. (e) Mō kekko desu. (f) Biiru o sambon kudasai. (g) Kampai.

Unit 16

Renshū

1 (a) nihyaku-en, sambyaku-en, yonhyaku-en (b) happyaku-en, roppyaku-en, gohyaku-en (c) yonhyaku gojū-en, nanahyaku gojū-en, kyūhyaku gojū-en (d) sen-en, nisen-en, sanzen-en (e) sen gohyaku-en, sen gojū-en, hassen gojū-en (f) ichiman-en, yonman-en, yonsen-en (g) niman gosen-en, niman gohyaku-en, niman gojū-en   **3** Bank: 9–3, not open on weekends. Post office: 9–5, 9–12, not open on Sundays.   **4** (a) Toraberāzu chekku o kaetai desu. (b) Toraberāzu chekku o genkin ni kaetai desu. (c) Gosen-en satsu de kudasai/onegaishimasu. (d) Koko ni sain shite kudasai. (e) Sumimasen, ryōgae-guchi wa doko desu ka. **5** (a) Over near the cashpoint machine. (b) 100 pounds. (c) £1 = 140 yen, 14,000 yen. (d) 3% (e) In 5000 and 1000 notes.   **7** (a) Hagaki o okuritai desu. (b) Kono hagaki o okuritai desu. (c) Tegami o okuritai desu. (d) Kono kozutsumi o okuritai desu. (e) Kono kozutsumi o funabin de okuritai desu. (f) Kono kozutsumi o kōkūbin de okuritai desu.   **8** The parcel is 1 kilo 700 grammes. She wants to send it by seamail. A Japanese kimono and various books. 5 × 70 yen stamps. 3350 yen. Order: (d), (j), (c), (g), (h), (l), (k), (e), (b), (i), (f), (a), (m)   **9** Kono kozutsumi o Igirisu ni okuritai desu./Kōkūbin de onegaishimasu./Nihon no omiyage to tegami desu./Earoguramu wa Igirisu made ikura desu ka./Hagaki no kitte o jūmai kudasai./Gosen-en de onegaishimasu.

10

11 Chotto itte, tsugi no shingō o migi ni magatte kudasai. Massugu itte, kōsaten o hidari ni magatte kudasai. Baiten wa ginkō no tonari ni arimasu.

Fukushū tesuto

1 (a) (iv), (b) (vii), (c) (vi), (d) (ii), (e) (viii), (f) (iii), (g) (i). Extra item: (h) Yōshoku **2** (a) (ii), (b) (i), (c) (iii), (d) (ii) **3** (a) Chotto chiisai desu. Motto ōkii no wa arimasu ka. (b) Sen-en de onegaishimasu. (c) Furaido poteto no esu o onegaishimasu/o kudasai. (d) Tempura teishoku ni shimasu. (e) Toraberāzu chekku o kaetai desu. (f) Jū doru o en ni kaetai desu. (g) Kono tegami o kōkūbin de okuritai desu.

Unit 17

Renshū

1

	Japanese inn	Hotel	Youth hostel
Price/night	From 6000 yen	From 5000	From 2000
Per person?	Y	N	Y
Per room?	N	Y (Twin)	N
Japanese room?	Y	N	N
Western room?	N	Y	Y
Japanese food?	Y	N	N
Western food?	N	Y	Y
Page number (in guide book)	2	3	4

2
(a) Hokkaidō no shukuhaku no annai ga arimasu ka. (b) Tōkyō no chizu ga arimasu ka. (c) Washitsu to yōshitsu to dochira ga yoroshii desu ka. (d) Tsuin no heya wa ikura desu ka. (e) Shinguru no heya wa ikura desu ka. (f) Watashi no uchi de kono annaisho o yomimashō. **3** (a) 3rd February (b) Three nights (c) 2500 yen (d) Breakfast: 600 yen; evening meal; 1000 yen (e) His name and phone number **4** Nigatsu muika ni yoyaku o shitai desu./Yonin desu./Nihaku desu./Ippaku wa ikura desu ka./Shokuji wa haitteimasu ka./Ja, chōshoku to yūshoku o onegaishimasu. **5** (a) Moshi moshi; de gozaimasu (b) Gogatsu tōka (c) Nannin-sama (d) Futari; ikura desu ka (e) Washitsu; yōshitsu (f) onegaishimasu (g) Yokushitsu; gohyaku-en; hassen-en (h) Shokuji (i) chōshoku; yūshoku (j) hassen-en; onegaishimasu (k) O-namae; O-denwa-bangō **6** Moshi   moshi,   Ryokan   Hanaya   desu/de gozaimasu./Nannin-sama desu ka/de gozaimasu ka./Washitsu desu/deshō ka. Yōshitsu desu/deshō ka (or: Washitsu to yōshitsu to dochira ga yoroshii desu ka)./Yokushitsu ga aru heya wa ichiman-en de/desu/de gozaimasu; yokushitsu ga nai heya wa niman yonsen-en desu/de gozaimasu./Iie, chōshoku wa sen-en de yūshoku wa nisen-en desu/de gozaimasu./O-namae to o-denwa-bangō o onegaishimasu.
7 (a) Iie (b) Hai (c) Iie (d) Iie (e) Hai

Tesuto

1 (a) (iii), (b) (ii), (c) (iii), (d) (iii), (e) (iii)   **2** (a) (v), (b) (vi), (c) (ii), (d) (vii), (e) (i), (f) (iii), (g) (iv); Per person = (h) Hitori (ni tsuki)

Unit 18

Renshū

1 (a) To Ueno station (b) The kanji (Japanese characters) for Ueno (c) 120 yen (d) 50 yen, because he can pay the rest at the fare adjustment office.   **2** (a) Sumimasen, Ueno (eki) made ikura desu ka. (b) Ano chizu o mimashō. (c) Ueno no kanji ga wakarimasu ka. (d) Ueno made 120-en desu. (e) Ueno eki no seisanjō de nokori o haraimasu.   **3** Sumimasen, Ginza made ikura desu ka./Sumimasen, mōichido itte kudasai./Hyaku gojū-en desu ne. Arigatō gozaimasu.   **4** (a) (iii), (b) (i), (c) (ii)   **5** (a) Sumimasen, Ueno ni ikitai desu. (b) Koko kara Asakusa ni itte kudasai. Soshite, Ginza-sen ni norikaete kudasai. (c) Asakusa de norikaemasu ne. (d) Hai, sō desu. Ginza-sen ni norikaemasu. (e) Wakarimashita. Arigatō gozaimasu.   **6** (a) T (b) F (c) F (d) F (e) F (f) T (g) T   **7** Doko de shinkansen no kippu o kaimasu ka. (b) Kyōto-yuki no kippu o yonmai kudasai. (c) Katamichi desu ka, ōfuku desu ka. (d) Shitei seki o onegaishimasu. (e) Waribiki kippu ga arimasu ka. (f) Pasupōto o misete kudasai.   **8** Sumimasen, Hiroshima-yuki no kippu o nimai kudasai./Katamichi o onegaishimasu (kudasai)./ Jiyūseki o onegaishimasu (kudasai). Kodomo no waribiki kippu ga arimasu ka.   **9** (c), (a), (d), (b), (e)   **10** Sumimasen, Hiroshima-yuki no densha wa nanban-sen desu ka./Tsugi no densha wa nanji desu ka/Yoji desu ne. Arigatō gozaimasu.   **11** Anne: Sumimasen, kono densha wa Hiroshima-yuki desu ka. Passer-by: Iie, sono densha wa Ōsaka-yuki desu. Tsugi no densha wa Hiroshma-yuki desu.   **12** (a) dono gurai (b) Jūjikan han (c) Tōi (d) kaimashō (e) O-cha; ikaga (f) nani ga arimasu ka (g) gozaimasu (h) Eigo de (i) Oishii (j) hitotsu; o kudasai (k) kyūhyaku-en (l) otsuri (m) tōchaku shimasu (n) Kuji han (o) ichiji (p) Nani o shimashō ka   **13** (b)   **14** (a) Takushii de ikimashō. (b) Takushii noriba wa doko desu ka. (c) Sapporo yūsuhosuteru ni ikitai desu. (d) Yūsuhosuteru no chizu ga arimasu ka. (e) Yūsuhosutero wa asoko desu. Ano resutoran no tonari desu.   **15** *Possible answer*: 'Plaza' hoteru ni ikitai desu./(Koko kara) massugu itte kudasai. (Soshite) kōsaten o hidari ni magatte kudasai./Hai, sō desu. (Sorekara) tsugi no shingō o migi ni magatte kudasai./'Plaza' hoteru wa asoko desu. Ano depāto no mukaigawa desu./Arigatō. Sen-en de onegaishimasu.

Tesuto

1 (a) Shinjuku (eki) made ikura desu ka. (c) Doko de norikaemasu ka. (b) Shibuya eki ni ikitai desu. (d) Doko de shinkansen no kippu o kaimasu ka. (e) Kyōto-yuki no kippu o ichimai kudasai. (f) Tsugi no shingō o hidari ni magatte kudasai. (g) Maebashi-yuki no densha wa nanban-sen desu ka.   **2** (a) (i), (b) (ii), (c) (iii), (d) (ii), (e) (i)

Unit 19

Renshū

1 (a) 2 (b) 1 (c) 5 (d) 4 (e) 3 (f) 11 a.m.–9 p.m. (g) 11 o'clock   **2** (a) Sapporo no chizu ga arimasu ka. (b) Yuki Matsuri wa doko desu ka. (c) Sapporo ni omoshiroi hakubutsukan ga arimasu ka. (d) Sapporo no kankō o shitai desu. (e) Yūmeina biiru-en wa doko ni arimasu ka (doko desu ka). (f) Konban disuko ni ikitai desu.   **3** Tōkyō no chizu ga arimasu ka./Tōkyō ni omoshiroi hakubutsukan ga arimasu ka./Meiji jingū wa doko desu ka (doko ni arimasu ka.) Nihon no omiyage o kaitai desu./Asakusa wa doko desu ka (doko ni arimasu ka.) Yūmeina Sunshine rokujū biru wa doko desu ka/(doko ni arimasu ka)./Konban kabuki o mitai desu. Kabuki-za wa doko desu ka. (doko ni arimasi ka.) Arigatō gozaimashita. National Museum/Tokyo Art Gallery: Ueno area, 9–4.30; Meiji shrine: in Yoyogi park, 9–4.30; Japanese souvenirs: Asakusa – near Ueno park; Sunshine 60 building; Ikebukuro area; Kabuki theatre: Near Higashi-Ginza, from 7.30.   **4** (a) Hai, totemo suki desu. (b) Sukii-jō ni ikimashita. (c) Gosen-en desu. (d) Sukii yōgu o karitai desu. (e) Rifuto de ikimashita. (f) Iie, amari shimasen deshita. (g) Iie, jōzu dewa arimasen. (h) Sukotto-san to An-san wa sukii no renshū o shimashita.   **5** (a) Kyō wa nani o shimashō ka. (b) Sumimasen, nyūjōken wa ikura desu ka. (c) Ichinichi no nyūjōken o yonmai kudasai. (d) Sore ni, sukii yōgu o karitai desu. (e) (Watashi wa) sukii ga amari jōzu dewa arimasen.   **6** Ichijikan wa gohyaku-en desu. Ichinichi wa nisen-en desu./Hitori ni tsuki sanbyaku-en desu./Ichijikan wa sen-en desu./Zembu de sen roppyaku-en desu./Yonhyaku-en no otsuri desu.   **7** (a) Moshi moshi (b) konshū no doyōbi (c) man-in; gogo; seki (d) ikura (e) Ikkai no; 7000; 6000; 10,000; Kodomo no seki (f) 7000; 4-mai; 1-mai (g) 31,500 yen (h) nanji kara (i) 2–6; sankai (j) gaido (k) gaido: iyahōn (l) o-namae; o-denwa-bangō (m) 3844-2329   **8** (a) (iv), (b) (vii), (c) (v), (d) (vi), (e) (i), (f) (iii), (g) (ii)   **9** Doyōbi wa man-in desu ga nichiyōbi wa mada seki ga arimasu./Ikkai no seki wa hachi pondo to jū pondo desu. Nikai no seki wa roku pondo to kyū pondo desu. Kodomo no seki wa hangaku desu./Zembu de nijūyon pondo desu./Shichiji han kara desu./(Sore dewa) o-namae to o-denwa-bangō o onegaishimasu.

Fukushū Tesuto

1

H	A	K	U	B	U	T	S	U	K	A	N
A	I	E	R	I	J	O	H	R	I	N	U
U	N	Y	U	J	O	K	E	N	R	E	S
K	I	S	Y	U	K	O	H	S	A	W	A
A	S	H	I	T	E	I	S	E	K	I	B
Y	O	W	A	S	H	I	T	S	U	K	O
O	F	U	K	U	N	Y	U	H	R	A	K
Y	U	S	H	K	A	U	K	A	H	I	N
A	R	U	W	A	R	I	B	I	K	I	A
J	O	H	N	N	E	B	I	K	E	S	K

2 (a) arimasu (b) shitai (c) haitteimasu (d) gomai (e) nanban-sen (f) kakarimasu (g) kūseki (h) ikura (i) onegaishimasu   **3** (a) Tōkyō no shukuhaku ga arimasu ka. (b) Daburu no heya wa ikura desu ka. (c) Konban heya ga arimasu ka. (d) Katamichi (no kippu) o kudasai. (e) Gakusei no waribiki kippu ga arimasu ka. (f) Kono hen ni bijutsukan ga arimasu ka. (g) Doko de norikaemasu ka.   **4** (a) (iii), (b) (i), (c) (ii), (d) (iii)

Unit 20

Renshū

1 (a) (vi), (b) (iii), (c) (iv), (d) (viii), (e) (v), (f) (i), (g) (ix), (h) (ii). (i) = Oishisō desu ne.   **3** (a) Gomen kudasai. (b) and (c) Shitsurei shimasu. (d) Tsumaranai mono desu ga, dōzo. (e) Itadakimasu. (f) Kōhii o onegaishimasu. (g) Mō kekkō desu. (h) Oishikatta desu. (i) Gochisōsama deshita.   **5** (a) (v), (b) (vii), (c) (viii), (d) (ix), (e) (x), (f) (ii), (g) (i), (h) (vi), (i) Kōhii no okawari wa ikaga desu ka. (j) (iii), (k) (iv).   **6** Yoku irasshaimashita; dōzo o-hairi kudasai./Kochira e dōzo; o-kake kudasai./Rondon wa dō deshita ka./Doko ni (e) ikimashita ka./Dōmo arigatō gozaimasu./Kōcha to kōhii to dochira ga ii desu ka/Sandoitchi wa ikaga desu ka./An-san wa genki desu ka./Kōcha no okawari wa ikaga desu ka/Mata asobi ni kite kudasai./O-ki o tsukete; sayōnara.   **7** Name: Mike Robinson; Place of work: Bank of England; Bank of Japan   **8** Example: Eikoku Ginkō no (*your name*) desu.   **9** (a) batsu (b) batsu (c) maru (d) batsu (e) maru (f) batsu   **10** (a) Moshi moshi, Rondon Hoken no Gates desu ga Suzuki-san wa irasshaimasu ka. (b) Sumimasen, ima gaishutsu-chū desu. Go-dengon ga arimasu ka. (c) Hai, watashi ni denwa o onegaishimasu. Kaisha no denwa-bangō wa zero ichi nana ichi no roku roku san no ni ichi kyū hachi desu. Goji han made koko ni imasu. (d) Hai, wakarimashita. (e) Yoroshiku onegaishimasu.   **11** Sunday–Wednesday: business trip to Ōsaka; Thursday: meeting at Mainichi newspaper company; Friday: free (going to Mr Yamaguchi's house); Saturday: returns to England

Tesuto

1 (a) Gomen kudasai. (b) Yoku irasshaimashita. (c) Konnichiwa. (d) Dōzo, o-hairi kudasai. (e) Shitsurei shimasu. (f) Surippa o dōzo.   **2** Yamaguchi-san no o-taku desu ka. (b) Dengon o onegai dekimasu ka. (c) Mata denwa o shimasu. (d) Watashi ni denwa o onegaishimasu. (e) Go-dengon ga arimasu ka. (f) Sumimasen, ima denwa-chū desu. (g) Yoroshiku onegaishimasu/shitsurei shimasu.

JAPANESE–ENGLISH VOCABULARY

The unit where each word first appears is given in brackets.

aisu (U13)	*ice*	aruite (U10)	*on foot, walking*
aisukōhii (U5)	*iced coffee*	asa (U8)	*morning*
aisukuriimu (U2)	*ice-cream*	asagohan (U8)	*breakfast*
aiteimasu (U14)	*is open*	ashita (U9)	*tomorrow*
akai (U14)	*red*	asoko (U6)	*over there*
aki (U11)	*Autumn*	atsui (U11)	*hot*
amari (U12)	*not very*		
ame (U11)	*rain*	bai bai (U1)	*goodbye* (casual)
Amerika (U2)	*America*	baiten (U16)	*kiosk*
Amerika-jin (U2)	*American person*	ban (U7)	*number*
anata (U18)	*you*	ban (U8)	*evening / night*
ane (U4)	(my) *older sister*	bangohan (U8)	*evening meal*
ani (U3)	(my) *older brother*	bangumi (U12)	*programme*
annai (U17)	*information*	banku kādo (U16)	*bank card*
annaijo (U17)	*information desk*	basu (U2)	*bus*
annaisho (U17)	*information guidebook*	basu noriba (U19)	*bus stop*
		beddo (U2)	*bed*
ano... (U1)	a hesitation word, like *er, erm*	benkyō shimasu (U8)	*study*
		benri(na) (U11)	*convenient, handy*
ano (U5)	*that* (*over there*)	bentō (U18)	*packed lunch*
aoi (U14)	*blue*	bideo (U2)	*video*
apuru pai (U15)	*apple pie*	biifu sutēki (U15)	*beef steak*
are! (U4)	*expression of surprise*	biiru (U5)	*beer*
		biiru-en (U19)	*beer garden*
are (U5)	*that one over there* (noun)	bijinesu hoteru (U17)	*business hotel*
		bijutsukan (U19)	*art gallery*
arigatō (U1)	*thanks*	biru (U19)	*building*
arimasu (U6)	*have, there is*	bōifurendo (U3)	*boyfriend*
aru (U17)	*have*		

bōshi (U14)	*hat*	depāto (U5)	*department store*
burausu (U14)	*blouse*	deshita (U3)	*was*
		deshō (U17)	*polite form of* **desu**
chichi (U3)	*Father*	desu (U1)	*am; is; are*
chiisai (U5)	*small*	dewa (U5)	*right!*
chiizu (U13)	*cheese*	dewa arimasen (U3)	*is not*
chiizubāgā (U15)	*cheeseburger*	dezāto (U15)	*dessert*
chiizukēki (U15)	*cheesecake*	do (U11)	*degrees*
chikai (U14)	*basement*	dō (U9)	*how?*
chika ikkai (U14)	*first floor of basement*	dochira (U15)	*which one?*
chikaku (U7)	*near* (to)	Doitsu (U2)	*Germany*
chikatetsu (U10)	*underground* (train)	Doitsugo (U2)	*German* (language)
chikin (U2)	*chicken*	Doitsujin (U2)	*German person*
chikinbāgā (U15)	*chickenburger*	doko (U7)	*where*
chizu (U17)	*map*	dokusho (U3)	*reading*
chōchin (U14)	*paper lantern*	dokyumentarii	
chōdo ii (U5)	*just right*	(U12)	*documentary*
chokoretto (U15)	*chocolate*	dōmo (U1)	*thanks*
chōshoku (U17)	*breakfast*	dōmo arigatō	
chotto (U5)	*a little*	(gozaimasu)	*thank you*
chotto matte		(U1)	(*very much*)
kudasai (U18)	*please wait*	donata (U3)	*who*
Chūgoku (U2)	*China*	dono (U5)	*which*
Chūgokugo (U2)	*Chinese* (language)	dono gurai (U10)	*how long? how much?*
Chūgokujin (U2)	*Chinese person*	doraibu (U9)	*drive*
chūmon (U15)	*an order*	dorama (U12)	*drama*
		dore (U5)	*which one* (noun)
daburu (U17)	*double*	doru (U16)	*dollars*
daidokoru (U12)	*kitchen*	dōshi (U12)	*verbs*
daigaku (U20)	*university*	dōshite (U15)	*why?*
daitai (U8)	*more or less;*	doyōbi (U8)	*Saturday*
	usually	dōzo (U2)	*go ahead; there*
dame (U7)	*no good*		*you are*
dansu (U3)	*dancing*	dōzo yoroshiku (U1)	*pleased to meet you*
dare (U3)	*who*		
de gozaimasu (U15)	*is* (formal)	e (U11)	*picture, drawing*
dekimasen (U7)	*can't*	ē (U4)	*yes* (softer than 'hai')
dekimasu (U7)	*can, able to*	ē? (U8)	*expression of*
demasu (U12)	*take part in*		*surprise*
demo (U14)	*even; also; but*	earoguramu (U16)	*aerogramme*
dengon (U20)	*message*	eiga (U8)	*film, movie*
denki (U6)	*lights; electricity*	eigakan (U7)	*cinema*
denki seihin (U14)	*electrical goods*	Eigo (U2)	*English* (language)
denkiya (U6)	*electrical shop*	Eikoku (U20)	*England*
densha (U10)	*train*	eki (U7)	*station*
denwa (U2)	*telephone*	ekiben (U18)	*train lunches*
denwa-bangō (U2)	*telephone number*	empitsu (U2	*pencil*
denwa-chū (U20)	*on the phone*	emu (U14)	*M* (medium)
denwa o shimasu		en (U6))	*yen*
(U8)	*make a phone call*		

engei (U3)	*gardening*	go-jūsho (U17)	*address*
erebētā (U14)	*elevator*		*(somebody else's)*
eru (U14)	*L* (large)	go-kazoku U3)	*family* (somebody
esu (U14)	*S* (small)		else's)
esukarētā (U14)	*escalator*	gomen kudasai	
ē to (U2)	*a hesitation word*	(U20)	*excuse me*
	(*er, erm*)	goro (U8)	*about* (with times)
firumu (U6)	*camera film*	gorufu (U3)	*golf*
fujinfuku (U14)	*women's clothes*	gorufu o shimasu	
funabin (U16)	*sea mail*	(U8)	*play golf*
fune (U10)	*boat, ship*	go-shujin (U4)	*husband*
furaido poteto (U15)	*chips*		*(somebody else's)*
furan (U16)	*franc* (French)	gozaimasu (U17)	*have* (formal)
Furansu (U2)	*France*	gozen (U5)	*am*
Furansugo (U2)	*French* (language)	gurai (U10)	*about*
Furansujin (U2)	*French person*	guramu (U16)	*gramme*
furo (U11)	*a bath*	hachi (U2)	*eight*
futari (U3)	*two people*	hachigatsu (U2)	*August*
futatsu (U6)	*two* (items)	hagaki (U6)	*postcard*
futon (U2)	*Japanese-style bed*	haha (U3)	*Mother*
futorimasu (U15)	*put on weight*	hai (U1)	*yes*
futsuka (U9)	*2nd* (of month)	hairimasu (U20)	*enter*
fuyu (U11)	*Winter*	haisha (U3)	*dentist*
ga (U11)	*but*	haitteimasu (U17)	*is included*
gaido (bukku)		hajimemashite	
(U19)	*guide* (book)	(U1)	*how do you do?*
gaishoku (U15)	*eating out*	haku (paku) (U17)	*counter for nights*
gaishutsu-chū	*out* (of the office)	hakubutsukan	
(U20)		(U19)	*museum*
gakkō (U5))	*school*	hambāgā (U13)	*hamburger*
gakusei (U3))	*student*	han (U5)	*half* (past)
gasu (U20)	*gas*	hana (U6))	*flower*
gekijō (U10)	*theatre*	hanaya (U6)	*flower shop*
genkan (U20)	*entrance porch*	hangaku (U19)	*half price*
genki(na) (U11)	*well; healthy;*	haraimasu (U18)	*pay*
	lively	hare (U11)	*fine* (weather)
genkin (U16)	*cash*	haru (U11)	*spring*
genzai (U15)	*these days*	hashi (U11)	*chopsticks*
getsuyōbi (U8)	*Monday*	hayai (U8)	*early*
ginkō (U7)	*bank*	hayai (U10)	*quick, fast*
ginkō-in (U16)	*bank clerk*	hayaku (U5)	*quickly*
go (U2)	*five*	he! (U10)	*hey; really!*
gochisōsama		hen (U19)	*area*
deshita (U20)	said after a meal	heya (U17)	*room*
gogatsu (U2)	*May*	hidari (U7)	*left*
gogo (U5)	*pm; afternoon* (U10)	hidarigawa (U7)	*left-hand side*
gohan (U8)	*rice* (cooked)	hidoi (U12)	*terrible*
		hikōki (U10)	*aeroplane*

hiru (U8)	*midday*	irasshaimasu	*polite form of*
hirugohan (U8)	*lunch*	(U20)	**imasu**
hisashiburi (U11)	*'long time, no see'*	iroiro (na) (U14)	*various*
hisho (U3)	*secretary*	isha (U3)	*doctor*
hitori (U3)	*one person; alone*	isu (U12)	*chair*
hitori ni tsuki		itadakimasu (U12)	*said before eating*
(U17)	*per person*	Itaria (U2)	*Italy*
hitotsu (U6)	*one* (item)	Itariago (U2)	*Italian* (language)
hoken (U20)	*insurance*	Itariajin (U2)	*Italian person*
hokkē (U12)	*hockey*	itsu (U8)	*when?*
hōmu (U18)	*platform*	itsuka (U9)	*5th* (of month)
hōmu dorama		itsutsu (U6)	*five* (items)
(U12)	*soap opera*	itte (U3)	*speak* (command)
hon (U2)	*book*	itte (U7)	*go* (command)
hon (bon, pon) (U6)	*counter for*	iyahōn (U19)	*earphones*
	cylindrical objects		
honbako (U12)	*bookcase*	ja arimasen (U3)	*is not*
hontō ni (U11)	*really; in truth*	ja mata ne! (U1)	*see you!* (casual)
hoteru (U17)	*hotel*	jazu (U12)	*jazz*
hyaku (U6)	*hundred*	ji (U5)	*o'clock*
		jidō kippu uriba	*automatic ticket*
ichi (U2)	*one*	(U18)	*machine*
ichiban (U7)	*number 1; most*	jikan (U10)	*hour*
ichigatsu (U2)	*January*	jikan-hyō (U5)	*timetable*
ichinichijū (U8)	*all day long*	jitensha (U10)	*bicycle*
ie (U20)	*house*	jiyū seki (U18)	*unreserved seat*
Igirisu (U2)	*England*	jōba (U3)	*horse riding*
Igirisujin (U2)	*English person*	jōdan (U4)	*joke*
ii (U9)	*good, fine, nice*	jōzu (U7)	*good at*
iie (U1)	*no*	jū (U2)	*ten*
ikaga (U18)	*how about?*	jūgatsu (U2)	*October*
ikebana (U3)	*flower arranging*	jūichigatsu (U2)	*November*
ikimasu (U9)	*go*	jūnigatsu (U2)	*December*
ikkai (U14)	*ground floor*	jūsho (U17)	*address*
ikura (U6)	*how much?*	jūsu (U5)	*juice*
ikura (U18)	*salmon roe*		
imasu (U12)	*is, there is*	kaban (U5)	*bag*
	(animate)	kabuki-za (U19)	*Kabuki theatre*
imōto (U4)	*younger sister*	kado (U7)	*corner*
	(own)	kaemasu (U16)	*to change*
imōto-san (U4)	*younger sister*	kaerimasu (U9)	*return; go back*
	(somebody else's)	kaetai (U16)	*want to change*
Indo (U2)	*India*	kai (U14)	*floor*
Indogo (U2)	*Indian*	kaidan (U14)	*stairs*
	(languages)	kaigi (U20)	*meeting*
Indojin (U2)	*Indian person*	kaigi-chū (U20)	*in a meeting*
inu (U12)	*dog*	kaimasu (U18)	*buy*
ippaku (U17)	*one night*	kaimono (U8)	*shopping*
irasshaimase (U5)	*welcome; may I*	kaisatsu-guchi	
	help you?	(U18)	*ticket gate*

kaisha-in (U3)	*company worker / employee*	kochira (U1)	*this person; this way*
kakari-in (U17)	*attendant*	kodomo (U19)	*child(ren)*
kakarimasu (U10)	*(It) takes*	kōen (U19)	*park*
kamera (U14)	*camera*	kōgyō (U19)	*performance*
kampai (U15)	*cheers!*	kōhii (U5)	*coffee*
kan (U10)	*(length of time)*	kōka (U16)	*coin*
ka na (U11)	*I wonder?* *(casual speech)*	koko (U6)	*here*
		kokonoka (U9)	*9th (of month)*
kanai (U4)	*(my) wife*	kokonotsu (U6)	*nine (items)*
kane (U6)	*money*	kōkūbin (U16)	*airmail*
kani (U18)	*crab*	kokuritsu (U19)	*national*
kanjō (U5)	*bill*	komedi (U12)	*comedy*
kankō (U19)	*sightseeing*	komisshon (U16)	*commission*
Kankoku (U10)	*Korea*	kompyūtā (U2)	*computer*
kappu nudoru (U10)	*cup noodles*	kompyūtā gēmu (U2)	*computer games*
kara (U2)	*from*	konban (U9)	*this evening*
karē (U13)	*curry*	konbanwa (U1)	*good evening*
karimasu (U19)	*rent, borrow*	kongetsu (U9)	*this month*
kashikomarimashita (U15)	*certainly, sir / madam*	konnichiwa (U1)	*hello; good afternoon*
		kono (U5)	*this*
kasshu mashiin (U16)	*cashpoint*	kono chikaki ni (U12)	*near here*
katamichi (U18)	*one way; single*	kono hito (U3)	*this person*
katsudon U15)	*pork cutlet dish*	kono yō (na) (U15)	*this type (of)*
kawaii (U4)	*pretty; cute*	konshū (U9)	*this week*
kawase rēto (U16)	*exchange rate*	kōra (U8)	*cola*
kayōbi (U8)	*Tuesday*	kore (U2)	*this one (noun)*
kazoku (U3)	*(own) family*	kōsaten (U7)	*crossroads*
keiken (U17)	*experience*	kōshū denwa (U16)	*public telephone*
keiyōshi (U11)	*adjective*	kōto (U2)	*coat*
kēki (U2)	*cake*	kotoshi (U10)	*this year*
kekkō (U14)	*enough*	kozutsumi (U16)	*parcel*
kesa (U10)	*this morning*	ku (U2)	*nine*
kimari (U15)	*decision*	kudasai (U5)	*please; could I have*
kimasu (U9)	*come*	kugatsu (U2)	*September*
kimeteimasen (U17)	*haven't decided*	kurashikku (U12)	*classical*
		kurejitto kādo (U16)	*credit card*
kinenkan (U19)	*memorial museum*	kuriketto (U12)	*cricket*
kinō (U10)	*yesterday*	kuroi (U14)	*black*
kinyōbi (U8)	*Friday*	kuruma (U10)	*car*
kippu (U6)	*ticket*	kūseki (U19)	*vacant seats*
kiro (U16)	*kilo*	kusuri (U6)	*medicine*
kissaten (U11)	*coffee shop*	kusuriya (U6)	*chemist's*
kitte (U6)	*stamp*	kutsu (U14)	*shoes*
kiteimasu (U14)	*try on (clothes)*	kyō (U9)	*today*
kōcha (U8)	*black tea*	kyōgijō (U12)	*playing field*

kyokuin (U6)	*post assistant*	mōshimasu (U20)	(I am) *called*
kyonen (U10)	*last year*	moshi moshi (U17)	*hello* (on phone)
kyōsō (U12)	*a race*	mō sugu (U5)	*soon, shortly*
kyū (U2)	*nine*	mottekaerimasu	
		(U15)	*take away*
mada (U7)	*not yet*	mottekimasu	
made (U5)	*until*	(U12)	*bring, get*
madoguchi (U18)	(ticket) *window*	motto (U5)	*more*
mae (U7)	*in front of*	muika (U9)	*6th* (of month)
magatte (U7)	*turn* (command)	mukaigawa (U7)	*opposite side*
mai (U6)	*counter for flat*	musuko (U1)	(my) *son*
	objects	musuko-san (U4)	*son* (someone
mainichi (U9)	*every day*		else's)
maishū (U9)	*every week*	musume (U4)	(my) *daughter*
maitsuki (U9)	*every month*	musume-san (U4)	*daughter*
makuai (U19)	*interval*		(someone else's)
man (U6)	*ten thousand*	muttsu (U6)	*six* (items)
manga (U8)	*comic book;*	muzukashii (U19)	*difficult*
	cartoon	muzukashisō	
man-in (U19)	*full house*	(U19)	*looks difficult*
maruku (U16)	*mark* (German)		
massugu (U7)	*straight on*	nai (U17)	*don't have*
mata (U10)	*again*	naka (U12)	*inside*
mata ashita (U1)	*see you tomorrow*	namae (U2)	*name*
matsuri (U19)	*festival*	nan/nani (U2)	*what*
meishi (U20)	*business card*	nanban (U18)	*what number?*
men (U14)	*cotton*	nan de (U10)	*how?*
menyū (U5)	*menu*	nana (U2)	*seven*
michi (U7)	*road; path*	nanatsu (U6)	*seven* (items)
midori (U18)	*green*	nanji (U5)	*what time?*
migi (U7)	*right*	nannichi (U8)	*what date?*
migigawa (U7)	*right-hand side*	nannin (U3)	*how many people?*
mikka (U9)	*3rd* (of month)	nanoka (U9)	*7th* (of month)
mimasu (U8)	*see; watch; look*	nansai (U4)	*how old?*
mina-san (U2)	*everybody*	nanyōbi (U8)	*what day?*
minshuku (U17)	*family-run inn*	narimasu (U16)	*become*
miruku (U5)	*milk*	natsu (U11)	*summer*
miruku shēku		nemasu (U8)	*sleep*
(U15)	*milk shake*	nen (U6)	*year*
misete (U5)	*show me; may*	ni (U2)	*two*
	I see?	ni (U8)	*on, at* (with
miso shiru (U15)	*miso soup*		time/dates)
mittsu (U6)	*three* (items)	niaimasu (U14)	*to suit*
mizu (U8)	*water*	nibanme (U7)	*second*
mo (U3)	*also; too*	nichi (U4)	*day* (date)
mō (U11)	*already*	nichiyōbi (U8)	*Sunday*
mōichido (U3)	*once more*	nichiyōhin (U14)	*everyday goods*
mokuyōbi (U8)	*Thursday*	nigatsu (U2)	*February*
mono (U20)	*thing*	nihaku (U17)	*two nights*

Nihon (U2)	*Japan*	o-namae wa? (U2)	*what's your name?*
Nihongo (U2)	*Japanese*	oneesan (U4)	*older sister*
Nihonjin (U2)	*Japanese person*		*(somebody else's)*
niku (U6)	*meat*	onegaishimasu	
nikuya (U6)	*butcher's*	(U14)	*please*
nin (U3)	*people*	ongaku (U12)	*music*
ningyō (U14)	*doll*	oniisan (U4)	*older brother*
ni shimasu U15)	*decide on*		*(somebody else's)*
nochi (U11)	*later*	onna no hito (U17)	*woman*
nodo ga kawaiteimasu		orenji (U15)	*orange*
(U12)	*I'm thirsty*	o-tearai (U11)	*toilet*
nokori (U18)	*the rest*	o-tera (U10)	*temple*
nomimasu (U8)	*drink* (verb)	otoko no hito (U17)	*man*
nomimono (U8)	*drinks* (noun)	otona (U19)	*adult*
noriba (U19)	*(bus/taxi) stop*	otōsan (U4)	*Father*
norikaemasu		otōto (U3)	*younger brother*
(U18)	*change; transfer*		*(own)*
nyūjōken (U19)	*admission ticket*	otōto-san (U4)	*younger brother*
nyūsu (U12)	*news*		*(somebody else's)*
		otsuri (U14)	*small change*
ocha (U8)	*green tea*	owarimasu (U12)	*end; finish*
odori (U10)	*dance*	oyasumi nasai (U1)	*good night*
ōfuku (U18)	*return* (ticket)		
o-genki de (U11)	*take care*	pan (U6)	*bread*
o-hairi kudasai		pantsu (U2)	*trousers*
(U20)	*please come in*	panya (U6)	*bakery*
ohayō gozaimasu		pāsento (U14)	*percent*
(U1)	*good morning*	pasokon (U14)	*PC*
oishii (U11)	*delicious*	pasupōto (U16)	*passport*
oishisō (U15)	*looks delicious*	pātii (U9)	*party*
okaasan (U1)	*Mother*	pēji (U17)	*page*
okagesama de (U11)	*I'm fine, thanks*	pen (U2)	*pen*
o-kake kudasai		penshon (U17)	*pension (lodgings)*
(U20)	*please sit down*	piza (U5)	*pizza*
o-kane (U6)	*money*	pondo (U16)	*pounds (sterling)*
ōkii (U5)	*big*	poppusu (U12)	*pop music*
okimasu (U8)	*wake up*		
okujō (U14)	*rooftop*	raigetsu (U9)	*next month*
okurimasu (U16)	*send*	rainen (U10)	*next year*
okusan (U4)	*wife* (somebody	raishū (U9)	*next week*
	else's)	raisu (U14)	*rice*
okyakusan (U5)	*customer; guest*	rajikase (U14)	*radio cassette*
omedetō (gozaimasu)		rajio (U14)	*radio*
(U18)	*congratulations*	reji (U14)	*cash desk*
o-meshiagari (U15)	*to eat in* (formal)	remon tii (U15)	*lemon tea*
omiyage (U14)	*souvenir*	ressun (U19)	*lesson*
o-mochikaeri (U15)	*to take away*	resutoran (U2)	*restaurant*
	(formal)	rifuto (U19)	*(ski) lift*
omoshiroi (U11)	*interesting*	ringo (U6)	*apple*
		rirakkusu (U8)	*relax*

rokku (U12)	*rock music*	shigatsu (U2)	*April*
roku (U2)	*six*	shigoto (U3)	*work*
rokugatsu (U2)	*June*	shii dii pureyā	
rusu (U20)	*not in* (the house)	(U2)	*CD player*
ryōgae-guchi (U16)	*exchange window*	shimasu (U8)	*do; make; play*
ryokan (U17)	*Japanese inn*	shimbun (U5)	*newspaper*
ryokō shimasu		shimpai (U18)	*worry*
(U10)	*travel; take a trip*	shingō (U7)	*traffic lights*
ryōri (U10)	*cooking, cuisine*	shinkansen (U10)	*bullet train*
		shinsetsu(na) (U11)	*kind, helpful*
sai (U4)	*years old*	shiroi (U14)	*white*
saikin (U12)	*recently*	shita (U12)	*below, under*
sain (U16)	*signature*	shitei seki (U18)	*reserved seat*
saisho (U17)	*first*	shitsurei shimasu	*pardon me for*
saizu (U14)	*size*	(U2)	*interrupting*
sakana (U7)	*fish*	shizuka(na) (U11)	*quiet*
sakanaya (U6)	*fishmonger's*	shōji (U20)	*trading*
sakaya (U6)	*wine shop*	shokuji (U17)	*meal*
sake (U6)	*rice alcohol*	shōshō omachi (U5)	*please wait a*
sakkā (U3)	*football*		*moment*
sampaku (U17)	*three nights*	shufu (U3)	*housewife*
samui (U11)	*cold*	shūgaku ryokō	
san (U1)	*Mr / Mrs / Miss / Ms*	(U10)	*school trip*
san (U2)	*three*	shujin (U4)	*husband* (own)
sandoitchi (U5)	*sandwich*	shūmatsu (U16)	*weekend*
sangatsu (U2)	*March*	shumi (U3)	*hobby*
sannin (U3)	*three people*	shutchō-chū (U20)	*on a business trip*
sarada (U13)	*salad*	soba (U15)	*noodles*
sashimi (U15)	*sliced raw fish*	sō desu (U1)	*that's right*
satsu (U16)	*note* (money)	soko (U6)	*there* (that place)
sayōnara (U1)	*goodbye*	soku (U19)	*pair* (counter)
sei (U14)	*made in*	sono (U5)	*that*
seifuku (U14)	*uniform*	sore (U5)	*that one* (noun)
seisanjō (U18)	*fare adjustment*	sorekara (U7)	*and then*
	office	sore ni (U8)	*and next*
seito (U3)	*pupil*	sorosoro (U20)	*soon, shortly*
seki (U18)	*seat*	soshite (U7)	*and*
sen (U6)	*thousand*	soto (U12)	*outside*
sen (U18)	(train) *line*	suiei (U3)	*swimming*
sengetsu (U10)	*last month*	suiyōbi (U8)	*Wednesday*
sensei (U3)	*teacher; professor*	sukāto (U14)	*skirt*
senshū (U10)	*last week*	sukēto gutsu (U19)	*skates*
sensu (U14)	*fan*	suki (U12)	*like*
sētā (U14)	*jumper*	sukii (U3)	*skiing*
shashin	*photo*	sukiijō (U19)	*ski ground*
shatsu (U14)	*shirt*	sukii tsuā (U5)	*ski tour*
shi (U2)	*four*	sukottorando (U2)	*Scotland*
shichi (U2)	*seven*	sumimasen (U1)	*excuse me; sorry*
shichigatsu (U2)	*July*	sūpā (U5)	*supermarket*

supagetti (U5)	spaghetti
supōtsu (U3)	sports
surippa (U20)	slippers
surōpu (U19)	(ski) slope
suteki (na) (U5)	smart, fashionable
sutēki (U13)	steak
sutereo (U2)	stereo
sutoa gaido (U14)	store guide
sutoroberii (U15)	strawberry
tabako (U5)	cigarettes
tabemasu (U8)	eat
tabemono (U8)	food
taberaremasu (U15)	can eat
taishikan (U20)	embassy
takai (U11)	expensive; high
takusan (U10)	many
takushii (U2)	taxi
takushii noriba (U18)	taxi tank
tamago (U8)	eggs
tanjōbi (U4)	birthday
tanoshii (U11)	pleasant, enjoyable
tatoeba (U14)	for example
tēburu (U12)	table
tegami (U6)	letter
teinei (U14)	polite
teishoku (U15)	set meal
tempura (U15)	Japanese fried food
ten'in (U3)	shop assistant
tenisu (U8)	tennis
tenisu kōto (U12)	tennis court
tenki (U11)	weather
tēpu rekōdā (U2)	tape-recorder
tera (Ul0)	temple
terebi (U2)	television
terehon kādo (U16)	telephone card
teriyakibāgā (U15)	teriyakiburger
to (U3)	and
tōchaku shimasu (U18)	arrive
tōi (U18)	far
tōka (U9)	10th (of month)
tokei (U2)	watch or clock
toki (U12)	time, when
tōki (U14)	pottery
tokidoki (U8)	sometimes
tokoro (U11)	place
tokui (U12)	good at
toku ni (U19)	in particular
tomodachi (U9)	friend
tonari (U7)	next to
toraberāzu chekku (U16)	travellers' cheques
toriniku (U2)	chicken, poultry
tōsuto (U8)	toast
totemo (U11)	very
T.shatsu (U14)	T-shirt
tsugi (U7)	next
tsuin (U17)	twin (room)
tsuitachi (U9)	1st (of month)
tsukemono (U15)	pickles
tsukue (U12)	desk
tsumaranai (U20)	boring
uchi (U8)	house, home
udon (U15)	noodles
ue (U12)	above, on top
uētoresu (U15)	waitress
uisukii (U2)	whiskey
untenshu (U18)	driver
uriba (U14)	(shop) department
ushiro (U12)	behind
utteimasu (U14)	sell
wakai (U4)	(looks) young
wakamono (U15)	young people
wakarimashita (U7)	I've understood
wanpisu (U14)	dress
wā puro (U2)	word processor
waribiki (U14)	discount
warui (U10)	bad
washi (U14)	Japanese paper
washitsu (U17)	Japanese-style room
washoku (U15)	Japanese cuisine
watashi (U2)	I
watashitachi (U18)	we
ya (U19)	and
yakitori (U15)	grilled meat on skewers
yakyū (U12)	baseball
yaoya (U6)	greengrocer's

— Index of grammatical structures —

(U= unit; S = setsumei)

kudasai (*may I have*) U5:S5
mō/mada (*already / not yet*) U11:S4
months U2
nan (*what*) plus:
   de U10:S3; **gatsu** (*month*) U9:S3; **ji** (*time*) U8:S5; **nichi** (*date*)
   U8:S5; **nin** (*people*) U3:S7; **sai** (*age*) U4:S1; **yōbi** (*day*) U8:S5;
numbers: see U2/3/4/5 and appendix; **hitotsu** system U6:S5
particles:
   ga (*but*) U11:S5; **ga** U12:S1; **goro** U8:S4; **kara/made** U2:S3,
   U5:S6; **mo** (*also*) U3:S3; **ni** U8:S4/8, U9:S1/3, U12:S3; **no** U2:S4,
   U9:S4; **o** U8:S2; **to** (*with*) U9:S8; **wa** U2:S1, U8:S3
plural U3:S6
question words:
   ka U1:S5; *how much?* U6:S3; *what day / date?* U8:S5; *what time?*
   U8:S5; *where?* U7, U9:S2; *who?* U3:S2; *how (by what)?* U10:S3
sentence pattern:
   wa/desu U3:S1; **o kudasai** U6:S6; with **masu** verbs U8:S1/2; with
   ni (*to*) U9:S1; with time expressions U9:S3; with adjectives
   U11:S2; with **suki/jōzu** U12:S1/2; with words of location U12:S4
time U5:S4, S5; length of time U10:S4
time expressions U8; U9:S3; U10:S5
this/that U5:S2; this place/that place U6:S8
verbs:
   arimasu (*have*) U6:S4; **arimasu/imasu** (*exist*) U12:S3; **masen ka**
   U9:S6; **mashō** U9:S5; **masu** verbs U8; negative U9:S6; negative
   with **amari/zenzen** U12:S5
past tense U10:S1; **tai desu** (*want to*) U10:S5

Appendix: Numbers

0	zero/rei	30	sanju	6000	rokusen
1	ichi	40	yonjū	7000	nanasen
2	ni	50	gojū	8000	hassen
3	san	60	rokujū	9000	kyūsen
4	shi/yon	70	nanajū	10,000	ichiman
5	go	80	hachijū	20,000	niman
6	roku	90	kyūjū	30,000	sanman
7	shichi/nana	100	hyaku	1,000,000	hyakuman
8	hachi	200	nihyaku	10,000,000	senman
9	kyū/ku	300	sambyaku	100,000,000	ichioku
10	jū	400	yonhyaku	1000,000,000	jūoku
11	jūichi	500	gohyaku	1000,000,000,000	itchō
12	jūni	600	roppyaku		
13	jūsan	700	nanahyaku		
14	jūshi/jūyon	800	happyaku		
15	jūgo	900	kyūhyaku		
16	jūroku	1000	sen/issen		
17	jūnana/jūshichi	2000	nisen		
18	jūhachi	3000	sanzen		
19	jūkyū/jūku	4000	yonsen		
20	nijū	5000	gosen		